电气自动化专业英语

ENGLISH IN ELECTRIC AUTOMATION

(修订版)

李久胜 马洪飞 陈宏钧 刘汉奎 编

哈尔滨工业大学出版社

内 容 提 要

本书分电子技术、电机控制技术、计算机控制技术、自动控制系统四部分,共十五章,每章后配有以专业术语为主的词汇表。本书从大学高年级学生科技英语阅读和写作的需要出发,选取的专业技术类文章覆盖了电气自动化领域的基础内容。

本书既可作为高等院校电气自动化类各专业的英语教材,也可作为有关工程技术人员从事英文科技阅读和写作的参考书。

图书在版编目(CIP)数据

电气自动化专业英语/李久胜等编. —3 版. —哈尔滨:哈尔滨工业大学出版社,2005.1(2023.1 重印)
ISBN 978-7-5603-1413-6

Ⅰ.电… Ⅱ.李… Ⅲ.电气化-英语-高等学校-教材 Ⅳ.H31

中国版本图书馆 CIP 数据核字(2005)第 001864 号

责任编辑	王桂芝 黄菊英
出版发行	哈尔滨工业大学出版社
社　　址	哈尔滨市南岗区复华四道街 10 号　邮编 150006
传　　真	0451-86414749
网　　址	http://hitpress.hit.edu.cn
印　　刷	哈尔滨市工大节能印刷厂
开　　本	880mm×1230mm　1/32　印张 11.25　字数 291 千字
版　　次	2005 年 1 月第 3 版　2023 年 1 月第 18 次印刷
书　　号	ISBN 978-7-5603-1413-6
定　　价	26.00 元

(如因印装质量问题影响阅读,我社负责调换)

修订版前言

《电气自动化专业英语》(第1版)自1999年5月出版发行以来,由于其专业知识覆盖面较广、所选文章有代表性,得到了许多国内工科院校相关专业的认同和支持,目前已重印多次,读者反馈意见较好,这对作者无疑是极大的鼓励和鞭策。

为了不辜负读者的厚爱,同时本着不断完善的宗旨,本次再版,我们结合新世纪专业英语教学改革的要求和广大学生英语水平普遍提高的实际,在总结教学经验和广泛征求读者意见的基础上,对本书的全部内容进行了系统的修改和补充,并在每章后增加了重点、难点句子的译文,以便于读者自学。另外,为了使本书的感观更加精美,在版式方面也进行了一些调整。

由于作者水平有限,虽是修订,但书中仍难免有不妥之处,再次恳请读者批评指正。

编　者
2005年1月

前　言

随着国际交流的日益增强,对于大学生英语能力的要求不断提高,阅读和撰写英文科技文章已成为在科学技术领域参与国际交流的重要手段。由于科技英语的表达方式、词汇范畴与公共英语差异较大,所以专业英语训练是大学高年级学生继公共英语课程之后的一个重要补充和提高。为此,编者根据培养高素质跨世纪人才对专业英语教学的要求、参考大量国外当代的教材、专著和教学参考书、结合自己的教学体会的基础上,编写了这本适合于电气自动化类各专业的英语教材。本书可作为高等院校电气自动化类各专业的英语教材(参考学时60),也可供工程技术人员阅读参考。本书从实用角度出发,结合电气自动化类各专业所学的内容,选取了该专业领域的大量科技文章,表述规范、专业词汇丰富、内容权威、结构完整,各部分后均配有词汇和短语。全书共分四个部分:

第一部分(1～4章)电子技术。包括电子测量、模拟和数字电子技术及电力电子技术。

第二部分(5～8章)电机控制技术。包括电机原理和结构、电机的基本控制系统及运动控制传感器。

第三部分(9～11章)计算机控制技术。包括计算机网络及可编程控制器的基础知识。

第四部分(12～15章)自动控制系统。包括电力分配技术、自动控制原理及电力拖动自动控制系统。

本书由哈尔滨工业大学工业自动化教研室的四位教师联合编写，1～4章由李久胜编写，5～8章由马洪飞编写，9～11章由陈宏钧编写，12～15章由刘汉奎编写。在编写过程中得到刘金琪老师的大力协助，并提出了许多宝贵意见，在此表示感谢。

由于编者水平和经验有限，书中难免存在不足和疏漏之处，敬请读者批评指正。

编　者
1999年4月

CONTENTS

PART 1 ELECTRONICS

1 Electrical Measuring Instruments 1
   1.1 SAFETY PRECAUTION 1
   1.2 BASIC METER CONSTRUCTION AND OPERATION 2
   1.3 USE OF MEASURING INSTRUMENT 5

2 Fundamentals of Solid-State Power Device 19
   2.1 INTRODUCTION 19
   2.2 SOLID-STATE POWER DEVICES 19
   2.3 POWER SEMICONDUCTOR CAPABILITIES 25
   2.4 PHYSICAL CHARACTERISTICS OF POWER SEMICONDUCTORS 26
   2.5 COMMUTATION 28
   2.6 SUMMARY 32

3 Analog Electronics 37
   3.1 INTRODUCTION 37
   3.2 OPERATIONAL-AMPLIFIER CIRCUITS 40

4 Digital Electronics 56
   4.1 THE DIGITAL IDEA 56
   4.2 ASYNCHRONOUS DIGITAL SYSTEMS 64
   4.3 SEQUENTIAL DIGITAL SYSTEMS 68

PART 2 ELECTRICAL MACHINE, CONTROL COMPONENT AND SENSOR

5 Introduction to Electrical Machines 81
   5.1 BRIEF HISTORY OF ELECTRICAL MACHINES 81

5.2 BASIC CONSTRUCTION OF ELECTRICAL MACHINES 83
5.3 CONSTRUCTION FEATURES OF ELECTRICAL MACHINES 85

6 DC Motor and Induction Motor 96
6.1 TYPES OF DC MOTORS 96
6.2 DC MOTOR ANALYSIS 101
6.3 DC MOTOR SPEED-TORQUE CHARACTERISTICS 103
6.4 THREE-PHASE INDUCTION MOTOR 109
6.5 INDUCTION MOTOR TORQUE-SPEED CHARACTERISTICS ... 111

7 Electrical Machine Control Systems 120
7.1 CONTROL SYMBOLS 120
7.2 MACHINE CONTROL WITH SWITCHES 120
7.3 CONTROL EQUIPMENT FOR ELECTRICAL MACHINES 124
7.4 MOTOR STARTING SYSTEMS 131
7.5 FORWARD AND REVERSE CONTROL 138
7.6 DYNAMIC BRAKING 140

8 Control Sensors 145
8.1 INTRODUCTION 145
8.2 SENSORS AND TRANSDUCERS 147
8.3 ANALOG SENSORS FOR MOTION MEASUREMENT 149
8.4 DIGITAL TRANSDUCERS 154

PART 3 COMPUTER CONTROL TECHNIQUES

9 Introduction of Computernets 166
9.1 USES OF COMPUTER NETWORKS 169
9.2 NETWORK HARDWARE 175
9.3 NETWORK SOFTWARE 187
9.4 EXAMPLE NETWORKS 203

10 Introduction of Programmable Controller 224
10.1 HISTORY 224
10.2 BASIC CONCEPTS 226
10.3 GENERAL APPLICATION AREAS 227
10.4 OPERATING ENVIRONMENT CONSIDERATIONS 232

10.5 DEDICATED MICROPROCESSOR BASED SYSTEM—A CONTRAST 235
10.6 PERSONAL COMPUTER IMPLICATIONS 236
10.7 FACTORY AUTOMATION AND PROGRAMMABLE CONTROLLERS 238

11 Foundation of PLC 242
11.1 THE CENTRAL PROCESSING UNIT 242
11.2 INSTALLATION AND MAINTENANCE 256
11.3 APPLICATIONS 262

PART 4 AUTOMATIC CONTROL SYSTEMS

12 Electrical Distribution 274
12.1 PRIMARY DISTRIBUTION SYSTEMS 274
12.2 CONSUMER DISTRIBUTION SYSTEMS 275
12.3 GROUNDING OF ELECTRICAL SYSTEMS 282
12.4 GROUNDING OF ELECTRICAL EQUIPMENT 283
12.5 GROUND-FAULT PROTECTION 283
12.6 THREE-PHASE SYSTEMS 285
12.7 HARMONIC EFFECT OF FLUORESCENT LIGHTING FIXTURES 287

13 Introduction to Control Engineering 291
13.1 INTRODUCTION 291
13.2 DEFINITIONS 294
13.3 THE POSITION-CONTROL SYSTEMS 298
13.4 PROCESS-CONTROL SYSTEMS 302
13.5 AUTONOMIC CONTROL SYSTEMS 305
13.6 REASONS WHY CONTROL SYSTEMS ARE PREFERRED TO HUMAN OPERATIONS 306
13.7 CONCLUDING REMARKS 307

14 Speed Control of DC Motor 312
14.1 REGULATOR SYSTEMS 312
14.2 ELECTRICAL BRAKING 312

- 14.3 DC MOTOR SPEED CONTROL ·············· 314
- 14.4 A SINGLE-QUADRANT SPEED CONTROL SYSTEM USING THYRISTORS ·············· 315
- 14.5 PROTECTION CIRCUITS OR LIMITING CIRCUITS ·········· 318
- 14.6 THE CLOSED-LOOP WARD-LEONARD METHOD OF SPEED CONTROL ·············· 319
- 14.7 TYPES OF PHASE-CONTROLLED THYRISTOR DC DRIVES ············· 323
- 14.8 DUAL-CONVERTER DRIVE ·············· 325
- 14.9 COMPUTER MONITORING OF SPEED PROFILE ············· 328
- 14.10 PULSE-WIDTH MODULATION SPEED CONTROL OF DC MOTORS ·············· 330

15 Frequency Controls for AC Motors ·············· 334

- 15.1 ADJUSTABLE-FREQUENCY CONCEPTS ·············· 334
- 15.2 TERMINOLOGY ·············· 336
- 15.3 PWM VERSUS AVI VERSUS CSI ·············· 337
- 15.4 PERFORMANCE COMPARISONS OF PWM, AVI, AND CSI ·············· 340
- 15.5 APPLICATIONS OF GENERAL-PURPOSE INVERTERS ······ 342

PART 1
ELECTRONICS

1

Electrical Measuring Instruments

Electrical personnel use many different types of measuring instruments. Some jobs require very accurate measurements while other jobs need only rough estimates. Some instruments are used solely to determine whether or not a circuit is complete. The most common measuring and testing instruments are voltage testers, voltmeters, ammeters, ohmmeters, continuity testers, megohmmeters, wattmeters, and watt-hour meters.

All meters used for measuring electrical values are basically current meters. They measure or compare the values of current flowing through them. The meters are calibrated and the scale is designed to read the value of the desired unit.

1.1 SAFETY PRECAUTION

Correct meter connections are very important for the safety precaution of the user and for proper maintenance of the meters. A basic knowledge of the construction and operation of meters will aid the user in making proper connections and maintaining them in safe working order.

Many instruments are designed to be used on DC or AC only, while others can be used interchangeably. Note: It is very important to use each meter only with the type of current for which the meter is designed. Using a meter with an incorrect type of current can result in damage to the meter and may cause injury to the user.

Some meters are constructed to measure very low values. Other meters can measure extremely high values.

CAUTION: Never allow a meter to exceed its rated maximum limit. The importance of never allowing the actual value to exceed the maximum value indicated on the meter can not be overemphasized. Exceeding maximum values can damage the indicating needle, interfere with proper calibration, and in some instances may cause the meter to explode, resulting in injury to the user. Some meters are equipped with over correct protection. However, a current many times greater than the instrument's design limit may still be hazardous.

1.2 BASIC METER CONSTRUCTION AND OPERATION

Many meters operate on the principle of electromagnetic interaction. This interaction is caused by an electric current flowing through a conductor which is placed between the poles of a permanent magnet. This type of meter is especially suitable for direct current.

Whenever an electric current flows through a conductor a magnetic force is developed around the conductor. The magnetic force caused by the electric current reacts with the force of the permanent magnet. This causes the indicating needle to move. The larger the amount of current, the farther the needle will move.

The conductor is formed into coil, which is placed on a pivot between the poles of the permanent magnet. The coil is connected to the terminals of the instrument through two spiral springs. These springs supply a reacting force proportional to the deflection. When no current is flowing, the springs cause the needle to return to zero.

The meter scale is designed to indicate the amount of current being measured. The movement of the coil (and thus the movement of the indicating needle) is proportional to the amount of current flowing in the coil. If it is necessary to measure larger currents than the coil can safely carry, a bypass circuit, or shunt, is included. The shunt many be contained within the meter housing or connected externally.

Example 1

A meter is constructed to measure 10 A on a maximum scale. The coil can safely carry 0.001 A. The shunt must be designed to carry 9.999 A. The meter is designed to indicate 10 A when 0.001 A flows in the coil.

Fig. 1.1(a) illustrates a permanent-magnet meter. Fig. 1.1(b) show an external shunt connected across the meter terminals. The permanent-magnet meter can be used as an ammeter or a voltmeter. When the scale is designed to indicate current and the internal resistance is kept to a minimum, the meter functions as an ammeter. When the scale is designed to indicate voltage, the internal resistance will be relatively high, depending upon the value of voltage for which the meter is designed. Note: Regardless of the design, the distance the needle moves is determined by the amount of current flowing in the coil.

A slight change must be made in the design in order to use this type of meter on AC. A rectifier is a device which changes AC to DC. It must be incorporated into the meter and the scale must be drawn to indicate the correct value of AC voltage. Rectifier-type AC meters cannot be used on DC and are generally designed as voltage meters.

The electrodynamometer, Fig. 1.2 is another design for both amme-

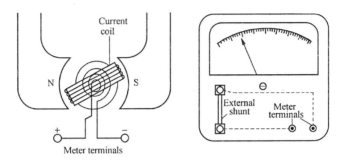

(a) Permanent-magnet meter (b) Permanent-magnet meter with external shunt

Fig. 1.1

ters and voltmeters that can be used on alternating current. This instrument consists of two stationary coils and one movable coil. The three coils are connected in series with each other through two spiral springs. The spring also support the movable coil. When current flows through the coils the movable coil moves in a clockwise direction.

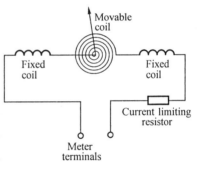

Fig.1.2 Voltmeter-type electrodynamometer instrument

In the electrodynamometer. The scale is not divided uniformly, as it is in permanent magnet-type meters. The force on the movable coil varies with the square of the current flowing through the coils. This requires that the divisions near the beginning of the scale be made closer together than those near end. The greater the distance between the divisions, the more accurately one can read the meter. It is important to strive for an accurate reading.

The moving-vane meter is another type of construction for meters. Current flowing in the coil causes two iron strips (the vanes) to become magnetized. One vane is movable; the other is suationary. The magnetic reaction between the two vanes causes the movable one to turn. The amount of movement depends upon the value of current flowing in the coil.

CAUTION: All of the instruments described depend upon magnetism for their operation, so it is important that they not be placed near other magnets. The magnetic force from another magnet may damage the meter and/or cause incorrect measurements.

1.3 USE OF MEASURING INSTRUMENT

A voltmeter is designed to measure the electrical pressure applied to a circuit and/or the voltage drop across a component. Voltmeters must always be connected in parallel with the circuit or the component being measured.

1.3.1 Voltage Testers

The AC-DC voltage tester is a rather crude but useful instrument for the electrician. This instrument is designed to indicate approximate values of voltage. The more common types indicate the following values of voltage: AC, 110, 220, 440, and 550 V; DC, 125, 250, and 600 V. Many of these instruments will also indicate the "polarity" of DC; i.e., which conductor of the circuit is positively or negatively charged.

The voltage tester is used to check common voltages, to identify the grounded conductor, to check for blown fuses, and to distinguish between AC and DC. The voltage tester is small and rugged, making it easier to carry and store than the average voltmeter. Fig. 1.3 and 1.4 depict methods for testing fuses with a voltage tester.

To determine which conductor of a circuit or a system is grounded, connect the tester between one conductor and a well established ground. If the tester indicates a voltage, the conductor is not grounded. Continue

6 English in Electric Automation

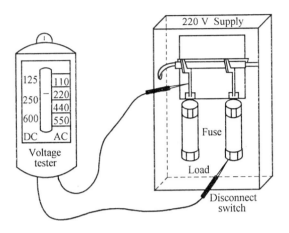

Fig.1.3 Testing cartridge fuses with a voltage tester. The tester indicates 220 V AC. The right-hand fuse is good. If the fuse is blown, the tester will indicate zero voltage

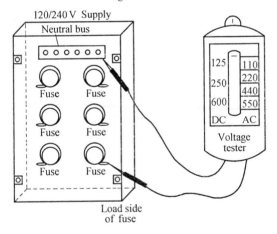

Fig.1.4 Testing plug fuses with a voltage tester. Tester value of zero volt indicates that the fuse is blown

this procedure with each conductor until zero voltage is indicated (see

Fig.1.5).

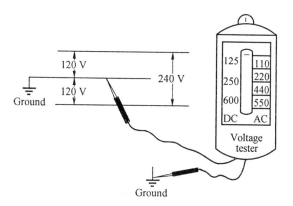

Fig.1.5 Testing to locate the grounded conductor. If the tester indicates zero, the conductor is grounded

To determine the approximate voltage between any two conductors, connect the tester between the two conductors.

CAUTION: Always read and follow the instructions that are supplied with the voltage tester.

1.3.2 Voltmeters

The voltmeter is a much more accurate measurement than the voltage tester. Because voltmeters are connected in parallel with the circuit or the component being considered, it is necessary that they have relatively high resistance. The internal resistance keeps the current through the meter to a minimum. The lower the value of current through the meter, the less effect it has on the electrical characteristics of the circuit.

The sensitivity (and therefore the accuracy) of the meter is stated in ohms per volt(Ω/V). The higher the ohms per volt, the better the quality of the meter. High values of ohms per volt minimize any change in circuit characteristics.

The average meter used by the electrician is generally between 95 percent and 98 percent accurate. This range of accuracy is satisfactory for most applications. It is very important, however, that the electrical worker strive to obtain the most accurate reading possible. An accurate reading can be obtained by standing directly in front of the meter face and looking directly at it. If the meter has a mirror behind the scale, adjust the angle of sight until there is no reflection of the indicating needle in the mirror. For extreme accuracy, a digital meter may be used.

Voltmeters can be used for the same applications as voltage testers. Voltmeters are much more accurate than voltage testers. Therefore, much more information can be obtained. For example, if the supply voltage to a building is slightly below normal, the voltmeter can indicate this problem. The voltmeter can also be used to determine the amount of voltage drop on feeder and branch circuit conductors.

Voltmeters sometimes have more than one scale. It is very important to select the scale that will provide the most accurate measurement. A range selector switch is provided for this purpose. Note: It is advisable to begin with a high scale and work down to the lowest scale so as not to exceed the range limit of any scale. Setting the selector switch on the lowest usable scale will provide the most accurate reading.

Before using the meter, check to be sure that the indicating needle is pointing to zero. An adjustment screw is provided just below the face of the meter. A very slight turn will cause the needle to move. The needle can be aligned with the zero line on the scale by turning the screw.

When using voltmeters on DC, it is very important to maintain proper polarity. Most DC power supplies and meters are color coded to indicate the polarity. Red indicates the positive terminal; black indicates the negative terminal. If the polarity of the circuit or component is unknown, touch the leads to the terminals while observing the indicating needle. If the indicating needle attempts to move backwards, the meter lead connections must be reversed.

CAUTION: Do not leave a meter connected with the polarity reversed.

1.3.3 Ammeters

Ammeters are designed to measure the amount of current flowing in a circuit or part of a circuit. They are always connected in series with the circuit component being considered. The resistance of the meter must be extremely low so it does not restrict the flow of current through the circuit. When measuring the current flowing through very sensitive equipment, even a slight change in current caused by the ammeter may cause the equipment to malfunction.

Ammeters, like voltmeters, have an adjustment screw to set the indicating needle to zero. Many meters have mirrors to assist the user in obtaining an accurate reading.

Ammeters are used to locate overloads and open circuits. They can also be used to balance the loads on multiwire circuits and to locate malfunctions.

Ammeters should always be connected in series with the circuit or component under consideration. If direct current is being used, always check the polarity. Fig.1.6(a) shows an ammeter measuring the current through a circuit. Fig.1.6(b) shows an AC ammeter.

1.3.4 Ohmmeter

An ohmmeter is used to measure resistance. Batteries located in the meter case furnish the power for its operation.

CAUTION: It is very important to be sure that the circuit or component is disconnected from its regular power source before connecting the meter. Connecting an ohmmeter to a circuit which has not been deenergized can result in damage to the meter and possible injury to the user.

The ohmmeter scale is designed to be read in the direction opposite

10　English in Electric Automation

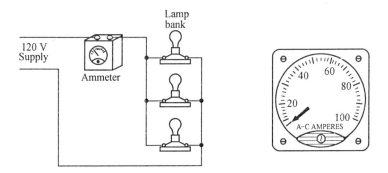

(a) Ammeter measuring current through a lamp bank　　(b) Alternating-current ammeter

Fig.1.6

to other meters. When the meter circuit is open the indicating needle should point to infinity. The needle can be aligned with the infinity mark by turning the adjustment screw.

Most ohmmeters have several ranges. The range selector switch must be set on the scale that will provide the most accurate measurement. The ranges are generally as follow: $r*1$, $r*100$, and $r*10\,000$. If the select switch is set on $r*1$, the value indicated on scale is the actual value. If the selector switch is set on $r*100$, the value indicated on the scale must be multiplied by 100. For $r*10\,000$, the value must be multiplied by 10 000.

Before measuring a resistance, it is important to check the zero adjustment. The procedure is as follows:

(1) Set the range selector switch on the desired range.

(2) Connect the test leads together. The indicating needle should point to zero.

(3) If the needle is not aligned with the zero line, turn the zero adjustment until the needle and the zero line are aligned. Note: Do not leave the test leads connected together, because under zero resistance the

batteries will deteriorate rapidly.

(4) **CAUTION**: Be sure the circuit is deenergized.

(5) Connect the test leads across (in parallel with) the component or circuit to be measured. The needle will indicate the resistance value.

The ohmmeter is an excellent continuity tester. Connect the ohmmeter across the circuit to be tested. If the circuit is complete, the needle will indicate the resistance of the circuit. A reading of zero generally indicates a short circuit. A reading of infinity indicates an open circuit.

1.3.5 Continuity Tester

A simple continuity tester can be constructed from a 6 V battery and bell. One terminal of the battery is connected to the bell and the other is connected to the circuit. The second terminal on the bell is connected to the other side of the circuit. If the current path is complete, the bell will ring.

Continuity testers can be used to check fuses and switches, Fig. 1.7 and 1.8.

CAUTION: Never attach a continuity tester to a circuit that is energized.

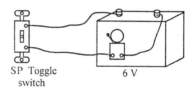

SP Toggle switch   6 V

Fig. 1.7 Continuity tester consisting of a 6 V bell and a 6 V battery. The tester is connected to a switch. When the circuit is complete (switch contacts closed), the bell will ring

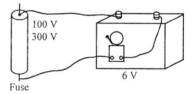

100 V
300 V

Fuse   6 V

Fig. 1.8 Continuity tester connected across a 100 A fuse. If the fuse is good, the bell will ring

1.3.6 Megohmmeter (MEGGER)

A megohmmeter, commonly known by the trade name MEGGER, is an instrument used to measure very high values of resistance. For example, it is used to measure the resistance of the insulation on circuit conductors and motor windings. A megohmmeter is designed to measure the resistance in megohms; one megohm (MΩ) is equal to one million ohms.

A small generator called a magneto is contained within the megohmmeter housing. The magneto furnishes the power for the instrument, just as batteries do for an ohmmeter. The magneto can be hand powered or driven by batteries or other sources of electricity. Megohmmeters have many different voltage ratings. Some of the most common are designed to operate on one of the following values: 500 V, 1 000 V, and 10 000 V. The amount of voltage the magneto should generate depends upon the ohmic value and the type of resistance being measured.

Because megohmmeters are designed to measure very high resistance, they are usually used for insulation tests. Visual inspection of insulation and leakage tests with voltmeters are not always reliable. A megohmmeter test is one of the most reliable tests available to the maintenance electrician.

CAUTION: Before a megohmmeter is connected to a conductor or a circuit, the circuit must be deenergized. When testing the insulation, the testing is generally done between each conductor and the ground. A good ground is a vital part of the testing procedure. The ground connection should be checked with the megohmmeter and with a low-range ohmmeter to ensure good continuity.

Insulation tests should be made at the time of the installation and periodically thereafter. For circuits and equipment rated at 600 V or less, the 1 000 V magneto can be used. A log (record) should be maintained, noting dates of tests, time of day, temperature, humidity, and resistance values.

Because atmospheric conditions affect the resistance of insulation, many different readings may be obtained over a period of time. This is because the resistance of insulation varies with temperature, humidity, and air quality.

The common enemies of insulation are moisture, dirt, oil, and chemicals. It is important to keep the equipment and conductors as clean and dry as possible. Good maintenance practices and periodic testing of the insulation should be the rule rather than the exception. Megohmmeter scales are usually drawn to indicate a minimum of 10 000 Ω and a maximum of 200 MΩ (200 000 000 Ω). (Megohm is abbreviated MΩ) Conductor insulation designed for 600 V should indicate a resistance of 600 000 Ω or higher. For motors, generators, transformers, and similar equipment the minimum resistance for those designed to operate at 1 000 V or less should be 1 MΩ (1 000 000 Ω). A good rule of thumb for wires and equipment rated at over 1 000 V is to divide the voltage rating by 1 000 to obtain the minimum value of insulation resistance in megohms.

Periodic testing of insulation should take place at least once every 2 months. The resistance values will vary according to temperature and other atmospheric conditions. However, a steady downward trend in the value of the resistance longer than 1 year to 18 months indicates trouble, and the circuit or equipment should be checked out.

1.3.7 Multimeters

Multimeters are designed to measure more that one unit. For example, the volt-ohm-milliammeter, measures DC and AC voltages, DC current, and resistance. The advantage of this type of meter is that measurements can be taken with or without deenergizing the circuit.

1.3.8 Wattmeter

Wattmeters are designed to measure electrical power. Because electrical power is the product of current and voltage, the wattmeter may be considered a combination ammeter-voltmeter. It is generally a dynamometer-type instrument constructed as shown in Fig.1.9. The coils are connected into the circuit, Fig.1.10. The stationary coils, called current coils, are connected in series with the load. The movable coil is connected in series with a high resistance. This series combination is connected in parallel with the load.

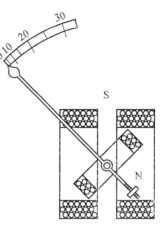

Fig.1.9 Basic construction of a dynamometer type wattmeter

The movable coil is known as the voltage coil. The magnetic reaction between the two coils causes the voltage coil to move. The indicating needle is attached to the voltage coil and moves according to the amount of current flowing through both coils. The scale is designed to indicate the power in watts.

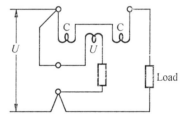

Fig.1.10 Dynamometer type wattmeter showing coil connection

Because of the two circuits in the wattmeter, either coil can burn out under overload. For this reason, current and voltage ratings are marked on instrument. Note: Care must be taken to not exceed these limits.

1.3.9 Watthour Meters

Electrical energy is the product of power and time. The watthour meter measures the amount of power expended in a specific amount of time. In a DC watthour meter, the speed is directly proportional to the power. It is a meter which registers the amount of watt-hours or kilowatt-hours delivered to the customer. Because most customers require a large amount of energy, the standard meter is designed to indicate kilowatt-hours. (One kilowatt-hour is equal to one thousand watt-hours)

The AC kilowatt-hour meter works on the principle of induction. Moving magnetic fields cause currents to flow in an aluminum disk. These currents, called eddy currents, produce magnetic fields that interact with the moving magnetic fields, causing the disk to rotate. The rotating disk drives a gear chain which, in turn, drives the indicating needles.

Kilowatt-hour meters have either four or five dials. Each dial has an indicating needle and a scale from 0 to 9. The dials are read from right to left. Beginning with the right-hand dial and working to the left, the dials indicate units, tens, hundreds, thousands, and ten-thousands. In Fig. 1.11, the dials of a four-dial meter are shown. The dials indicate 1 238 kW·h. If the indicating needle is between two numbers, the smaller of the two numbers is always read.

Fig. 1.11 Kilowatt-hour meter dials

Vocabulary

1. personnel   n.   人员,职员
2. voltmeter   n.   电压表,伏特计(表)
3. ohmmeter   n.   欧姆计,电阻表
4. megohmmeter   n.   兆欧表
5. wattmeter   n.   瓦特表(计),电表,功率(W)
6. watt-hour   n.   瓦时,瓦特小时(能量单位)

7. ammeter	n.	安培计,电流表
8. calibrate	v.	校正(准)
9. scale	n.	刻度,量程
10. rated	adj.	额定的
11. interfere with		有害于……
12. indicating needle		(仪表)指针
13. hazardous	adj.	危险的
14. pivot	n.	支点
15. terminal	n.	接线端子
16. spiral	adj.	螺旋形的
17. spring	n.	弹簧
18. shunt	n.	分流;分路(流)器;并联,旁路
19. rectifier	n.	整流器
20. electrodynamometer	n.	电测力计
21. strive for	v.	争取
22. vane	n.	(机器的)叶,叶片
23. strip	n.	条,带,(跨接)片
24. crude	n.	不精细的,粗略的
25. polarity	n.	极性
26. fuse	n.	保险丝,熔丝
27. rugged	adj.	坚固的
28. depict	v.	描绘,描写
29. cartridge fuse		盒式保险丝
30. blow	v.	(保险丝)烧断
31. plug fuse		插头式保险丝
32. malfunction	n.	故障
33. deenergize	v.	不给……通电
34. insulation	n.	绝缘
35. generator	n.	发电机
36. magneto	n.	磁发电机

37. humidity   n.   湿度
38. moisture   n.   潮湿，湿气
39. abbreviate   v.   缩写，缩写为
40. transformer   n.   变压器
41. thumb   v.   检查，查阅
42. milliammeter   n.   毫安表
43. multimeter   n.   万用表
44. dynamometer   n.   测力计，功率计
45. aluminum   n.   铝
46. deteriorate   v.   (使)恶化
47. eddy current   涡流
48. gear   n.   齿轮，传动装置
49. dial   n.   刻度盘

Notes:

1. The meters are calibrated and the scale is designed to read the value of the desired unit.
这些仪表可以被校准并且设计了不同的量程，以便读出期望的数值。

2. Note: It is very important to use each meter only with the type of current for which the meter is designed.
注意：每种仪表只能用来测量符合设计要求的电流类型。

3. The importance of never allowing the actual value to exceed the maximum value indicated on the meter can not be overemphasized.
不允许被测的实际数值超过仪表最大允许值的要求再强调也不过分。

4. These springs supply a reacting force proportional to the deflection.
这些弹簧提供了与偏差成正比的恢复力。

5. The force on the movable coil varies with the square of the current flowing through the coils.
作用在动线圈上的力根据流过该线圈的电流平方来变化。

6. The lower the value of current through the meter, the less effect it has on the

electrical characteristics of the circuit.

流过仪表的电流越小,对电路特性的影响越小。

7. Good maintenance practices and periodic testing of the insulation should be the rule rather than the exception.

良好的保养和定期的绝缘检测应成为制度而不是偶尔为之。

2

Fundamentals of Solid-state Power Device

2.1 INTRODUCTION

In this chapter we focus on solid-state power devices, or power semiconductors, only as they are being used in the power leads or power circuits to three-phase 460 V AC squirrel cage induction motors for either phase (voltage) control or frequency (speed) control.

2.2 SOLID-STATE POWER DEVICES

The five major types of power semiconductors used in solid-state AC motor control are:

(1) Diodes
(2) Thyristors [e.g., silicon-controlled rectifiers (SCRs)]
(3) Transistors
(4) Gate-turn-off thyristors
(5) Triacs

SCRs and triacs are commonly used for phase controls. Various combinations of diodes, SCRs, transistors, and GTOs are used for speed controls. The commonality of these devices is the use of crystals of silicon in the form of wafers that are layered so as to form various combinations of P-N junction. The P junction is usually called the anode and N junction is usually called the cathode for diodes, SCRs, and GTOs; the corresponding terms for transistors are collector and emitter. The differences among these devices relate to how they go into and out of conduction and in their available ampere and voltage capabilities.

Let's take a brief look at each of these devices in terms of these parameters.

2.2.1 Diodes

Fig. 2.1 shows a single diode. The left portion shows a PN junction within the silicon crystal. The right portion shows the schematic symbol for a single diode.

When the anode (P) is positive with respect to the cathode (N), forward current will flow, with a relatively low voltage drop in the diode itself. When the polarity is reversed, only a slight reverse leakage current will flow. This is illustrated in Fig. 2.2. The forward voltage drop is usually about 1 V, independent of the current rating.

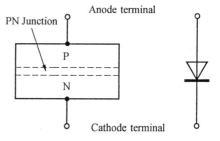

Fig. 2. 1 Single-diode P-N junction and schematic symbol

The forward current rating of a diode depends on its size and design, both of which are predicted on the need to dissipate the heat generated within the device so that the maximum junction temperature (usually 200℃) is not exceeded.

The reverse breakdown voltage (see Fig. 2.2) is the other important parameter of a diode. Its value depends more on the internal design of the diode than on its physical size.

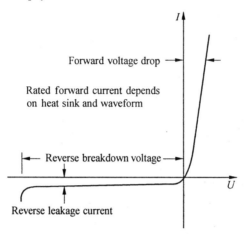

Fig.2.2 Steady-state volt-ampere characteristic of a diode

Note that a diode will conduct in the forward direction only when a forward voltage is applied. It does not have any inherent means to control the ampere or voltage value of this conduction.

Diodes are used in AC power circuits primarily as rectifiers, which means that they rectify the alternating current into direct current, with no inherent means of controlling the values of the resulting DC ampere or DC voltage. Single diodes are available with ratings up to 4 800 A and 1 200 V PRV (peak reverse voltage) and to 2 000 A with 4 400 V PRV.

2.2.2 Thyristors

Fig.2.3 shows the P-N junction arrangement and schematic symbol for a thyristor, also commonly known as a silicon-controlled rectifier (SCR). Note that the series junctions from anode to cathode are P-N-P-N, with a gate terminal connected to the inner P layer.

If there is no connection to the gate terminal, and the anode is negative with respect to the cathode, no current will flow from anode to cathode (see Fig. 2.3). This is because the inner P junction acts as a blocking circuit since it is deenergized. This is true even if the anode is positive with respect to the cathode. However-

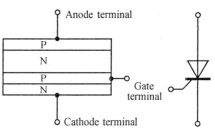

Fig. 2.3 Single-thyristor P-N junctions and schematic symbol

er, when the anode is positive and a positive signal is applied to the gate, current will flow from anode to cathode as long as the anode is positive, even though the positive signal is removed from the gate.

In other words, the gate can turn the thyristor on, but not off. The only way that the thyristor can be turned off is by forcing a current zero at the terminals of the anode by external means. Thus a thyristor is similar to a diode in that its forward conduction can be stopped only by forcing a current zero. However, a thyristor differs from a diode in that forward conduction can be initiated only ① if the anode is positive and ② if the gate is momentarily positive. This characteristic is implied in the term "silicon-controlled rectifier."

Fig.2.4 illustrates the steady-state volt-ampere characteristic of a thyristor. Note that the reverse breakdown voltage and reverse leakage current are similar in shape to those of a diode. The forward voltage drop, when in conduction, is higher, usually about 1.4 V, than for a diode. There is also a slight forward leakage current when in the blocked state.

As in the case of diodes, the value of on-state current is determined by the ability of the device and its mounting (heat sink) to dissipate the internal heat. Maximum junction temperatures of thyristors are considerably lower than for diodes, usually on the order of 125 ℃. This, plus the 1.4 V forward drop, means that thyristors are considerably larger than

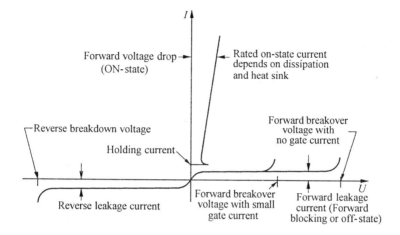

Fig.2.4 Steady-state volt-ampere characteristic of a thyristor

diodes for the same ampere rating. Single thyristors are available with ratings in excess of 2 000 A at 2 200 V PRV, and 1 400 A at 4 000 V PRV.

2.2.3 Transistors

Fig.2.5 shows the junction arrangement, schematic symbol, and volt-ampere characteristic for a typical power transistor. If the collector (anode) is positive with respect to emitter (cathode), no current will flow from collector to emitter until current flows from the base (gate) to the emitter. Also, in contrast to thyristors, transistors are not self-latching. Current flows from collector to emitter only as long as base current flows. Opening the base circuit will block current flow from collector to emitter.

A power transistor is similar to a thyristor in that it can control the initiation of forward conduction. It differs from a thyristor in that it can also control the turn-off or commutation requirements for frequency control of AC motors.

Note that the volt-ampere characteristic (see Fig.2.5) does not show

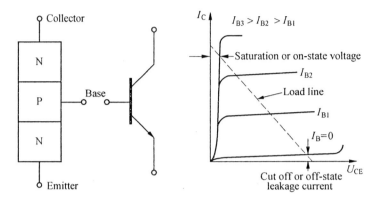

Fig 2.5 NPN transistor junction geometry, symbol, and volt-ampere characteristic

any reverse characteristic. Normally, a reverse shunting diode (not shown in Fig.2.5) is connected between the emitter and the collector, to protect the transistor from reverse voltages. Power transistors are available with ratings up to 400 A and 1 000 V PRV.

2.2.4 Gate-Turn-Off Thyristors

Fig.2.6 shows the schematic symbol for a GTO. GTOs are similar to thyristor s in P-N-P-N junction arrangement and in forward current operation. If the anode is positive, conduction is initiated by application of a positive pulse to the gate. However, the silicon wafers and junctions are designed with special characteristics so that the application of a strong negative current pulse to the gate "squeezes" the forward current to turn-off, even though the anode remains positive. GTOs are often used with momentary ratings

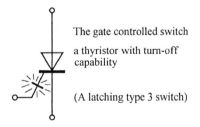

The gate controlled switch a thyristor with turn-off capability

(A latching type 3 switch)

Fig. 2. 6 Schematic symbol of a gate-turn-off thyristor

up to 2 400 A at 1 200 V PRV.

2.2.5 Triac

Fig. 2.7 shows the schematic symbol for a triac. A triac consists of a special thyristor package with forward and reverse thyristors operated from a single gate lead. They are commonly used in light-dimmer circuits and as on-off relays where slight leakage currents in the off-state will not cause misoperation of other controls. The availability of triacs with increased ampere capabilities has led to their use in phase control of AC motors.

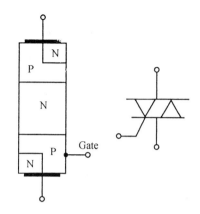

Fig.2.7 Schematic symbol of a triac

2.3 POWER SEMICONDUCTOR CAPABILITIES

Table 2.1 is a summary of how and where these power devices are used in solid-state AC motor motors up to 600 V AC, by horsepower ranges. The horsepower ratings are based on the devices not being used in parallel.

Table 2.1 Typical Usage of Power Semiconductors in Solid-State AC Motor Control, Up to 600 V, Without Paralleling Devices

Device	Phase control Horsepower range	Frequency Control		
		Horsepower range	Input stage	Output stage
Diode	—	1 ~ 500	Yes	No
Thyristor	5 ~ 1 000	1 ~ 500	Yes	Yes
Transistor	—	1 ~ 500	No	Yes
GTO	—	5 ~ 500	No	Yes
Triac	1 ~ 5	—	—	—

2.4 PHYSICAL CHARACTERISTICS OF POWER SEMICONDUCTORS

In terms of physical characteristics, the three most commonly used types of power semiconductors are the ① studmounted, ② wafer or "hockey puck," and ③ isolated heat sink types. Their common feature is the need to create physical contact with other devices, called heat sinks, so as to remove internal heat in order to keep the junction temperature within design values. The heat sink absorbs the junction heat and dissipates it via fins, fans, or by liquid cooling. (Liquid cooling is seldom, if ever, used in 600 V-class solid-state AC motor control and will not be covered in this discussion) The differences among the three physical types of power semiconductors have largely to do with how they are mounted and connected to their heat sinks.

2.4.1 Stud mounted Devices

The threaded portion may be a part of the P-N junction or may be electrically isolated from the active electrical parts. In any event, the threaded portion is usually inserted into a threaded hole in the heat sink.

Stud-mounted devices are used as direct power control devices in the smaller-horsepower ratings, and quite often as auxiliary protective devices in larger ratings. In the latter case they are usually mounted directly on the heat sinks that are used with the larger devices, such as the hockey puck design.

2.4.2 Hockey Puck Devices

Typical hockey puck power devices can be diodes, thyristors, or GTOs. Sizes range in diameter from approximately 25 mm(1 in.) up to 100 mm(4 in.). Each flat surface is either the P or the N junction. Both heat transfer and electrical conduction take place from these surfaces.

Hockey puck devices are typically mounted between extruded aluminum heat sinks. Special clamping, joint compounds, and torque wrenches are required to assure optimum heat transfer as well as electrical conductivity.

Since the heat sinks for both stud-mounted and hockey puck devices can also carry the electric current, they must be electrically isolated from their mechanical mountings. Fans can be added to heat sinks to further increase heat removal and allow larger continuous ratings to be achieved.

Since the heat sinks can be at the same voltage level as the power devices, hockey puck and stud-mounted solid-state AC motor controls must be supplied with enclosures. The enclosures must have suitable ventilation openings or heat exchangers so that heat can be removed. It is not usually practical to use these designs in totally enclosed, sealed-off boxes such as NEMA 12 or similar enclosures.

2.4.3 Isolated Heat Sink Devices

Isolated heat sink power semiconductors can be diodes, SCRs. GTOs, transistors, or triacs. Several of the packages contain combinations of devices, internally wired. The distinguishing feature is the term "isolated heat sink." This is the aluminum mounting plate on the bottom of each package. This plate is electrically, but not thermally isolated from the active power devices. Most of the junction heat is transferred to the aluminum plate. The plate, in turn is mounted on a second, larger heat sink plate, which has a finned surface on the opposite side.

Isolated heat sink designs lead themselves to totally enclosed designs. They also have the advantage of prepackaged multiple devices already internally wired. Their chief disadvantage is that the ability to dissipate heat is limited by the bottom mounting plate, so that continuous ratings must be substantially less than the open heat sink-mounted hockey puck devices. Nevertheless the use of isolated heat sink devices is increasing rapidly, both in general applications and in device capabilities.

The arrangement in the upper left corner is unique, as it combines the advantages of the hockey puck (e.g., easy replacement, easy change in rating) with the isolated heat sink concept for totally enclosed designs. It has quite aptly been called the "open brick" model.

2.5 COMMUTATION

Prior to in-depth discussions of actual solid-state AC motor controls, it is important that the concept of commutation and its variations be demystified. The various types of commutation are alluded to throughout all discussions of solid-state motor controls.

Commutation is the process by which load current in a power semiconductor is caused to cease, or to stop flowing, or to be transferred to an alternative path. There are three basic methods of achieving commutation: ① natural or line commutation, ② load commutation, and ③ forced commutation.

2.5.1 Natural or Line Commutation

Fig.2.8 shows a power semiconductor circuit arranged to convert AC to DC. This particular circuit can be shown mathematically to convert three-phase 60 Hz 460 V AC to 600 V DC with a 360 Hz ripple.

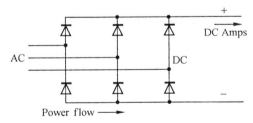

Fig.2.8 AC-to-DC conversion with line commutation

Since the AC line 60 Hz sine wave of voltage passes through zero at the end of each positive and negative half-cycle, the power semiconductors are automatically commutated (turned off) at the end of each half cycle of linevoltage. This is natural or line commutation.

Suppose for the moment that the DC voltage of Fig. 2.8 is imposed on the circuit from a DC source, is of reverse polarity (as in Fig. 2.9),

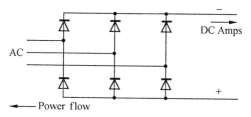

Fig. 2.9 DC-to-AC conversion with line commutation

and that the DC voltage is somewhat higher than 600 V. If the power semiconductors were diodes, a short circuit would result. However, if the devices were thyristors, transistors, or GTOs, since they are in the blocking state until gated on, no power flow would occur, nor would there be a short circuit as in the case of diodes. The devices would see zero voltage (from the line) once each half cycle, so that if they were gated on at any time during each half cycle, the AC line voltage would commutate the devices off at the end of the cycle. This is also natural or line commutation, with power flow from DC to AC.

Fig. 2.10 shows a set of power semiconductors connected in the AC power leads of an AC squirrel cage induction motor. As in Fig. 2.8 and 2.9, the power devices in Fig. 2.10 see a current zero from each cycle of the AC line sine wave. Therefore, the devices can be diodes, thyristors, transistors, GTOs, or triacs. Diodes would be redundant, since they

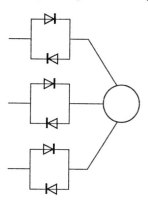

Fig. 2.10 Power semiconductors in the line circuit of an AC squirrel cage motor

act a short between line and motor. Thyristors and triacs would be practical in Fig.2.10, for phase control, because they would be turned off, or commutated, each half cycle of the line voltage. GTOs and transistors would not be required in Fig.2.10 because their inherent turn-off ability is not needed. Fig.2.10 is another example of the use of natural or line commutation.

2.5.2 Load Commutation

Load commutation occurs when the load has certain characteristics that can result in automatic AC voltage zeros, which will cause device commutation or turn-off once each half cycle. A synchronous motor with its DC field supplied from a separate source has the capability of generating the effect of load commutation. To visualize, imagine for the moment that the synchronous motor is being turned by the load and that the DC field is energized.

The motor rotation plus the effect of the DC field results in the generation of sine-wave voltages at the input terminals of the motor. These sine-wave voltages, if connected to power semiconductors, provide commutation or turn-off once each half cycle. This is load commutation and is illustrated in Fig.2.11.

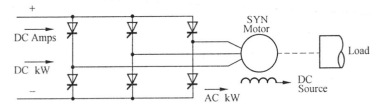

Fig.2.11 Separately excited synchronous motor providing load commutation

The arrangement as shown in Fig.2.11. will not work with a squirrel cage induction motor because the excitation or magnetizing current of the motor comes from the same source as the power component of the line amperes. Special circuitry can be added to the power semiconductor control system to provide a form of load commutation for induction motors once the motor speed has reached a certain value. This can be cost-effective for large induction motors but not generally for motors up to 373 kW at 600 V. Forced-commutation techniques are used with these motors.

2.5.3 Forced commutation

Fig.2.12 shows a squirrel cage induction motor being fed from power semiconductors, which in turn are fed from a DC source. As noted above, the AC squirrel cage motor does not generate a commutation or turn-off sine wave. Suppose that it is desired to switch the power semiconductors on and off in sequence to provide the effect of adjustable frequency to the motor. Forced commutation must then be used to turn off the devices.

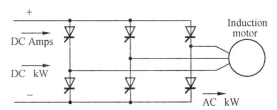

Fig.2.12 Squirrel cage motor fed from a DC source with power semiconductors

If the devices are transistors, the application of a base signal will turn the transistors on. Removal of the base signal will cause commutation turn-off. No other power devices are required for this forced commutation with transistors.

With GTOs, a positive gate pulse will cause turn-on and a negative gate plus will cause commutation or turn-off. As with transistors, no other auxiliary power devices are required for forced commutation.

As noted previously with thyristors, the gate circuit has no effect on turn-off. The forcing of current zero in the anode-cathode circuit must be done by auxiliary power devices in parallel with the anode-cathode circuit. A typical arrangement might include a capacitor and an auxiliary thyristor, as shown in Fig. 2.13. Capacitor C becomes charged when the main thyristor is gated on. The auxiliary thyristor is gated on at the same time as the main thyristor is gated off, so that the capacitor discharge forces a current zero in the anode circuit of the main thyristor.

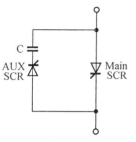

Fig.2.13 Simplified forced commutation circuit for thyristors

2.6 SUMMARY

The three important items to keep in mind when considering the use of power semiconductors in solid-state AC motor control are:

(1) Power semiconductors (diodes, thyristors, GTOs, transistors, and triacs) can be used to control AC voltages, convert AC to DC, change DC back to AC, and to switch DC on and off.

(2) Which type or types of devices are to be used depends on the functions desired and the characteristics of the power circuits on the input and output sides of the devices. The decisions are based largely on the type of commutation that can be used—line, load, or forced.

(3) The physical nature of the devices (stud mounted, hockey puck, or isolated heat sink) and the associated cooling requirements are dictated largely by cost trade-offs and the type of controller enclosure that is required.

With these three criteria and capabilities in mind, let us look next at which devices can do the best job, starting with their use as phase controls for solid-state motor starters.

Vocabulary

1. semiconductor   *n*.   半导体
2. squirrel   *n*.   鼠笼式
3. diode   *n*.   二极管
4. thyristor   *n*.   晶闸管
5. transistor   *n*.   (电子)晶体管
6. triac   *n*.   双向可控硅
7. phase   相位控制
8. silicon   *n*.   硅
9. crystal   *n*.   晶体
10. wafer   *n*.   薄片
11. anode   *n*.   阳极,正极
12. cathode   *n*.   阴极
13. collector   *n*.   集(电)极
14. emitter   *n*.   (发)射极
15. schematic   (电路)原理图符号
16. leakage   漏电流
17. rating   *n*.   额定值,标称值;定额
18. dissipate   *v*.   散发
19. breakdown   *n*.   击穿
20. heat sink   *n*.   散热器
21. self-latching   自锁
22. commutation   *n*.   换向
23. geometry   *n*.   几何结构
24. squeeze   *v*.   压榨,挤,挤榨
25. light-dimmer   调光
26. capability   *n*.   容量
27. studmounted   *adj*.   栓接式
28. hockey puck   *n*.   冰球
29. fin   *n*.   飞边

30. active	adj.	有源的
31. horsepower	n.	马力
32. diameter	n.	直径
33. in.	abbr.	英寸（inch, inches）
34. extruded	adj.	型材的
35. clamp	v.	夹住,夹紧
36. compound	n.	紧密结合
37. wrench	n.	扳手
38. torque	n.	扭矩,转矩
39. enclosure	n.	外(机)壳
40. ventilation	n.	通风,流通空气
41. sealed-off	adj.	密封的
42. thermal	adj.	热的,热量的
43. substantially	adv.	主要地,实质上地
44. aptly	adv.	适当地,适宜地
45. brick	n.	砖,砖块,砖形物
46. demystify	v.	阐明
47. allude	vi.	暗指,间接提到
48. cease	v.	停止,终了
49. line	n.	线电压
50. ripple	n.	脉动,波动
51. redundant	adj.	多余的
52. separately	ad.	单独励磁地
53. synchronous		同步电动机
54. circuitry	n.	电路,线路
55. cost-effective		花费大的
56. capacitor	n.	电容器
57. dictate	v.	确定
58. trade-off		权衡,折衷
59. criteria	n.	标准,判据

Notes:

1. In this chapter we focus on solid-state power devices, or power semiconductors, only as they are being used in the power leads or power circuits to three-phase 460-V ac squirrel cage induction motors for either phase (voltage) control or frequency (speed) control.

本章将集中讨论固态功率器件或功率半导体器件,并且只研究它们在采用相控(电压控制)或频率控制(速度控制)的三相交流鼠笼式感应电机的功率电路中的应用。

2. The commonality of these devices is the use of crystals of silicon in the form of wafers that are layered so as to form various combinations of P - N junction.

这些器件的共性是:利用硅晶体形成的薄片构成 P - N 结的各种组合。

3. The differences among these devices relate to how they go into and out of conduction and in their available ampere and voltage capabilities.

这些器件的区别在于导通和关断的方法及电流和电压的容量。

4. The forward current rating of a diode depends on its size and design, both of which are predicted on the need to dissipate the heat generated within the device so that the maximum junction temperature(usually 200℃)is not exceeded.

二极管正向导通电流的额定值取决于其尺寸和设计,而这二者是根据器件散热的要求来确定的,以保证器件不超过最大结温(通常为 200℃)。

5. This plate is electrically, but not thermally isolated from the active power devices.

这个底板与功率器件之间是导热并绝缘的。

6. Prior to in-depth discussions of actual solid-state AC motor controls, it is important that the concept of commutation and its variations be demystified.

在深入地讨论实际的固态交流电机的控制之前,将换流的概念和种类阐述清楚是必要的。

7. Commutation is the process by which load current in a power semiconductor is caused to cease, or to stop flowing, or to be transferred to an alternative path. There are three basic methods of achieving commutation:(a) natural or line commutation, (b) load commutation, and (c) forced commutation.

换流是功率半导体器件中负载电流被截止或停止流动或转换到另一回

路的过程。有以下三种换流方式:(a)自然或线电压换流、(b)负载换流和(c)强制换流。

8. Which type or types of devices are to be used depends on the functions desired and the characteristics of the power circuits on the input and output sides of the devices.

采用哪种类型的器件取决于要实现的功能和器件输入和输出侧功率电路的特性。

9. The physical nature of the devices (stud mounted, hockey puck, or isolated heat sink) and the associated cooling requirements are dictated largely by cost trade-offs and the type of controller enclosure that is required.

器件的物理特性(栓接式,冰球式,或绝缘散热式)和相关的冷却要求,在很大程度上取决于对成本的权衡考虑和控制器外壳的要求。

3

Analog Electronics

3.1 INTRODUCTION

3.1.1 The Contrast between Analog and Digital Electronics

We have already explored how transistors and diodes are used as switching devices to process information which is represented in digital form. Digital electronics uses transistors as electrically controlled switches: transistors are either saturated or cut off. The active region is used only in transition from one state to the other.

By contrast, analog electronics depends on the active region of transistors and other types of amplifiers. The Greek roots of "analog" mean "in due ratio", signifying in this usage that information is encoded into an electrical signal which is proportional to the quantity being represented.

In Fig.3.1 our information is some sort of music, originating physically in the excitation and resonance's of a musical instrument. The radiated sound consists in the ordered movement of air molecules and is best understood as acoustic waves. These produce motion in the diaphragm of

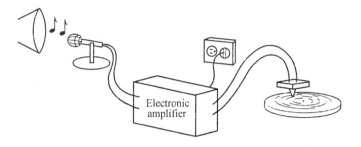

Fig.3.1 Analog system

a microphone, which in turn produces an electrical signal. The variation in the electrical signal are a proportional representation of the sound waves. The electrical signal is amplified electronically, with an increase in signal power occurring at the expense of the input AC power to the amplifier. The amplifier output drives a recording head and produces a wavy groove on a disk. If the entire system is good, every acoustic variation of the air will be recorded on the disk and, when the record is played back through a similar system and the signal reradiated as sound energy by a loudspeaker, the resulting sound should faithfully reproduce the original music.

Electronic systems based on analog principles form an important class of electronic devices. Radio and TV broadcasting are common examples of analog systems, as are many electrical instruments used in monitoring deflection (strain gages, for example), motion (tachometers), and temperature (thermocouples). Many electrical instruments—voltmeters, ohmmeters, ammeters, and oscilloscopes-utilize analog techniques, at least in part.

Analog computers existed before digital computers were developed. In an analog computer, the unknowns in a differential equation are modeled with electrical signals. Such signals are integrated, scaled, and summed electrically to yield solutions with modest effort compared with analytical or numerical techniques.

3.1.2 The Contents Of This Chapter

Analog techniques employ the frequency-domain viewpoint extensively. We begin by expanding our concept of the frequency domain to include periodic, nonperiodic, and random signals. We will see that most analog signals and processes can be represented in the frequency domain. We shall introduce the concept of a spectrum, that is, the representation of a signal as the simultaneous existence of many frequencies. Bandwidth (the width of a spectrum) in the frequency domain will be related to information rate in the time domain.

This expanded concept of the frequency domain also helps us distinguish the effects of linear and nonlinear analog devices. Linear circuits are shown to be capable of "filtering" out unwanted frequency components. By contrast, new frequencies can be created by nonlinear devices such as diodes and transistors. This property allows us to shift analog signals in the frequency domain through AM and FM modulation techniques, which are widely used in public and private communication systems. As an example we shall describe the operation of an AM radio.

Next we study the concept of feedback, a technique by which gain in analog systems is exchanged for other desirable qualities such as linearity or wider bandwidth. Without feedback, analog systems such as audio amplifiers or TV receivers would at best offer poor performance. Understanding of the benefits of feedback provides the foundation for appreciating the many uses of operational amplifiers in analog electronics.

Operational amplifiers (op amps, for short) provide basic building blocks for analog circuits in the same way that NOR and NAND gates are basic building blocks for digital circuits. We will present some of the more common applications of op amps, concluding with their use in analog computers.

3.2 OPERATIONAL-AMPLIFIER CIRCUITS

3.2.1 Introduction

(1) The Importance of OP Amps. An operational amplifier is a high-gain electronic amplifier which is controlled by negative feedback to accomplish many functions or "operations" in analog circuits. Such amplifiers were developed originally to accomplish operations such as integration and summation in analog computers for the solving of differential equations. Applications of op amps have increased until, at the present time, most analog electronic circuits are based on op amp techniques. If, for example, you required an amplifier with a gain of 10, convenience, reliability, and cost considerations would dictate the use of an op amp. Thus op amps form the basic building blocks of analog circuits much as NAND and NOR gates provide the basic building blocks of digital circuits.

(2) An OP-Amp Model Typical Properties. The typical op amp is a sophisticated transistor amplifier utilizing a dozen or more transistors, several diodes, and many resistors. Such amplifiers are mass-produced on semiconductor chips and sell for less than $1 each. These parts are reliable, rugged, and approach the ideal in their electronic properties.

Fig.3.2 shows the symbol and the basic properties of an op amp. The two input voltages, u_+ and u_-, are subtracted and amplified with a large voltage gain, A, typically $10^5 \sim 10^6$. The input resistance, R_i, is large, 100 kΩ ~ 100 MΩ. The output resistance, R_o, is small, 10 ~ 100 Ω. The amplifier is often supplied with DC power from positive ($+U_{CC}$) and negative($-U_{CC}$) power supplies. For this case, the output voltage lies between the power supply voltages, $-U_{CC} < U_o < +U_{CC}$. Sometimes one power connection is grounded (i.e., " $-U_{CC}$" = 0). In this case the output lies in the range, $0 < U_o < +U_{CC}$. The power connections are seldom drawn in circuit diagrams; it is assumed that

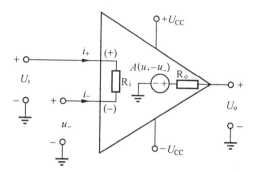

Fig.3.2 Op-amp model

one connects the op amp to the appropriate power source. Thus the op amp approximates an ideal voltage amplifier, having high input resistance, low output resistance, and high gain.

The high gain is converted to other useful features through the use of strong negative feedback. All the benefits of negative feedback are utilized by op-amp circuits. To those listed earlier in this chapter, we would for op-amp circuits add three more: low expense, ease of design, and simple construction.

(3) The Contents of This Section. We begin by analyzing two common op-amp applications, the inverting and the uninverting amplifiers. We derive the gain of these amplifiers by a method that may be applied simply and effectively to any op-amp circuit. We then discuss active filters. which are op amp amplifiers with capacitors added to shape their frequency response. We then deal briefly with analog computers and conclude by discussing some nonlinear applications of op-amps.

3.2.2 Op-Amp Amplifiers

(1) The Inverting Amplifier. The inverting amplifier, shown in Fig. 3.3, uses an op-amp plus two resistors. The positive(+)input to the op-amp is grounded (zero signal); the negative(−)input is connected to the input signal (via R_1) and to the feedback signal from the output (via

R_F). One potential source of confusion in the following discussion is that we must speak of two amplifiers simultaneously. The op amp is an amplifier which forms the amplifying element in a feedback amplifier which contains the op-amp plus the associated resistors. To lessen confusion, we shall reserve the term "amplifier" to apply only to the overall, feedback amplifier. The op-amp will never be call an amplifier; it will be called the op-amp. For example, if we refer to the input current to the amplifier, we are referring to the current through R_1, not the current into the op-amp.

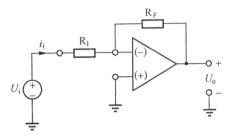

Fig.3.3 Inverting amplifier

We could solve for the gain of the inverting amplifier in Fig.3.3 either by solving the basic circuit laws (KCL and KVL) or by attempting to divide the circuit into main amplifier and feedback system blocks. We shall, however, present another approach based on the assumption that the op-amp gain is very high, effectively infinite. In the following, we shall give a general assumption, which may be applied to any op-amp circuit; then we will apply this assumption specifically to the present circuit. As a result, we will establish the gain and input resistance of the inverting amplifier.

① We assume that the output is well behaved-does not try to go to infinity. Thus we assume that the negative feedback stabilizes the amplifier such that moderate input voltages produce moderate output voltages. If the power supplies are +10 and -10 V, for example, the output would have to lie between these limits.

② Therefore, the input voltage to the op-amp is very small, essentially zero, because it is the output voltage divided by the large voltage gain of the op-amp

$$u_+ - u_- \approx 0 \Rightarrow u_+ \approx u_-$$

For example, if $|U_o| < 10$ V and $A = 10^5$, then $|u_+ - u_-| < 10/10^5 = 100\ \mu$V. Thus normally u_+ and u_- are equal within 100 μV or less, for any op-amp circuit. For the inverting amplifier in Fig.3.3, u_+ is grounded; therefore, $u_- \approx 0$. Consequently, the current at the input to the amplifier would be

$$i_1 = \frac{U_i - u_-}{R_1} \approx \frac{U_i}{R_1} \qquad (3.1)$$

③ Because $u_+ \approx u_-$ and R_i is large, the current into the + and − op-amp inputs will be very small, essentially zero

$$|i_+| = |i_-| = \frac{|u_- - u_+|}{R_i} \approx 0 \qquad (3.2)$$

For example, for $R_i = 100$ kΩ, $|i_-| < 10^{-4}/10^5 = 10^{-9}$ A.

For the inverting amplifier, Eq.(3.2) implies that the current at the input, i_i, flows through R_F, as shown in Fig.3.4. This allows us to compute the output voltage. The voltage across R_F would be $i_i R_F$ and, because one end of R_F is connected to $u_- \approx 0$

$$U_o = -i_i R_F = -\frac{U_i}{R_1} \cdot R_F$$

Thus the voltage gain would be

$$A_u = \frac{U_o}{U_i} = -\frac{R_F}{R_1} \qquad (3.3)$$

The minus sign in the gain expression means that the output will be inverted relative to the input: a positive signal at the input will produce a negative signal at the output, Eq.(3.3) shows the gain to depend

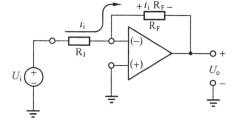

Fig.3.4 The input current flows through the feedback circuit

on the ratio of R_F to R_1. This would imply that only the ratio and not the individual values of R_F to R_1 matter. This would be true if the input resistance to the amplifier were unimportant, but the input resistance to an amplifier is often critical. The input resistance to the inverting amplifier would follow from Eq.(3.1);

$$R_i = \frac{U_i}{i_i} \approx R_1 \tag{3.4}$$

For a voltage amplifier, the input resistance is an important factor, for if R_i were too low the signal source (of U_i) could be loaded down by R_i. Thus in a design, R_1 must be sufficiently high to avoid his loading problem. Once R_1 is fixed, R_F may be selected to achieve the required gain. Thus the values of individual resistors become important because they affect the input resistance to the amplifier.

Let us design an inverting amplifier to have a gain of -8. The input signal is to come from a voltage source having an output resistance of 100 Ω. To reduce loading, the input resistor, R_1, must be much larger than 100 Ω. For a 5% loading reduction, we would set $R_1 = 2\ 000\ \Omega$. To achieve a gain of -8 (actually 95% of -8, considering loading), we require that $R_F = 8 \times 2\ 000 = 16\ k\Omega$.

Feedback effects dominate the characteristics of the amplifier. When an input voltage is applied, the value of u_- will increase. This will cause U_o to increase rapidly in the negative direction. This negative voltage will increase to the value where the effect of U_o on the $-$ input via R_F cancels the effect of U_i through R_1. Put another way, the output will adjust itself to withdraw through R_F any current that U_i injects through R_1, since the input current to the op-amp is extremely small. In this way the output depends only on R_F and R_1.

(2) The Noninverting Amplifier. For the noninverting amplifier shown in Fig.3.5 the input is connected to the + input. The feedback

from the output connects still to the − op amp input, as required for negative feedback. To determine the gain, we apply the assumptions outlined above.

① Because $u_+ \approx u_-$, it follows that

$$u_- \approx U_i \quad (3.5)$$

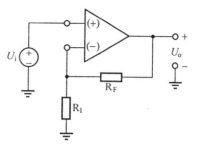

Fig.3.5 Noninverting amplifier

② Because $i_- \approx 0$, R_F and R_1 carry the same current. Hence U_o is related to u_- through a voltage-divider relationship

$$u_- = U_o \frac{R_1}{R_1 + R_F} \quad (3.6)$$

Combining Eqs.(3.5) and (3.6), we establish the gain to be

$$U_i = U_o \frac{R_1}{R_1 + R_F} = A_u = +(1 + \frac{R_F}{R_1}) \quad (3.7)$$

The + sign before the gain expression emphasizes that the output of the amplifier has the same polarity as the input: a positive input signal produces a positive output signal. Again we see that the ratio of R_F and R_1 determines the gain of the amplifier.

When a voltage is applied to the amplifier, the output voltage increases rapidly and will continue to rise until the voltage across R_1 reaches the input voltage. Thus little input current will flow into the amplifier, and the gain depends only on R_F and R_1. The input resistance to the noninverting amplifier will be very high because the input current to the amplifier is also the input current to the op-amp, i_+, which must be extremely small. Input resistance values exceeding 1 000 MΩ are easily achieved with this circuit. This feature of high input resistance is an important virtue of the noninverting amplifier.

3.2.3 Active Filters

(1) What Are Active Filters? An active filter combines amplification

with filtering. The RC filters we investigated earlier are called passive filters because they provide only filtering. An active filter uses an op-amp to furnish gain but has capacitors added to the input and feedback circuits to shape the filter characteristics.

We derived earlier the gain characteristic of an inverting amplifier in the time domain. In Fig. 3.6 we show the frequency-domain version. We may easily translate the earlier derivation into the frequency domain

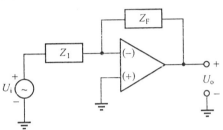

Fig.3.6 Active filter circuit.

$$U_i \Rightarrow \underline{U}_i(\omega) \qquad U_o \Rightarrow \underline{U}_o(\omega)$$

$$A_u = -\frac{R_F}{R_1} \Rightarrow \underline{F}_u(\omega) = -\frac{\underline{Z}_F(\omega)}{\underline{Z}_1(\omega)}$$

The filter function, $F_u(\omega)$, is thus the ratio of the two impedances, and in general will give gain as well as filtering. We could have written the minus sign as 180°, for in the frequency domain the inversion is equivalent to a phase shift of 180°.

(2) Low-Pass Filter. Placing a capacitor in parallel with R_F (see Fig.3.7) will at high frequencies tend to lower Z_F and hence the gain of the amplifier; consequently, this capacitor converts an inverting amplifier into a low-pass filter with gain. We may write

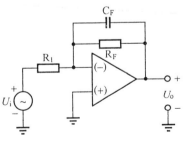

Fig.3.7 Low-pass filter circuit

$$\underline{Z}_F(\omega) = R_F \parallel \frac{1}{j\omega C_F} = \frac{1}{(1/R_F) + j\omega C_F} = \frac{R_F}{1 + j\omega R_F C_F} \quad (3.8)$$

Thus the gain would be

$$\underline{F}_u = -\frac{R_F}{R_1}\frac{1}{1 + j\omega R_F C_F} = A_u \frac{1}{1 + j(\omega/\omega_c)} \quad (3.9)$$

where $A_u = -R_F/R_1$, the gain without the capacitor, and $\omega_c = 1/R_F C_F$ would be the cutoff frequency. The gain of the amplifier is approximately constant until the frequency exceeds ω_c, after which the gain decreases with increasing ω. The Bode plot of this filter function is shown in Fig. 3.8 for the case where $R_F = 10$ kΩ, $R_1 = 1$ kΩ, and $C_F = 1$ μF.

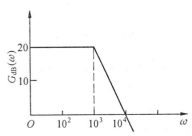

Fig. 3.8 Bode plot for active low-pass filter

(3) High-Pass Filter. The high-pass filter shown in Fig. 3.9 uses a capacitor in series with R1 to reduce the gain at low frequencies. The details of the analysis will be left to a problem. The gain of this filter is

$$\underline{F}_u(\omega) = -\frac{R_F}{R_1}\frac{j(\omega/\omega_c)}{1 + j(\omega/\omega_c)} = A_u \frac{j(\omega/\omega_c)}{1 + j(\omega/\omega_c)}$$

where $A_u = -R_F/R_1$ is the gain without the capacitor and $\omega_c = 1/R_1 C_1$ is the cutoff frequency, below which the amplifier gain is reduced. The Bode plot of this filter characteristic is shown in Fig. 3.10.

(4) Other Active Filter. By using more advanced techniques, one can simulate RLC narrowband filters and, by using additional op-amps, many sophisticated filter charac-

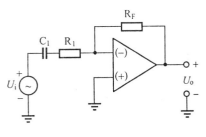

Fig. 3.9 High-pass filter circuit

teristics can be achieved. Discussion of such applications lies beyond the scope of this text, but there exist many handbooks showing circuits and giving design information about active filters.

3.2.4 Analog Computers

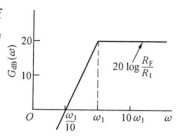

Fig. 3.10 Bode plot for active high-pass filter

Often a differential equation is solved by integration. The integration may be accomplished by analytical methods or by numerical methods on a digital computer. Integration may also be performed electronically with an op-amp circuit. Indeed, op-amps were developed initially for electronic integration of differential equations.

(1) An Integrator. The op-amp circuit in Fig.3.11 uses negative feedback through a capacitor to perform integration.

We have charged the capacitor in the feedback path to an initial value of U_1, and then removed this prebias voltage at $t = 0$. Let us examine the initial state of the circuit before investigating what will happen after the switch is opened. Since u_+ is approximately zero, so will be u_-,

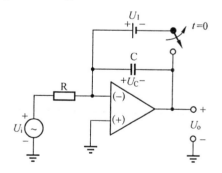

Fig.3.11 Integrator circuit

and hence the output voltage is fixed at $-U_1$. The input current to amplifier, U_i/R, will flow through the U_1 voltage source and into the output of the op-amp. Thus the output voltage will remain at $-U_1$ until the switch is opened.

After the switch is opened at $t = 0$, the input current will flow through the capacitor and hence the U_C will be

$$U_C(t) = U_o(0) + \int_0^t \frac{U_i(t')}{RC} dt'$$

Thus the output voltage of the circuit is

$$U_o(t) = - U_C(t) = - U_1 - \frac{1}{RC}\int_0^t U_i(t')dt' \quad t \gg 0 \quad (3.10)$$

Except for the minus sign, the output is the integral of U_i scaled by $1/RC$, which may be made equal to any value we wish by proper choice of R and C.

(2) Scaling and Summing. We need two other circuits to solve simple differential equations by analog computer methods. Scaling refers to multiplication by a constant, such as

$$U_2 = \pm KU_1$$

where K is a constant. This is the equation of an amplifier, and hence we would use the inverting amplifier in Fig.3.3 for the $-$ sign or the noninverting amplifier in Fig.3.5 for the $+$ sign.

A summer produces the weighted sum of two or more signals. Fig.3.12 shows a summer with two inputs. We may understand the oper-

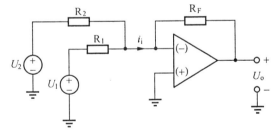

Fig.3.12 Summer circuit

ation of the circuit by applying the same reasoning we used earlier to understand the inverting amplifier. Since $u_- \approx 0$, the sum of the currents through R_1 and R_2 is

$$i_i = \frac{U_1}{R_1} + \frac{U_2}{R_2} \quad (3.11)$$

The output voltage will adjust itself to draw this current through RF, and hence the output voltage will be

$$U_o = -i_i R_F = -\left(U_1 \cdot \frac{R_F}{R_1} + U_2 \cdot \frac{R_F}{R_2}\right)$$

The output will thus be the sum of U_1 and U_2, weighted by the gain factors, R_F/R_1 and R_F/R_2, respectively. If the inversion produced by the summer is unwanted, the summer can be followed by an inverted, a scalier with a gain of -1. Clearly, we could add other inputs in parallel with R_1 and R_2. In the example to follow, we shall sum three signals to solve a second order differential equation.

(3) Solving a DE. Let us design an analog computer circuit to solve the differential equation

$$2\frac{d^2 u}{dt^2} + 4\frac{du}{dt} + u = 6\cos 10t \quad t > 0$$

$$u(0) = -2 \quad \text{and} \quad \frac{du}{dt} = +3 \text{ at } t = 0$$

(3.12)

Moving everything except the highest-order derivative to the right side yields

$$\frac{d^2 u}{dt^2} = -2\frac{du}{dt} - \frac{u}{2} + 3\cos 10t \quad (3.13)$$

The circuit which solves Eq. (3.12) is shown in Fig. 3.13. The circuit consists of two integrators to integrate the left side of Eq. (3.13), a summer to represent the right side, and two inverts to correct the signs. The noninverting inputs are grounded, and the inputs and feedback are connected to the inverting input of the op-amps. Hence we have shown only the inverting inputs. With $d^2 u/dt^2$ the input to the integrators, the output of the first integrator will be $-du/dt$ [with the battery giving the initial condition of 3 V, as in Eq. (3.13)], and hence the output of the second integrator will be $+u$ (with an initial condition of -2 V). This output is fed into the summer, along with du/dt after inversion, and the driving function $\cos 10\ t$, which must also be inverted to cancel the in-

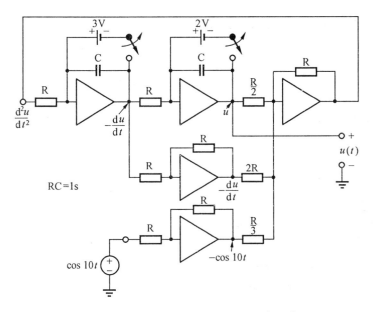

Fig.3.13 Analog computer to solve Eq.(3.12)

version in the summer. The input resistors connecting the three signals into the summer produce the weighting factors in Eq.(3.13), and hence the output of the summer represents the right side of Eq.(3.13). We therefore connect that output to our "input" of d^2u/dt^2 to satisfy Eq. (3.12). To observe the solution to Eq.(3.12), we merely open the switches at $t = 0$.

Clearly, these techniques can be applied to higher-order equations. Sophisticated use of analog computer requires a variety of refinements. Often, the equations being solved are scaled in time (time is sped up or slowed down on the computer) to accommodate realistic resistor and capacitor values. Also, voltage and current values can be scaled to bring the unknowns within the allowable range of the computer. In the next section we show how nonlinear operations can be introduced to solve nonlinear differential equations by analog methods.

3.2.5 Nonlinear Applications of Op-amps

Op-amps can be combined with nonlinear circuit elements such as diodes and transistors to produce a variety of useful circuits. Below we discuss a few such applications. Many more circuits are detailed in standard handbooks and manufacturers' application literature for their products.

An Improved Half-Wave Rectifier. The op-amp in Fig 3.14 drives a half-wave rectifier. When the input voltage is negative the output of the op amp will be negative and the diode will be OFF;

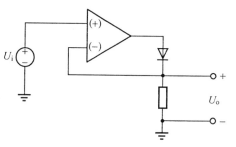

Fig.3.14 Improved half-wave rectifier

hence the output will be zero. When the output is positive the diode will turn ON and the output will be identical to the input, because the circuit will perform as a non-inverting amplifier shown in Fig.3.5 with $R_F = 0$. Use of the op amp effectively reduces the diode turn-on voltage. If the input voltage is greater than $0.7/A$, where A is the voltage gain of the op-amp, the output voltage exceed 0.7 V and turn on the diode. Hence the turn-on voltage is effectively reduced from $0.7 \sim 0.7/ A$.

This circuit would not be used in a power supply circuit; rather, it would be used in a detector or other circuit processing small signals. where the turn-on voltage of the diode would be a problem.

Vocabulary

1. analog electronics 　　　　　模拟电子学
2. explore　　　　　 v. 　　　研究
3. digital electronics　　　　　　数字电子学
4. switch　　　　　　 n. 　　　开关

5. saturate	v.	使饱和
6. active region		动态区域
7. due	adj.	应得的
8. ratio	n.	比,比率
9. signify	v.	表示
10. encode	v.	编码
11. resonance	n.	共鸣
12. radiated	v.	传播
13. molecule	n.	分子
14. acoustic wave		声波
15. diaphragm	n.	振动膜
16. wavy groove		起伏的沟槽
17. disk	n.	磁盘,磁碟片
18. loudspeaker	n.	扩音器,喇叭
19. microphone	n.	扩音器,麦克风
20. deflection	n.	挠度,挠曲
21. strain gage		应变计量器
22. tachometer	n.	转速计
23. thermocouple	n.	热电偶
24. oscilloscope	n.	示波器
25. analytical	adj.	解析的
26. numerical	adj.	数值的
27. integrate	v.	求……的积分
28. scale	v.	改变比例
29. frequency-domain		频域
30. random	adj.	随机的
31. audio	adj.	音频的
32. operation amplifier		运算放大器
33. summation	n.	求和,加法
34. sophisticated	adj.	复杂的,完善的

35. mass-produce　　　　v.　　大量生产
36. subtract　　　　　　v.　　减去，减
37. inverting amplifier　　　　反相放大器
38. uninverting amplifier　　　同相放大器
39. derive　　　　　　　v.　　推导
40. active filter　　　　　　　有源滤波器
41. stabilize　　　　　　v.　　使稳定
42. moderate　　　　　　adj.　适度的，适中的
43. virtue　　　　　　　n.　　优点
44. amplification　　　　n.　　扩大
45. capacitor　　　　　　n.　　电容器
46. impedance　　　　　n.　　阻抗
47. bode plot　　　　　　　　波特图
48. simulate　　　　　　v.　　模拟，仿真
49. narrowband filter　　　　　带通滤波器
50. low-pass filter　　　　　　低通滤波器
51. high-pass filter　　　　　 高通滤波器
52. differential equation　　　 微分方程
53. prebias　　　　　　　n.　　预偏置
54. summer　　　　　　　n.　　加法器
55. weighted　　　　　　adj.　加权的
56. refinement　　　　　　n.　　改进
57. accommodate　　　　　v.　　适应

Notes:

1. The Greek roots of "analog" mean "in due ratio", signifying in this usage that information is encoded into an electrical signal which is proportional to the quantity being represented.

希腊词根"analog"的含义是"以一定的比例"，在这里表示信息被编码成为与被表达量成比例的电信号。

2. The electrical signal is amplified electronically, with an increase in signal power occurring at the expense of the input ac power to the amplifier.

电信号被用电子的方法放大,即利用输入放大器的交流电能将信号的功率放大。

3. Radio and TV broadcasting are common examples of analog systems, as are many electrical instruments used in monitoring deflection (strain gages, for example), motion (tachometers), and temperature (thermocouples).

收音机和电视的播放是模拟系统的典型例子,许多电子仪器也是模拟系统,它们的应用领域包括偏差检测(应变计量器)、运动控制(测速机)和温度测量(热电耦)。

4. In an analog computer, the unknowns in a differential equation are modeled with electrical signals. Such signals are integrated, scaled, and summed electrically to yield solutions with modest effort compared with analytical or numerical techniques.

在模拟计算机中,微分方程的未知量被用电信号来模拟。这些信号被用电子的方法积分、比例变换和求和以获得方程的解,比起解析或数值运算的求解方法要容易一些。

5. We shall introduce the concept of a spectrum, that is, the representation of a signal as the simultaneous existence of many frequencies.

我们将介绍频谱的概念,也就是,用同时存在的许多频率来表达一个信号。

6. Operational amplifiers (op amps, for short) provide basic building blocks for analog circuits in the same way that NOR and NAND gates are basic building blocks for digital circuits.

运算放大器(缩写为 op amps)是模拟电路的基本构成单元,正如 NOR 和 NAND 门电路为数字电路的基本单元一样。

7. An operational amplifier is a high-gain electronic amplifier which is controlled by negative feedback to accomplish many functions or "operations" in analog circuits.

运算放大器是一个受负反馈控制的高增益的电子放大器,用来在模拟电路中完成许多运算功能。

8. An active filter uses an op-amp to furnish gain but has capacitors added to the input and feedback circuits to shape the filter characteristics.

有源滤波器用一个放大器来提供增益,同时在输入和反馈电路中加入电容以改变滤波特性。

4

Digital Electronics

4.1 THE DIGITAL IDEA

4.1.1 What Is a Digital Signal

(1) A Historical Example. "Listen my children and you shall hear/ Of the midnight ride of Paul Revere..." According to Longfellow's poem, Paul Revere was sent riding through the New England countryside by a signal from the bell tower of the Old North Church in Boston. "One if by land and two if by sea." That is, one light was to be displayed if the British forces were advancing toward Concord by the road from Boston, and two lights were to be displayed if they were crossing the Mystic River to take an indirect route.

The message received by the Patriot was coded in digital form. We would say today that the two "bits" of information were conveyed by the code (strictly speaking, two bits could indicate four possible message and would require distinguishable lights, say one red and one white). The first light signaled that the British were advancing. The second light indicated by what route they were coming. Because only two routes of advance were envisioned, this second bit of information could be interpreted as indicating one of the two routes.

Information can be communicate in digital form if the massage is capable of being defined by a series of yes/no statements. There can be only two states of each variable used in conveying the information. Reducing information to a series of yes/no statements might appear to be a severe limitation on this method, but the method is in fact quite powerful. Numbers can be represented in base 2 and the alphabet by a digital code. Indeed, any situation with a finite number of outcomes can be reduced to a digital code. Specifically, n digital bits can represent 2^n states of possible outcomes. Digital communication takes a well-defined code known to the parties at both ends, as in our historical example.

(2) Analysis of the Revere Communication Code. In order to fix further the idea of digital information, we shall define two digital variables which describe the Paul Revere communication system, Let B describe whether the British are coming, and L describe the route by which they are coming, provide that they are coming. The mathematical variables, B and L, are unusual mathematical variables because each can have only two values. We may call those two values by any names we wish: yes/no, true/false, one/zero, high/low, even black/white. When this type of mathematics was used primarily for analysis of philosophical arguments through symbolic logic, the values of the variables were called true or false, according to the validity of the logical propositions being represented. Recently, the names one/zero have come to be preferred by engineers and programmers dealing with digital codes. These names have the obvious advantage of fitting with the binary (base2) number system for representation of numerical information, but these names occasionally lend confusion to the discussion of digital systems. Nevertheless, we shall use

1/0 of one/zero as our two possible states of the digital variables B and L. Thus the definitions of B and L are

$B = 1$ if the British are coming

$B = 0$ if the British are not coming

$L = 1$ if coming by sea

$L = 0$ if coming by land

The first light (B) uniquely determines if he should ride. When the first light appears, he mounts his horse. But he cannot leave until the second light (L) appears (or fails to appear), for the second light reveals the route of the British and hence defines in part the message to be announced.

(3) Representing Digital Information Electrically. In digital electronics, digital variables are represented by logic levels. At any given time, a voltage is expected to have one value or another, or more precisely to lie within one region or another. In a typical system, a voltage between 0 and 0.8 V would be considered a digital zero, a voltage between 0.8 ~ 2 V would be forbidden; that is if the voltage fell within this range, you would know that the digital equipment needs repair. These definitions are shown in Fig.4.1.

As an illustration of a digital circuit, we shall consider the amplifier-switch as a NOT circuit. The output of a NOT circuit is the digital complement, or the opposite, of the input. First we shall represent the definition of the NOT circuit with a truth table. This is shown in Fig.4.2: A represents the input, which may be either 1 or 0; B represents the output, which may also be 1 or 0, but depends upon the input. The NOT, or logical complement, operation is indicated algebraically by the equation under the truth table.

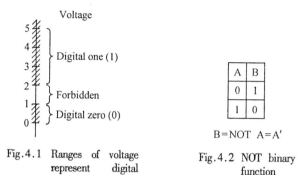

Fig.4.1 Ranges of voltage represent digital ones and zeros

Fig.4.2 NOT binary function

We shall now define logic levels for the amplifier-switch such that it performs the NOT function. The input-output characteristic of the circuit is repeated in Fig.4.3. Clearly, we wish 10 V to be in the region for a 1 and 0.7 V to be in the region for a 0. That is if the input were 10 V (digital 1), the output should be less than 0.7 V (digital 0), and vice versa. Hence we might consider making the region for a digital 0 to be from 0 ~ 1 V, and the region for a digital 1 to be, say, from 8 ~ 10 V. This will work but leaves insufficient range for a working digital system. That is, it is desirable to broaden the range of values in the regions for 1 and 0 to allow for variations in transistors, power supply voltage, noise that might get mixed in with the signal, and the like. In the present case, we can by trail and error determine that the region 0 ~ 1.5 V as a digital 0 works well with 5 ~ 10 V as a digital 1; with these definitions the circuit operates as a NOT circuit, that is, it performs the logical complement. These logic levels are shown in Fig.4.4.

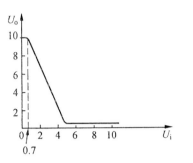 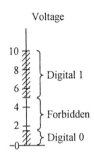

Fig.4.3 Amplifier-switch input-output characteristic

Fig.4.4 Digital definitions for amplifier-switch

4.1.2 Digital Representation of Information

(1) An Elevator Door Controller. Having explained the nature of digital signals, how digital information is represented electrically, and how transistor circuits have the possibility of performing digital operations, we turn to a more complete example showing how to represent a situation in digital form. Our purpose is to introduce the AND and OR digital functions and to illustrate further the language and mathematics of the digital approach.

The door on a typical elevator has a timer on it which closes the door automatically if no one enters the elevator and pushes a button for another floor. It also has an "electric eye" to prevent the door from closing on a passenger. Let us represent a command to the door-closing mechanism with the binary variable D (D = 1 if the door is to close). The state of the door(D) will be controlled by three binary variables: T represents the state of the timer (T = 1 means that the timer is running, time has not yet elapsed); B represents the results of someone's pushing a button for another floor (B = 1 means that a button has been pushed); and S represents the state of the safety device (S = 1 means that someone is in the door). We see that D is the dependent variable and is a function of three independent variables (T, B, and S). Keep in mind that these are all binary variables and hence can be only 1 or 0.

$$D = f(T,B,S)$$

How might such a mathematical function be described? One useful method for describing a binary function is a truth table, as shown in Fig. 4.5. Here we have enumerated all possible combination of the independent variables and shown the appropriate value of the dependent variable. In general, when there are n independent variables, each having two possible states, there will be 2^n possible combinations (2^3 in this case), which may be enumerated to define the function. The truth table offers a systematic form for displaying such an enumeration. The name truth table originated historically from the application of this type of representation to the systematic investigation of logical arguments. Because of these association, digital circuits are often called logic circuits.

(2) A Truth-Table Representation. Fig.4.5 presents the truth table for the elevator door function. Let us see how we determined the 1's and 0's in Fig.4.5. The 1's and 0's in the first three columns resulted from a systematic counting of the eight possibilities, or states. We call it "counting" because the pattern we have used constitute counting in the base 2 number system. However you think of it, the pattern is clear: we alternated the 1's and 0's fastest for S, slower for B, and slowest for T, thus covering all possible combinations. These represent the values of our independent variables. For filling out the 1's and 0's in the last column, we looked first at the S column, which represents the safety switch. We do not want the door to close when the safety switch indicates that someone stands in the door (S = 1), so we put 0 in the D column (D = 0

T	B	S	D
0	0	0	1
0	0	1	0
0	1	0	1
0	1	1	0
1	0	0	0
1	0	1	0
1	1	0	1
1	1	1	0

Fig .4.5 Truth table for elevator door controller

means do not close the door) for every 1 in the S column. This accounts of four of the eight states. The other four states depend on the button and the timer. If $S = 0$ (nothing blocking the door), the door should close if either the button is pushed ($B = 1$) or the timer expires ($T = 0$). We examine the remaining four states and put a 1 in column D if there is a 1 in the B column or a 0 in the T column. Using this rule, we find three combinations leading to the closing of the door. The first, all 0's, represents the timer running out to close of the door. The second represents a button being pushed and the timer running out simultaneously, and the third represent a button being pushed before the timer runs out. Of course, in all three cases the safety mechanism allows the door to close.

(3) The NOT Function. The truth-table method is a brute-force way for describing a binary function. The same information can be represent algebraically through the AND, OR, and NOT binary functions. Consider first the NOT function, the logical complement, described in the truth table of Fig.4.2. The NOT function is involved in this problem because NOT S allows the door to close, and NOT T prompts the closing of the door by timers. The NOT S function is represented algebraically by a prime added to the variable or expression to be NOTed: S' means NOT S. We need the NOT when a 0 is to trigger the OR or AND combinations because these trigger on a 1.

(4) The OR Function. The OR binary function is defined in Fig.4.6. The dependent variable, $C = A$ OR B , is 1 when either A or B (or both) is (are) 1. This is thus the inclusive OR because it includes the case where both A and B are 1. The OR function is involved in our elevator problem in describing the combined effect on the timer and the button. We wish the door to get the signal to close when the timer elapses ($T = 0$)

C=A OR B

A	B	C
0	0	0
0	1	1
1	0	1
1	1	1

Fig .4.6 OR function

OR the button is pushed (B = 1) or both. The way to express this algebraically is T' OR B. The truth table for this function is shown in Fig. 4.7. In constructing the truth table in Fig. 4.7, we added a NOT T column. Then we put a 1 in the last column wherever there was a 1 in either of the previous two columns because these are the variables we are ORing.

(5) The AND Function. Next we need to account for the safety switch. The AND function is required because we must express the simultaneous occurrence of an impulse to close the door and the lack of an obstacle in the door. The truth table for the AND function appeared in Fig. 4.8. Here we get a 1 only when both A and B are 1. To complete the truth table for our door-closing variable (D), we must AND S' with the last column in Fig. 4.7 in order to cover all the possibilities. Thus we may state the door-closing function as

T' OR B

T	T'	B	
0	1	0	1
0	1	1	1
1	0	0	0
1	0	1	1

Fig. 4.7 Binary function T' OR B

C = A AND B

A	B	C
0	0	0
0	1	0
1	0	0
1	1	1

Fig. 4.8 AND function

$$D = (T' \text{ OR } B) \text{ AND } (S') \qquad (4.1)$$

When interpreted as a binary or logical function, Eq. (4.1) states algebraically the same information as the truth table in Fig. 4.5, which we worked out by considering all possible combinations. We have now introduced a method of representing information in digital form and we have defined some basic logic relationships. We turn next to describing how electrical circuits can perform logical operations such as AND and OR.

4.2 ASYNCHRONOUS DIGITAL SYSTEMS

4.2.1 Logic Symbols and Logic families

(1) Logic Symbols. Digital systems consist of vast numbers of NAND, NOR, and NOT gates, plus memory and timing circuits which we will discuss later, all interconnected to perform some useful task, such as count and display time, measure a voltage, or perform arithmetic operations. If we were to draw a circuit diagram for such a system, including all the resistors, diodes, transistors, and interconnections, we would face an overwhelming task, and an unnecessary one. The task would be unnecessary because anyone who read the circuit diagram would in their mind group the components together into standard circuits and think in terms of the "system" functions of the individual gates. For this reason, we design and draw digital circuits with standard logic symbols, as shown in Fig.4.9(The + (OR) and · (AND) markings in the gates are optional. The shape of the gate symbol defines its function). The small circle at the output indicates the inversion of the signal. Thus without the small circle, the triangle would represent an amplifier (or buffer) with a gain of unity, and the second symbol would indicate an OR gate. As shown above, however, the common circuits are those which invert. These logic symbols show only the input and output connections. The actual gates, when wired into a digital circuit, would have power supply (U_{CC}) and grounding connections as well. Fig.4.10 shows the connections for a quadruple, two-input NAND gate. Notice that the output power is applied between pins 14 and 7 with

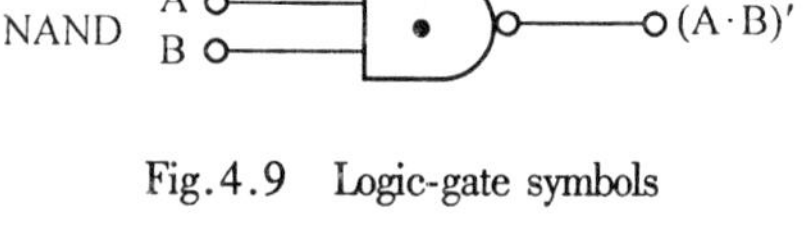

Fig.4.9 Logic-gate symbols

7 grounded.

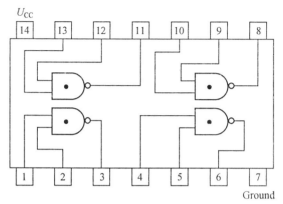

Fig.4.10 Quad-NAND chip

(2) Logic Families. If you wished to construct a digital circuit, you would not assemble a pile of diodes, resistors and proceed to wire them together, first into standard gate circuits, then into larger functions. You would purchase the gates already fabricated on an integrated circuit(IC), and packaged within a plastic capsule. This commercial IC "chip" includes four NAND gates packaged together. An important part of the design would be to select a particular "logic family," depending on the nature and working environment of your eventual product. The logic families are composed of a large selection of compatible circuits which can be connected together to make digital systems. The logic families differ in the details of circuits used to perform the logical operations. Here are some of the logic families.

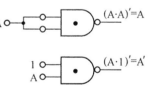

Fig.4.11 NOT from a NAND

① Diode-transistor logic (DTL) circuits are now obsolete. We used this simple type of logic only to illustrate the principles of logic gates.

② High threshold logic (HTL) circuits are similar to DTL gates but include a zener diode in place of the two series diodes, and use a larger power supply voltage, U_{CC}. The zener diode raises the threshold level for switching the transistor and hence separates the voltage regions for a 1 and 0 by a large margin, say 10 V. This logic family is useful where electrical noise is a problem, to prevent moderate noise signals, which might leak into the circuit, from affecting the circuit as valid digital signals. If, for example, your circuit must operate adjacent to a large dc motor or an arc welding machine, you would use HTL circuits.

③ Transistor-transistor logic (TTL) circuits use special-purpose transistors in place of the diodes. These circuits are widely used because they switch rapidly, require modest power to operate, and are inexpensive. The circuits used in this logic family are considerably more complicated than the DTL circuits.

④ Complementary metal-oxide semiconductor (CMOS) logic circuits use field-effect transistors (FETs), which differ from the type of transistors. These circuits require very little power to operate and are used where low power consumption is an important requirement, as in battery-operated calculators.

⑤ Emitter-coupled logic (ECL) gates switch very fast and are used in high-speed circuits such as high-frequency counters.

There are even more logic families than these. The design of logic circuits is highly sophisticated, and specialists in this area must become intimately familiar with all the possible products and logic families which are available at a given time.

4.2.2 Realization of Logic Functions

(1) The NOT Function. Often when a NOT circuit is required, the designer will make one out of a NOR or a NAND circuit. Fig. 4.11 shows the two ways to make a NOT (or inverter) out of a NAND circuit. The input to be fixed at a digital 1 in the lower realization would be attached to

the U_{CC} power supply through a resistor. Similarly, if one required an input to be fixed at 0, this input would be grounded. Grounding an input can be used to realize the NOT function with a NOR gate, which we will leave for a practice problem at the end of the chapter.

(2) Realizing the Elevator Door Function. In Section 4.1.2 we derived a logical expression for closing an elevator door (D = 1 means close) based on a timer (T = 1 means the timer is still running, do not close the door), a button switch (B = 1 means someone has pushed the button for another floor, close the door), and a safety device (S = 1 means that someone is blocking the door, do not close the door). The logical expression, recast into the notation we have developed, is given in Fig.4.12. We first shall realize the function with NAND and/or NOR gates. The realization in Fig.4.12 utilizes six gates: one NOR, one NAND, and four NOTs, which were accomplished with NANDs. This realization is based on direct translation of the logical expression into logic-gate symbols.

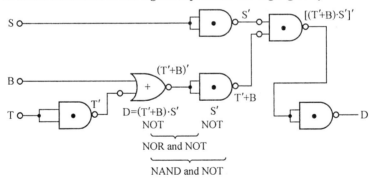

Fig.4.12 Straight forward realization of elevator door function using NAND and NOR gates

We may accomplish a simpler realization by manipulating the expression for D into a more convenient form. Eq.(4.2) shows such a manipulation.

$$D = [[(T' + B) \cdot S']']' = [(T' + B)' + S'']' =$$

$$[(T'+B)'+S]' \quad (4.2)$$

In Eq. (4.2) the first form is the same expression for D as in Fig.4.12, except that we NOTed it twice. We do this because we want the final result for D to be primed, that is, to be the NOT of something. This is required if we are to realize the final operation with a NOR or NAND gates. The second form results from using De Morgan's theorem to distribute one of the NOTs to the individual terms. The third form is the same as the second, except that we have removed the double complement from S. This final form proves convenient for realization with NOR gates. Fig.4.13 shows the realization. Note that we made a NOT out of NOR similar to the way we realized a NOT with a NAND earlier. De Morgan's theorem thus leads to a simpler realization.

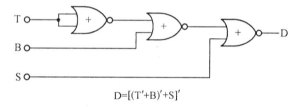

$D=[(T'+B)'+S]'$

Fig.4.13 Simple realization of the elevator door function using NOR gates

4.3 SEQUENTIAL DIGITAL SYSTEMS

The logic circuits in Sec. 4.2 are called combinational circuits because the output responds immediately to the inputs and there is no memory. When memory is a part of a logic circuit, the system is called sequential because its output depends on the input plus its history. In this section we show how memory is developed in logic circuits and how memory elements increase greatly the possible applications of logic circuits.

4.3.1 The Bitable Circuit

The basic memory circuit is the bitable circuit, which we examine in this section. In Fig. 4.14 we show two amplifier-switch circuits in cascade, the output of the first (T_1) providing the input to the second (T_2). This is called a two-stage amplifier, for amplification takes place in two distinct stages. Each of these stages is identical to the original amplifier-switch.

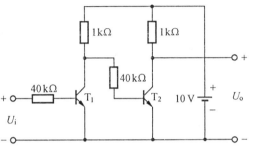

Fig. 4.14 Two-stage amplifier

Placing the two stages of amplification in cascade requires that we consider the output of the first stage as the input of the second stage. In Fig. 4.15 we have shown the overall input-output characteristic of input voltage starting with zero volts. With zero volts input, the first transistor (T_1) will be cut off and the second transistor (T_2) will be saturated.

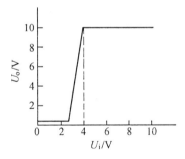

Fig. 4.15 Input-output characteristic of two-stage amplifier

As the input voltage rises, the first transistor will leave cutoff as the input voltage rises above 0.7 V, but the second transistor will remain saturated until the output of the first stage drops to about 4 V. This output of 4 V requires an input of about 3 V; hence the input must increase to approximately 3 V before come out of saturation and the output voltage of the entire two-stage amplifier begins to rise. In this region, both transistors are in the active region and the output rises rapidly. The second transistor will reach cutoff when the output of the first transistor falls below 0. 7 V, which will occur when the input of exceeds about 4 V. Thus both transistors are in the active region for the range of input voltages between 3 and 4 V.

What will happen if we connect the output of the two-stage amplifier to its input? Fig.4.16(a) shows the circuit redrawn with this connection

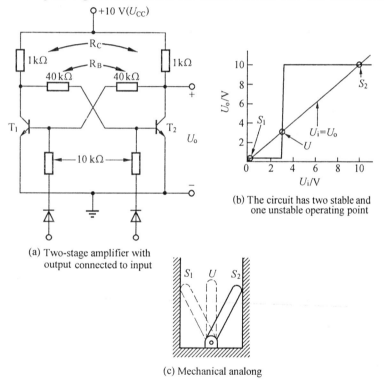

(a) Two-stage amplifier with output connected to input

(b) The circuit has two stable and one unstable operating point

(c) Mechanical analong

Fig.4.16

made and with turned around to emphasize the symmetry of the resulting circuit. We have also added inputs, which we shall discuss presently. Mathematically, this connection requires $U_i = U_o$, which defines a straight lines passing through the origin and having a slope of unity. In

Fig.4.16(b) we have drawn this line on the amplifier characteristic, which also has to be satisfied. This straight line is not a load line, but the same reasoning applies here as we followed in thinking about load lines: to satisfy both characteristics, the solution must lie at their intersection(S). Consequently, we have marked and labeled the three intersections on the graph. The two intersections labeled S_1 and S_2 are stable solutions, but the intersection labeled U is unstable. In Fig.4.16(c) we suggest a mechanical analog: the lever will have stable equilibria when resting against either wall but with a frictionless pivot the balanced position will be unstable and will not occur in practice. The stable position marked S_1 occurs with transistor T_2 saturated and transistor T_1 cutoff, and the stable position marked S_2 has transistor T_2 cutoff and transistor T_1 saturated. The circuit will remain in one of these stable states forever unless an external signal is applied to forced it to the other stable state, just as the lever in Fig.4.16(c) will lean against one wall unless an external force moves it to other wall. By applying sufficient positive voltage to the input of the transistor which is cut off, we can switch the state of the circuit. The diodes are placed in the inputs to ensure that the state of the circuit will not affect the input drivers.

The circuit shown in Fig.4.16(a) is called a bistable (or latch) circuit and it can serve as electronic memory. When you depress a button on your calculator for example, the signal sets latch circuits in the calculator to retain the keyed information after you release the button. The information thus retained is then available for processing after all numerical information is entered.

4.3.2 Flip-Flops

(1) The R-S Flip-Flop. We can realize the latch function with standard logic gates. Fig.4.17 shows a latch constructed from two NOR gates. The output of each NOR provides one of the inputs for the other

NOR. The other inputs are labeled S(for SET) and R(for RESET). The outputs are labeled Q and Q' because the latch provides complementary outputs. This circuit, called an R-S flip-flop, is similar in its operation to the bistable in Fig.4.16(b).

Let us consider that R and S are both 0 but that Q' is 1. In this case of the inputs to NOR_1 is 1 and hence its output(Q) is 0. This is consistent with the assumption that Q' is 1, which implies that both inputs to NOR_2 are 0. By symmetry, the latch will also be stable with Q = 1 and Q' = 0.

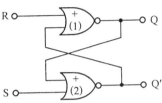

Fig.4.17 Latch from NOR gates

If now S momentarily becomes 1, the output of NOR_2(Q') will drop to 0, resulting in NOR_1 having 0 at both inputs. This will force Q to 1, and this 1 will keep Q' at 0 after S returns to the 0 state. Thus Q is SET by a 1 at S. Similarly, we can RESET the latch (Q = 0) with a 1 at R. The truth table for the R-S flip-flop is shown in Fig.4.18 together with the logic symbol for an R-S flip-flop. The logic symbol covers the various types of realizations for the R-S flip-flop, as well as the variety of logic

S	R	Q
0	0	No change
0	1	0
1	0	1
1	1	Not allowed

Fig.4.18 Flip-flop truth table and logic symbol

families which might be used. Seldom would individual gates be used for constructing a flip-flop; rather the logic designer would use one of the special types of flip-flop packaged on a single chip. In the following section we discuss the more popular types of flip-flops.

(2) Gated and Clocked Flip-Flops. The R-S flip-flop requires a

number of refinements to achieve its full potential for memory and digital signal processing. One problem is that the R-S flip-flop responds to its input signals at R and S immediately and at all times. Timing problems can occur when logic signals which are supposed to arrive at the same time actually arrive at slightly different times due to separate delays. Such timing problems can create short, unwanted pulses called "glitches."

The gated flip-flop in Fig.4.19(a) will respond to the R or S inputs

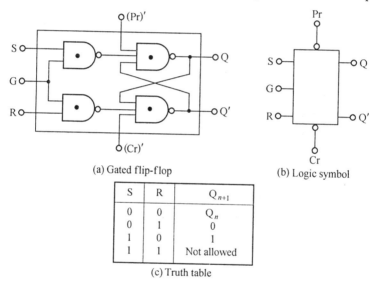

(a) Gated flip-flop

(b) Logic symbol

S	R	Q_{n+1}
0	0	Q_n
0	1	0
1	0	1
1	1	Not allowed

(c) Truth table

Fig.4.19

only when a gating signal arrives at the G(gate) input. Note that here we have built the flip-flop out of NAND gates. In this form, the forbidden state at the inputs to the cross-coupled NANDs is 00, which corresponds to 11 at the R and S inputs as before. This flip-flop also has Present (Pr) and Clear (Cr) inputs which set the latch independent of the gate. These are active when in the 0 state, as indicated by the circle at their inputs on the logic symbol (in Fig.4.19(b)). The truth table in (Fig.4.19(c)) now lists the output state after the gating pulse (Q_{n+1}) as a function of the R and S inputs and the state prior to the gating pulse(Q_n). Specifically, with RS = 00, the gating signal produces no change in the output state ($Q_{n+1} = Q_n$). Notice that by using an inverter on the gate input, we could have the gating occur at G = 0. This would be indicated by a circle at the gating input of the flip-flop symbol in Fig.4.19(b).

The R and S input are thus active when the signal at the gate input is 1. Normally, such timing, or synchronizing, signals are distributed throughout a digital system by clock pulses, as shown in Fig.4.20. The symmetrical clock signal provides two times each period when switching may be accomplished (i.e., when CK $\Rightarrow$ 1 and when (CK)' $\Rightarrow$ 1).

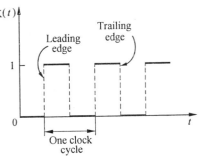

Fig.4.20 Clock signal

The gating time of the inputs can be further reduced by differentiating the clock signal in an RC circuit as shown in Fig.4.21 and applying

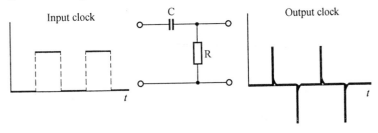

Fig.4.21 The RC circuit differentiates the clock signal to limit the time during which state changes can occur

the result to the input gate. This edge triggering is accomplished by building small coupling capacitors into the input of the integrated circuit. The circuit can be designed to trigger at the leading or trailing edge of the clock.

The symbol for an edge triggered flip-flop is shown in Fig.4.22 for both leading and lagging edge triggering. The distinguishing mark for edge triggering is triangle at the clock input. Triggering at the edges of the waveforms limits the time during which the inputs are active and thus server to eliminate glitches. By using circuits that trigger at either the leading or trailing edges, the designer can pass signals in a circuit at two times in each clock cycle.

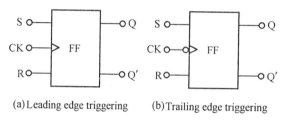

(a) Leading edge triggering   (b) Trailing edge triggering

Fig.4.22   Logic symbols for edge triggered flip-flops

(3) The J-K Flip-Flop. Another problem with the basic R-S flip-flop is the forbidden state at the input. This can be eliminated by ANDing the inputs with the output of the flip-flop, thus blocking one of the inputs, as shown in Fig. 4.23. The added gates here have the effect of inhibiting the 1 input to the gate whose output is 1. Therefore, the input (J or K) which is passed will always change the state of the output. Thus the truth table for the J-K flip-flop (see Fig.4.24) is the same as the truth table in Fig.4.19, except that we indicate a change of output state $(Q_n + 1 = Q_n')$ for the hitherto forbidden input state. The J-K flip-

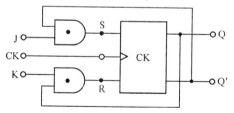

Fig.4.23   J-K flip-flop

flop thus gives us, in addition to a latched memory of the input, the capacity to "toggle"(A lever-actuated switch, like the ordinary light on-off switch, is called a toggle switch. Thus to toggle means to switch from one state to another) when both inputs are 1. This toggle feature reveals why we must use edge triggering for this flip-flop; for if the clock pulse were extended in time, thestate would oscillate back and forth and the eventual output would be indeterminent. The toggle mode of the J-K flip-flop is useful in counters and frequency dividers.

(4) The D- and T-Type Flip-Flops. The J-K (or R-S) flip-flop can be converted to a D-type flip-flop (D for delay) by connecting an inverter between the inputs as shown in Fig.4.25. This effectively eliminates the

J	K	Q_{n-1}
0	0	Q_n
0	1	0
1	0	1
1	1	Q'_n

Fig.4.24 Truth table for J-K flip-flop. Q_n represents the stage before the clock pulse and Q_{n+1} the stage after the clock pulse

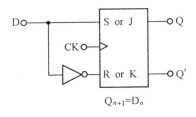

$Q_{n+1}=D_n$

Fig.4.25 D-type flip-flop

forbidden state for the R-S flip-flop and has the effect of delaying the output by one clock cycle, as shown by Fig.4.26. Although the input signal and the clock appear here to change at the same time, the clock transition occurs before the input transition marked with the arrow on the leading edge. Thus the output is

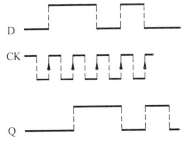

Fig.4.26 The output is delayed one clock cycle

assured have the value which was present at the input during the previous clock cycle (i.e., the output is delayed one clock cycle).

Tying the J and K inputs together produces a T-type flip-flop (T for toggle). The T-type flip-flop toggles with the clock pulse when its input is 1 and does not toggle when its output is 0. This is useful, as stated above, for counters and devide-by-2 applications. The logic symbol and truth table for the T-type flip-flop is shown in Fig.4.27.

(5) The Master-Slave Flip-Flop. Timing problems in logic circuits can be further eliminated through the use of the master-slave configuration shown in Fig.4.28. In this configuration, two J-K flip-flops are used: the first receives the input state at the trailing edge of the clock pulse and passes that state to the "slave" flip-flop at the leading edge

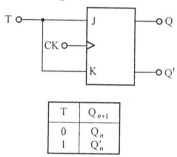

Fig.4.27 T-type flip-flop with truth table

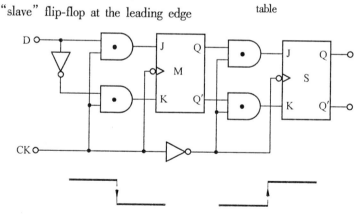

Fig.4.28 Master-slave flip-flop

of the next clock pulse. Notice that the clock pulse also gates the output of the master flip-flop to ensure that signals will be passed only at the correct time.

Vocabulary

1. patriot	n.	爱国者
2. envision	v.	预见
3. alphabet	n.	字母表
4. validity	n.	正确性
5. proposition	n.	命题
6. binary	n.	二进制
7. nevertheless	conj.	然而
8. reveal	v.	展现,揭示
9. complement	n.	补码
10. truthtable		真值表
11. algebraical	adj.	代数的
12. trial and error		试错法,试凑法
13. mechanism	n.	机械装置,机构
14. elapse	v.	(时间)流逝
15. enumerate	v.	列举
16. expire	v.	期满,终止
17. brute	adj.	僵化的
18. prime	n.	上撇号
19. trigger	v.	引起,触发
20. inversion	n.	反相,反转
21. quadruple	adj.	四合一
22. fabricate	v.	制造
23. integrated circuit		集成电路
24. capsule	n.	封装
25. compatible	adj.	兼容的
26. obsolete	adj.	废弃的
27. threshold	n.	阈值,门限
28. zener diode		齐纳二极管

29. adjacent	*adj.*	邻近的,接近的
30. arc welding		电弧焊
31. intimately	*adv.*	密切地
32. recast	*v.*	重做
33. bistable circuit		双稳电路
34. cutoff		截止,关闭
35. symmetry	*n.*	对称
36. label	*v.*	为……标号
37. equilibria	*n.*	平衡
38. lever	*n.*	杆,杠杆
39. latch circuit		锁存电路
40. memory	*n.*	存储器
41. depress	*v.*	压下
42. set	*v.*	置位
43. calculator	*n.*	计算器
44. flip-flop	*n.*	触发器
45. glitch	*n.*	干扰
46. synchronize	*v.*	同步
47. leading edge		上升沿
48. lagging(trailing)edge		下降沿
49. inhibit	*v.*	禁止
50. hitherto	*adv.*	迄今,至今
51. toggle	*v.*	(来回)切换
52. impulse	*n.*	推动力

Notes:

1. That is, it is desirable to broaden the range of values in the regions for 1 and 0 to allow for variations in transistors, power supply voltage, noise that might get mixed in with the signal, and the like.

也就是希望扩展区域 1 和 0 的有效范围,以允许晶体管和电源电压的变化以及混杂在信号中的噪声等因素的影响。

2. The door on a typical elevator has a timer on it which closes the door automatically if no one enters the elevator and pushes a button for another floor.

典型的电梯门上有一个定时器,其作用是当没有人进入电梯且按下去其它楼层的按钮时可自动关闭电梯门。

3. This accounts of four of the eight states.

这考虑到八个状态中的四个。

4. The truth-table method is a brute-force way for describing a binary function.

真值表是一种描述二进制功能的僵化方法。

5. The NOT S function is represented algebraically by a prime added to the variable or expression to be NOTed: S' means NOT S.

对 S 取反的代数表达法是在变量或要取反的表达式上加撇号号:S' 表示对 S 取反。

6. The task would be unnecessary because anyone who read the circuit diagram would in their mind group the components together into standard circuits and think in terms of the "system" functions of the individual gates.

这个工作是不必要的,因为任何阅读电路图的人在心里总会将元件组合成标准电路并且从每个门电路的"系统"功能角度来考虑问题。

7. This logic family is useful where electrical noise is a problem, to prevent moderate noise signals, which might leak into the circuit, from affecting the circuit as valid digital signals.

当电噪声成为问题时这个系列的逻辑器件可用于抑制适度的进入电路的噪声信号,以避免其成为有效数字信号而影响电路的性能。

8. We may accomplish a simpler realization by manipulating the expression for D into a more convenient form.

通过将表达式 D 变换为一种更方便的形式可以获得一个更简单的实现方法。

PART 2
ELECTRICAL MACHINE, CONTROL
COMPONENT AND SENSOR

5

Introduction to Electrical Machines

5.1 BRIEF HISTORY OF ELECTRICAL MACHINES

Electrical machinery has been in existence for many years. The applications of electrical machines have expanded rapidly since their first use many years ago. At the present time, applications continue to increase at a rapid rate.

Thomas Edison is given credit for developing the concept of widespread generation and distribution of electrical power. He performed developmental work on direct-current (DC) generators which were driven by steam engines. Edison's work with electrical lights and power production led the way to the development of DC motors and associated control equipment.

Most early discoveries related to electrical machinery operation dealt with direct-current systems. Alternating-current (AC) power generation and distribution became widespread a short time later. The primary reason for converting to AC power production and distribution was that transformers could be used to increase AC voltage levels for long-distance distribution of electrical power. Thus the discovery of transformers allowed the conversion of power production and distribution systems from DC to AC systems. Presently, almost all electrical power systems produce and distribute three-phase alternating current. Transformers allow the voltage produced by an AC generator to be increased while decreasing the current level by a corresponding amount. This allows long-distance distribution at a reduced current level, reduces power losses, and increases system efficiency.

The use of electrical motors has increased for home appliances and industrial and commercial applications for driving machines and sophisticated equipment. Many machines and automated industrial equipment now require precise control. Thus motor design and complexity has changed since early DC motors which were used primarily with railroad trains. Motor control methods have now become more critical to the efficient and effective operation of machines and equipment. Such innovations as servo control systems and industrial robots have led to new developments in motor design.

Our complex system of transportation has also had an impact on the use of electrical machines. Automobiles and other means of ground transportation use electrical motors for starting and generators for their battery-charging systems. There has recently been emphasis in the development of electric motor-driven automobiles. Aircraft use electrical machines in ways similar to automobiles. However, they also use sophisticated synchro and servo-controlled machines while in operation.

5.2 BASIC CONSTRUCTION OF ELECTRICAL MACHINES

Rotating electrical machines accomplish electromechanical energy conversion. Generators convert mechanical energy into electrical energy, while motors convert an electrical energy input into a mechanical energy output. Generators and motors have basic construction characteristics which are common among many types of machines. The functions of various machines differ even though their construction is similar. Generators have rotary motion supplies by prime movers which provide mechanical energy input. Relative motion between the conductors and a magnetic field of generators produces an electrical energy output. Motors have electrical energy supplied to their windings and a magnetic field that develops an electromagnetic interaction to produce mechanical energy or torque.

The construction of most rotating electrical machines is somewhat similar. Most machines have a stationary part called the stator and a rotating set of conductors called the rotor. The stator consists of a yoke or frame which serves as a support and a metallic path for magnetic flux developed in a machine.

5.2.1 Field poles and windings

Rotating machines have field poles which are part of the stator assembly. Field poles are constructed of laminated sheets of steel and secured to the machine frame. They are usually curved on the portion near the rotor to provide a low-reluctance path for magnetic flux. The field windings or field coils are placed around the poles. The field coils are electromagnets that develop an electromagnetic field interaction with the rotor to generate a voltage or to produce torque in a machine.

5.2.2 Rotor construction

In the study of electrical machines, there is a need to understand the electromagnetic fields produced by the rotating section of a motor or a generator. This section is called armature or rotor. Some types of machines use solid metal rotors called squirrel-cage rotors.

5.2.3 Slip rings, split rings, and brushes

In order for electrical energy to be supplied to a rotating device such as the armature, some sort of sliding brush contact must be established. Sliding brush contacts are either slip rings or split rings. Slip rings are constructed of a cylinder of insulating material with two separate solid metal rings glued to it. Sliding brushes made of carbon and graphite ride on the metal rings and permit application or extraction of electrical energy from the rings during rotation. The split-ring commutator is similar to the slip ring except a solid metal ring is cut into two or more separate sections. As a general rule, slip rings are used in AC motors and generators, while DC machines employ the split-ring commutating device. The gap or split in the commutator is kept at a minimum to reduce sparking of the brushes. Slip rings and split rings are shown in Fig.5.1.

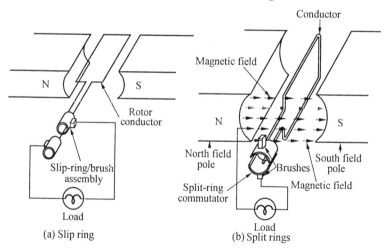

Fig. 5.1

5.2.4 Other machine parts

There are several other parts used in the construction of rotating machines. Among these are the rotor shaft, while rotates between a set of bearings. Bearings may be either the ball, roller, or sleeve type. Bearing seals, often made of felt material, are used to keep lubricant around the bearing and keep dirt out. A rotor core is usually constructed of laminated steel to provide a low-reluctance magnetic path between the field poles of a machine and to reduce eddy currents. Internal and external electrical connections provide a means of delivering or extracting electrical energy.

5.3 CONSTRUCTION FEATURES OF ELECTRICAL MACHINES

The energy-conversion process usually involves the presence of two important features in a given electromechanical device. These are the field winding, which produces the flux density, and the armature winding, in which the "working" emf is induced. In this section the salient construction features of the principal types of electric machines are described to show the location of these windings, as well as to demonstrate the general composition of such machines.

5.3.1 Three-Phase Induction Motor

This is one of the most rugged and most widely used machines in industry. Its stator is composed of laminations of high-grade sheet steel. The inner surface is slotted to accommodate a three-phase winding. In Fig.5.2(a) the three-phase winding is represented by three coils, the axes of which are 120 electrical degrees apart. Coil aa' represents all the coils assigned to phase a for one pair of poles. Similarly coil bb' represents phase b coils, and coil cc' represents phase c coils. When one end of each phase is tied together, as depicted in Fig.5.2(b), the three-

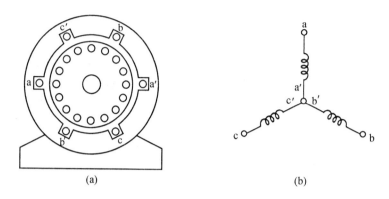

Fig.5.2 Three-phase induction motor

phase stator winding is said to be Y-connected. Such a winding is called a three-phase winding because the voltages induced in each of the three phases by a revolving flux density field are out of phase by 120 electrical degrees—a distinguishing characteristic of a balanced three-phase system.

The rotor also consists of laminations of slotted ferromagnetic material, but the rotor winding may be either the squirrel-cage type or the wound-rotor type. The latter is of a form similar to that of the stator winding. The winding terminals are brought out to three slip rings. This allows an external three-phase resistor to be connected to the rotor winding for the purpose of providing speed control. As a matter of fact, it is the need for speed control which in large measure accounts for the use of the wound-rotor type induction motor. Otherwise the squirrel-cage induction motor would be used. The squirrel-cage winding consists merely of a number of copper bars embedded in the rotor slots and connected at both ends by means of copper end rings. (In some of the smaller sizes aluminum is used.) The squirrel-cage construction is not only simpler and more economical than the wound-rotor type but more rugged as well. There are no slip rings or carbon brushes to be bothered with.

In normal operation a three-phase voltage is applied to the stator winding at points a-b-c in Fig.5.2. Magnetizing currents flow in each phase which together create a revolving magnetic field having two poles. The speed of the field is fixed by the frequency of the magnetizing currents and the number of poles for which the stator winding is designed. Fig.5.2 shows the configuration for two poles. If the pattern a-c'-b-a'-c-b' is made to span only 180 mechanical degrees and then is repeated over the remaining 180 mechanical degrees, a machine having a four-pole field distribution results. For a p-pole machine the basic winding pattern must be repeated $p/2$ times within the circumference of the inner surface of the stator.

The revolving field produced by stator winding cuts the rotor conductors, thereby inducing voltages. Since the rotor winding is short-circuited by the end rings, the induced voltages cause currents to flow which in turn react with the field to produce electromagnetic torque—and so motor action results.

Accordingly, on the basis of the foregoing description, it should be clear that for the three-phase induction motor the field winding is located on the stator and the armature winding on the rotor. Another point worth noting is that this machine is singly excited, i.e., electrical power is applied only to the stator winding. Current flows through the rotor winding by induction. As a consequence both the magnetizing current, which sets up the magnetic field, and the power current, which allows energy to be delivered to the shaft load, flow through the stator winding. For this reason, and in the interest of keeping the magnetizing current as small as possible in order that the power component may be correspondingly larger for a given current rating, the air gap of induction motors is made as small as mechanical clearance will allow. The air-gap lengths vary from about 0.02 in. for smaller machines to 0.05 in. for machines of higher rating and speed.

5.3.2 Synchronous Machines

The essential construction features of the synchronous machine are depicted in Fig.5.3. The stator consists of a stator frame, a slotted stator core, which provides a low-reluctance path for the magnetic flux, and a three-phase winding imbedded in the slots. Note that the basic two-pole pattern of Fig.5.2(a) is repeated twice, indicating that the three-phase winding is designed for four poles. The rotor either is cylindrical and equipped with a distributed winding or else has salient poles with a coil wound on each leg as depicted in Fig.5.3. The cylindrical construction is used exclusively for turbo-generators, which operate at high speeds. On the other hand the salient-pole construction is used exclusively for synchronous motors operating at speeds of 1 800 $r \cdot min^{-1}$ or less.

When operated as a generator the synchronous machine receives mechanical energy from a prime mover such as a steam turbine and is driven at some fixed speed. Also, the rotor winding is energized from a DC source, thereby furnishing a field distribution along the air gap. When the rotor is at standstill and DC flows through the rotor winding, no voltage is induced in the stator winding because the flux is not cutting the stator coils. However, when the rotor is being driven at full speed, voltage is induced in the stator winding and upon application of a suitable load electrical energy may be delivered to it.

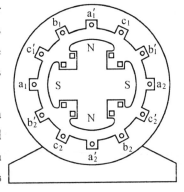

Fig. 5. 3   Salient-pole synchronous machine

For the synchronous machine the field winding is located on the rotor; the armature winding is located on the stator. This statement is valid even when the synchronous machine operates as a motor. In this mode AC power is applied to the stator winding and DC power is applied to the rotor winding for the purpose of energizing the field poles. Mechanical energy is then taken from the shaft. Note, too, that unlike the induction motor, the synchronous motor is a doubly excited machine; i.e., energy is applied to the rotor as well as the stator winding. In fact it is this characteristic which enables this machine to develop a nonzero torque at only one speed—hence the name synchronous.

Because the magnetizing current for the synchronous machine originates from a separate source (the DC supply), the air-gap lengths are larger than those found in induction motors of comparable size and rating. However, synchronous machines are more expensive and less rugged than induction motors in the smaller horsepower ratings because the rotor must be equipped with slip rings and brushes in order to allow the direct current to be conducted to the field winding.

5.3.3 DC Machines

Electromechanical energy-conversion devices that are characterized by direct current are more complicated than the AC type. In addition to a field winding and armature winding, a third component is needed to serve the function of converting the induced AC armature voltage into a DC voltage. Basically the device is a mechanical rectifier and is called a commutator.

Appearing in Fig.5.4 are the principal features of the DC machine. The stator consists of an unlaminated ferromagnetic material equipped with a protruding structure around which coils are wrapped. The flow of direct current through the coils establishes a magnetic field distribution along the periphery of the air gap in much the same manner as occurs in the rotor of the synchronous machine. Hence in the DC machine the field winding is located on the stator. It follows then that the armature winding is on the

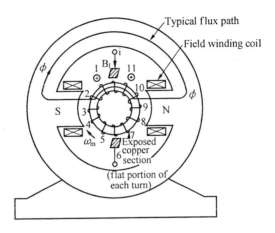

Fig. 5.4 Construction features of the DC machine showing the Grammering armature winding

rotor. The rotor is composed of a laminated core, which is slotted to accommodate the armature winding. It also contains the commutator—a series of copper segments insulted from one another and arranged in cylindrical fashion. Riding on the commutator are appropriately placed carbon brushes while serve to conduct direct current to or from the armature winding depending upon whether motor or generator action is taking place.

In Fig. 5.4 the armature winding is depicted as a coil wrapped around a toroid. This is merely a schematic convenience. In an actual winding, no conductors are wasted by placing them on the inner surface of the rotor core where no flux penetrates. In Fig. 5.3 those parts of the armature winding which lie directly below the brush width are assumed to have the insulation removed, i.e., the copper is exposed. This allows current to be conducted to and from the armature winding through the brush as the rotor revolves. In a practical winding each coil is made accessible to the brushes by connecting the coils to individual commutator segments and then placing the brushes on the commutator.

For motor action direct current is made to flow through the field winding as well as the armature winding. If current is assumed to flow into brush B_1 in Fig.5.4, then note that on the left side of the rotor for the outside conductors current flows into the paper while the opposite occurs for the conductors located on the outside surface of the right side of the rotor. A force is produced on each conductor, thereby producing a torque causing clockwise rotation. Now the function of the commutator is to assure that as a conductor such as 1 in Fig.5.4 revolves and thus goes from the left side of brush B_1 to the right side, the current flowing though it reverses, thus yielding a continuous unidirectional torque for the entire armature winding. Recall that a reversed conductor current in a flux field of reversed polarity keeps the torque unidirectional. The reversal of current comes about because the commutator always allows current to be conducted in the same directions in either side of the armature winding whether or not it is rotating.

Another point of interest in Fig.5.4 concerns the location of the brushes. By placing the brushes on a line perpendicular to the field axis all conductors contribute in producing a unidirectional torque. If, on the other hand, the brushes were placed on the same line as the field axis, then half of the conductors would produce clockwise torque and the other half of the counterclockwise torque, yield a zero net torque.

Vocabulary

1. air gap		气隙
2. aircraft	n.	飞机
3. alternating current, AC	n.	交流
4. armature	n.	电枢
5. automobile	n.	汽车
6. bearing	n.	轴承
7. brush	n.	电刷
8. carbon	n.	碳

9. circumference   *n.*   圆周
10. clearance   *n.*   间隙
11. coils   *n.*   线圈,绕组
12. commutator   *n.*   换向器
13. connection   *n.*   接线端
14. copper bar   铜导条
15. copper end rings   铜端环
16. core   *n.*   铁心
17. cylindrical   *a.*   圆柱式的
18. direct current, DC   直流
19. doubly excited   双边励磁
20. electric/electrical machine   电机
21. electromechanical   *a.*   机电的
22. felt   *n.*   毡
23. ferromagnetic   *a.*   铁磁的
24. field pole   磁极
25. flux density   磁通密度,磁密
26. frame   *n.*   机座,机壳
27. generator   *n.*   发电机
28. glue   *v.*   胶合,粘贴
29. graphite   *n.*   石墨
30. induction motor   感应电动机
31. laminate   *v.*   叠制,叠压
32. lubricant   *n.*   润滑剂,润滑油
33. magnetic flux   磁通
34. magnetizing current   磁化电流,励磁电流
35. mechanical rectifier   机械式换向器
36. metallic   *a.*   金属的
37. motor   *n.*   电动机
38. penetrate   *v.*   透过,渗透

39. periphery	n.	圆周,周围
40. perpendicular	a.	垂直的,正交的
41. polarity	n.	极性
42. protrude	v.	使伸出,突出
43. reluctance	n.	磁阻
44. revolving magnetic field		旋转磁场
45. rotor	n.	转子
46. salient	a.	突出的
47. salient-pole		凸极式
48. servo	n.	伺服
59. singly excited		单边励磁
50. slip rings		滑环
51. slot	n. & v.	槽,开槽
52. squirrel-cage		鼠笼式,笼型
53. stator	n.	定子
54. synchronous machine		同步电机
55. toroid	n.	环状物
56. torque	n.	转矩
57. transformer	n.	变压器
58. unidirectional	a.	单方向的,方向不变的
59. winding	n.	绕组
60. wound-rotor		绕线式
61. wrap	v.	捆,缠,环绕
62. yoke	n.	轭

Notes:

1. The primary reason for converting to AC power production and distribution was that transformers could be used to increase AC voltage levels for long-distance distribution of electrical power.

转变为交流电能产生与传输的主要原因是变压器能升高交流电压以便于电能的远距离传输。

2. Automobiles and other means of ground transportation use electrical motors for starting and generators for their battery-charging systems.

汽车及其他地面交通工具采用电动机启动,并用发电机对蓄电池充电。

3. Motors have electrical energy supplied to their windings and a magnetic field that develops an electromagnetic interaction to produce mechanical energy or torque.

电能供给电动机绕组和磁场,产生电磁感应作用,使电动机产生机械能或者转矩。

4. Such a winding is called a three-phase winding because the voltages induced in each of the three phases by a revolving flux density field are out of phase by 120 electrical degrees—a distinguishing characteristic of a balanced three-phase system.

这种绕组被称为三相(对称)绕组的原因是旋转磁场在三相绕组中的感应电动势互差120°电角度——三相对称系统的特点。

5. If the pattern a - c' - b - a' - c - b' is made to span only 180 mechanical degrees and then is repeated over the remaining 180 mechanical degrees, a machine having a four-pole field distribution results.

如果 a - c' - b - a' - c - b'仅占180°机械角度,并在剩余的180°机械角度内重复一次,则该电机有4个极。

6. Since the rotor winding is short-circuited by the end rings, the induced voltages cause currents to flow which in turn react with the field to produce electromagnetic torque? and so motor action results.

由于转子绕组通过端环短路,则感应电动势形成(转子)电流,电流与磁场相互作用产生电磁转矩,结果使电动机旋转起来。

7. Riding on the commutator are appropriately placed carbon brushes while serve to conduct direct current to or from the armature winding depending upon whether motor or generator action is taking place.

在换向器上适当(位置)放置碳刷,其作用是当电机作为电动机或发电机运行时,使直流电流流入或流出电枢绕组。

8. In a practical winding each coil is made accessible to the brushes by connecting the coils to individual commutator segments and then placing the brushes on the commutator.

在实际绕组中,通过把线圈和换向片相连并把电刷放在换向器上,使得每个线圈与电刷都是相接。

9. If current is assumed to flow into brush B_1 in Fig.5.4, then note that on the

left side of the rotor for the outside conductors current flows into the paper while the opposite occurs for the conductors located on the outside surface of the right side of the rotor.

如图 5.4 所示,如果假定电流由电刷 B_1 流入,则应注意的是转子左侧的外部导体电流是流入纸面的,而位于转子右侧的外部导体电流方向是相反的。

10. Now the function of the commutator is to assure that as a conductor such as 1 in Fig. 5.4 revolves and thus goes from the left side of brush B_1 to the right side, the current flowing though it reverses, thus yielding a continuous unidirectional torque for the entire armature winding.

现在,换向器的作用就是保证当图 5.4 所示的导体(如导体 1)由电刷 B_1 的左侧旋转至右侧时,电流的方向也随之改变,这样对整个电枢绕组而言就可产生一个方向不变的连续转矩。

11. The reversal of current comes about because the commutator always allows current to be conducted in the same directions in either side of the armature winding whether or not it is rotating.

无论电枢是否旋转,由于换向器使电流总是以同样的方向流入电枢绕组两侧,则电流反向。

12. If, on the other hand, the brushes were placed on the same line as the field axis, then half of the conductors would produce clockwise torque and the other half of the counterclockwise torque, yield a zero net torque.

另一方面,如果电刷与磁场轴线放在同一条线上,则一半的导体产生顺时针方向转矩,另一半的导体产生逆时针方向转矩,使有效转矩为零。

6

DC Motor And Induction Motor

6.1 TYPES OF DC MOTORS

The types of commercially available DC motors basically fall into four categories: ① permanent-magnet DC motors, ② series-wound DC motors, ③ shunt-wound DC motors, and ④ compound-wound DC motors. Each of these motors has different characteristics due to its basic circuit arrangement and physical properties.

6.1.1 Permanent-magnet DC motors

The permanent-magnet DC motor, shown in Fig.6.1, is constructed in the same manner as its DC generator counterpart. The permanent-magnet motor is used for low-torque applications. When this type of motor is used, the DC power supply is connected directly to the armature conductors through the brush/commutator assembly. The magnetic field is produced by permanent magnets mounted on the stator. The rotor of permanent magnet motors is a wound armature.

This type of motor ordinarily uses either alnico or ceramic permanent

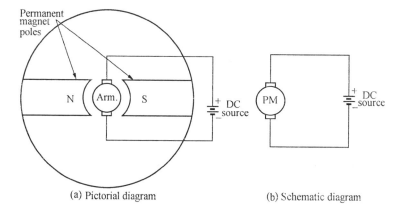

Fig.6.1 Permanent-magnet DC motor

magnets rather than field coils. The alnico magnets are used with high-horsepower applications. Ceramic magnets are ordinarily used for low-horsepower slow-speed motors. Ceramic magnets are highly resistant to demagnetization, yet they are relatively low in magnetic-flux level. The magnets are usually mounted in the motor fame and then magnetized prior to the insertion of the armature.

The permanent-magnet motor has several advantages over conventional types of DC motors. One advantage is reduced operational cost. The speed characteristics of the permanent-magnet motor are similar to those of the shunt-wound DC motor. The direction of rotation of a permanent-magnet motor can be reversed by reversing the two power lines.

6.1.2 Series-wound DC motors

The manner in which the armature and field circuits of a DC motors are connected determines its basic characteristics. Each of the types of DC motors are similar in construction to the type of DC generator that corresponds to it. The only difference, in most cases, is that the generator acts as a voltage source while the motor functions as a mechanical power conversion device.

The series-wound motor, shown in Fig.6.2, has the armature and field circuits connected in a series arrangement. There is only one path for current to flow from the DC voltage source. Therefore, the field is wound of relatively few turns of large diameter wire, giving the field a low resistance. Changes in load applied to the motor shaft causes changes in the current through the field. If the mechanical load increases, the current also increases. The increased current creates a stronger magnetic field. The speed of a series motor varies from very fast at no load to very slow at heavy loads. Since large currents may flow through the low-resistance field, the series motor produces a high-torque output. Series motors are used where heavy loads must be moved and speed regulation is not important. A typical application is for automobile starter motors.

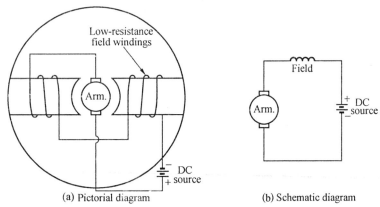

Fig.6.2 Series-wound DC motor

6.1.3 Shunt-wound DC motors

Shunt-wound DC motors are more commonly used than any other type of DC motor. As shown in Fig.6.3, the shunt-wound DC motor has field

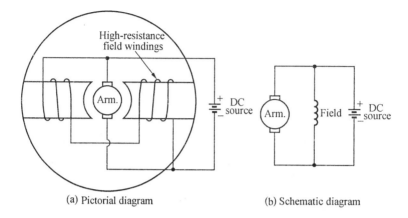

(a) Pictorial diagram (b) Schematic diagram

Fig.6.3 Shunt-wound DC motor

coils connected in parallel with its armature. This type of DC motor has field coils which are wound of many turns of small-diameter wire and have a relatively high resistance. Since the field is a high-resistant parallel path of the circuit of the shunt motor, a small amount of current flows through the field. A strong electromagnetic field is produced due to the many turns of wire that form the field windings.

A large majority (about 95%) of the current drawn by the shunt motor flows in the armature circuit. Since the field current has little effect on the strength of the field, motor speed is not affected appreciably by variations in load current. The relationship of the currents that flow through a DC shunt motor is as follows:

$$I_L = I_a + I_f$$

where I_L—total current drawn from the power source;

I_a—armature current;

I_f—field current.

The field current may be varied by placing a variable resistance in series with the field windings. Since the current in the field circuit is low, a low-wattage rheostat may be used to vary the speed of the motor due to the variation in field resistance. As field resistance increases, field current will decrease. A decrease in field current reduces the strength of the electromagnetic field. When the field flux is decreased, the armature will rotate faster, due to reduced magnetic-field interaction. Thus the speed of a DC shunt motor may be easily varied by using a field rheostat.

The shunt-wound DC motor has very good speed regulation. The speed does decrease slightly when the load increases due to the increase in voltage drop across the armature. Due to its good speed regulation characteristic and its ease of speed control, the DC shunt motor is commonly used for industrial applications. Many types of variable-speed machine tools are driven by DC shunt motors.

6.1.4 Compound-wound DC motors

The compound-wound DC motos shown in Fig.6.4 , has two sets of field windings, one in series with the armature and one in parallel. This motor combines the desirable characteristics of the series- and shunt-wound motors. There are two methods of connecting compound motors: cumulative and differential. A cumulative compound DC motor has series and shunt fields that aid each other. Differential compound DC motors have series and shunt fields that oppose each other. There are also two ways in which the series windings are placed in the circuit. One method is called a short shunt (see Fig.6.4), in which the! shunt field is placed across the armature. The long-shunt method has the shunt field winding placed across both the armature and the series field (see Fig.6.4).

Compound motors have high torque similar to a series-wound motor, together with good speed regulation similar to a shunt motor. Therefore, when good torque and good speed regulation are needed, the compound-wound dc motor can be used. A major disadvantage of a compound-wound motor is its expense.

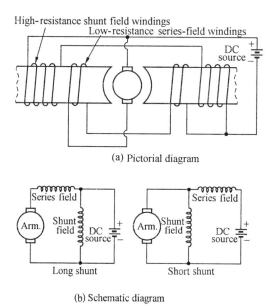

Fig.6.4 Compound-wound DC motor

6.2 DC MOTOR ANALYSIS

A DC motor is a DC generator with the power flow reversed. In the DC motor electrical energy is converted to mechanical form. On the basis of foregoing discussion, there are three types of DC motors: the shunt motor, the cumulatively compounded motor, and the series motor. The compound motor is prefixed with the word cumulative in order to stress that the connections to the series field winding are such as to ensure that the series field flux aids the shunt-field flux. The series motor, unlike the series generator, finds wide application, especially for traction-type loads. Hence due attention is given to this machine in the treatment that follows.

The performance of the DC motor operating in any one of its three modes can conveniently be described in terms of an equivalent circuit, a set of performance equations, a power-flow diagram, and the magnetization curve. The equivalent circuit is depicted in Fig.6.5. It is worthwhile to note that now the armature induced voltage is treated as a reaction or counter emf. By imposing some constraints, we obtain the correct equivalent circuit for the desired mode of operation. For example, for a series motor the appropriate equivalent circuit results upon removing R_f from the circuitry of Fig.6.5.

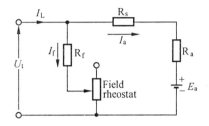

Fig.6.5 Equivalent circuit of the DC motor

The set of equations needed to compute the performance is listed below.

$$E_a = K_E \Phi n \qquad (6.1)$$

$$T = K_T \Phi I_a \qquad (6.2)$$

$$U_t = E_a + I_a(R_a + R_s) \qquad (6.3)$$

$$I_L = I_f + I_a \qquad (6.4)$$

Note that the last two equations are modified to account for the fact that for the motor U_t is the applied or source voltage and as such must be equal to the sum of the voltage drops. Similarly the line current is equal to the sum rather than the difference of the armature current and field currents.

The power-flow diagram is illustrated in Fig.6.6. The electrical power input $U_t I_L$ originating from the line supplies the field power needed to establish the flux field as well as the armature-circuit copper loss needed to maintain the flow of I_a. This current flowing through the armature conductors imbedded in the flux field causes torque to be developed. The law of conservation of energy then demands that the electromagnetic power, $E_a I_a$, be equal to $T\omega_m$, where ω_m is the steady-state operating speed. Removal of the rotational losses from the developed mechanical

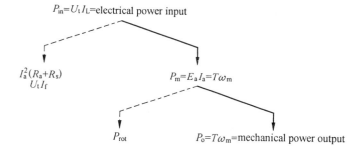

Fig.6.6 Power-flow diagram of the DC motor

power yields the mechanical output power.

The DC motor is often called upon to do the really tough jobs in industry because of its high degree of flexibility and ease of control. These features cannot easily be matched by other electromechanical energy-conversion devices. The DC motor offers a wide range of control of speed and torque as well as excellent acceleration and deceleration. For example, by the insertion of an appropriate armature-circuit resistance, rated torque can be obtained at starting with no more than rated current flowing. Also, by special design of the shunt-field winding, speed adjustments over a range of 4:1 are readily obtainable. If this is then combined with armature-voltage control, the range of speed adjustment spreads to 6:1. In some electronic control devices that are used to provide the DC energy to the field and armature circuits, a speed range of 40:1 is possible. The size of the motor being controlled, however, is limited.

6.3 DC MOTOR SPEED-TORQUE CHARACTERISTICS

How does the DC motor react to the application of a shaft load? What is the mechanism by which the DC motor adapts itself to supply to the load the power it demands? The answers to these questions can be obtained by reasoning in terms of the performance equations. Initially our remarks are confined to the shunt motor, but a similar line of reasoning applies for the others. For our purposes the two pertinent equations are those for torque and current. Thus

$$T = K_T \Phi I_a$$

and

$$I_a = \frac{U_t - K_E \Phi n}{R_a} \qquad (6.5)$$

Note that the last expression results form replacing E_a by Eq. (6.1) in Eq. (6.3). With no shaft load applied, the only torque needed is that which overcomes the rotational losses. Since the shunt motor operates at essentially constant flux, Eq. (6.2) indicates that only a small armature current is required compared to its rated value to furnish these losses. Eq. (6.5) reveals the manner in which the armature current is made to assume just the right value. In this expression U_t, R_a, K_E, and Φ are fixed in value. Therefore the speed is the critical variable. If, for the moment, it is assumed that the speed has too low a value, then the numerator of Eq. (6.5) takes on an excessive value and in turn makes I_a larger than required. At this point the motor reacts to correct the situation. The excessive armature current produces a developed torque which exceeds the opposing torques of friction and windage. In fact this excess serves as an accelerating torque, which then proceeds to increase the speed to that level which corresponds to the equilibrium value of armature current. In other words, the acceleration torque becomes zero only when the speed is at that value which by Eq. (6.5) yields just the right I_a needed to overcome the rotational losses.

Consider next that a load demanding rated toque is suddenly applied to the motor shaft. Clearly, because the developed torque at this instant is only sufficient to overcome friction and windage and not the load torque, the first reaction is for the motor to lose speed. In this way, as Eq. (6.5) reveals, the armature current can be increased so that in turn the electromagnetic torque can increase. As a matter of fact the applied load torque causes the motor to assume that value of speed which yields a current sufficient to produce a developed torque to overcome the applied shaft torque and the frictional torque. Power balance is thereby achieved, because an equilibrium condition is reached where the electromagnetic power, $E_a I_a$, is equal to the mechanical power developed, $T\omega_m$.

A comparison of the DC motor with the three-phase induction motor indicates that both are speed-sensitive devices in response to applied shaft loads. An essential difference, however, is that for the three-phase induction motor developed torque is adversely influenced by the power-factor angle of the armature current. Of course no analogous situation prevails in the case of the DC motor.

On the basis of the foregoing discussion it should be apparent that the speed-torque curve of DC motors is an important characteristic. Appearing in Fig.6.7 are the general shapes of the speed-torque characteristics as they apply for the shunt, cumulatively compounded, and series motors. For the sake of comparison the curves are drawn through a common point of rated torque and speed. An understanding of why the curves take the shapes and relative positions depicted in Fig.6.7 readily follows from an examination of Eq. (6.1), which involves the speed. For the shunt motor the speed equation can be written as

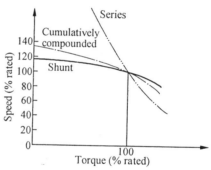

Fig.6.7 Typical speed-torque curves of DC motors

$$n = \frac{E_a}{K_E \Phi_{sh}} = \frac{U_t - I_a R_a}{K_E \Phi_{sh}} \quad (6.6)$$

The only variables involved are the speed n and the armature current I_a. At rated output torque the armature current is at its rated value and so, too, is the speed. As the load torque is removed, the armature current becomes correspondingly smaller, making the numerator term of Eq. (6.6) larger. This results in higher speeds. The extent to which the speed increases depends upon how large the armature circuit resistance drop is in comparison to the terminal voltage. It is usually around 5% ~ 10%. Accordingly, we can expect the percent change in speed of the shunt motor to be about the same magnitude. This change in speed is identified by a figure of merit called the speed regulation. It is defined as follows

$$\text{percent speed regulation} = \frac{(\text{no load speed}) - (\text{full load speed})}{\text{full load speed}} \times 100$$

(6.7)

The speed equation as it applies to the cumulatively compounded motor takes the form

$$n = \frac{U_t - I_a(R_a + R_s)}{K_E(\Phi_{sh} + \Phi_s)} \quad (6.8)$$

A comparison with the analogous expression for the shunt motor bears out two differences. One, the numerator term also includes the voltage drop in the series-field winding besides that in the armature winding. Two, the denominator term is increased to account for the effect of the series-field flux Φ_s. Starting at rated torque and speed, Eq. (6.7) makes it clear that as load torque is decreased to zero there is an increase in the numerator term which is necessarily greater than it is for the shunt motor. At the same time, moreover, the denominator term decreases because Φ_s reduces to zero as the torque goes to zero. Both effects act to bring about an increase in speed. Therefore the speed regulation of the cumulatively compounded motor is greater than for the shunt motor. Fig. 6.7 presents this information graphically.

The situation regarding the speed-torque characteristic of the series motor is significantly different because of the absence of a shunt-field winding. Keep inmind that the establishment of a flux field in the series motor comes about solely as a result of the flow of armature current through the series-field winding. In this connection, then, the speed equation for the series motor becomes

$$n = \frac{E_a}{K_E \Phi_s} = \frac{U_t - I_a(R_a + R_s)}{K_E' I_a} \qquad (6.9)$$

where K_E' denotes a new proportionality factor which permits Φ_s to be replaced by the armature current I_a. When rated torque is being developed the current is at its rated value. The flux field is therefore abundant. However, as load torque is removed less armature current flows. Now since I_a appears in the denominator of the speed equation, it is easy to see that the speed will increase greatly. In fact, if the load were to be disconnected from the motor shaft, dangerously high speeds would result because of the small armature current that flows. The centrifugal forces at these high speeds can easily damage the armature winding. For this reason a series motor should never have its load uncoupled.

Because the armature current is directly related to the air-gap flux in the series motor, Eq. (6.1) for the developed torque may be modified to read as

$$T = K_T \Phi I_a = K_T' I_a^2 \qquad (6.10)$$

Thus the developed torque for the series motor is a function of the square of the armature current. This stands in contrast to the linear relationship of torque to armature current in the shunt motor. Of course in the compound motor an intermediate relationship is achieved. It is interesting to note, too, that as the series motor reacts to develop greater torques, the speed drops correspondingly. It is this capability which suits the series motor so well to traction-type loads.

One of the attractive features the DC motor offers over all other types is the relative ease with which speed control can be achieved. The various schemes available for speed control can be deduced from Eq. (6.6), which is repeated here with one modification

$$n = \frac{U_t - I_a(R_a + R_e)}{K_E \Phi} \tag{6.11}$$

The modification involves the inclusion of an external armature-circuit resistance R_e. Inspection of Eq. (6.11) reveals that the speed can be controlled by adjusting any one of the three factors appearing on the right side of the equation: U_t, R_e, or Φ. The simplest is adjust Φ. A field rheostat such as that shown in Fig. 6.5 is used. If the field-rheostat resistance is increased, the air-gap flux is diminished, yielding higher operating speeds. General-purpose shunt motors are designed to provide a 200% increase in rated speed by this method of speed control. However, because of the weakened flux field the permissible torque that can be delivered at the higher speed is correspondingly reduced, in order to prevent excessive armature current.

A second method of speed adjustment involves the use of an external resistor R_e connected in the armature circuit as illustrated in Fig. 6.8. The size and cost of this resistor are considerably greater than those of the field rheostat because R_e must be capable of handling the full armature current. Eq. (6.11) indicates that the larger R_e is made, the greater will be the speed change. Frequently the external resistor is selected to furnish as much as a 50% drop in speed from the rated value. The chief disadvantage of this method of control is the poor efficiency of operation. For example, a 50% drop in

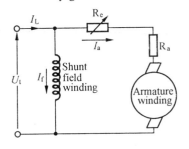

Fig. 6.8 Speed adjustment of a shunt motor by an external armature-circuit resistance

speed is achieved by having approximately half of the terminal voltage U_t appear across R_e. Accordingly, almost 50% of the line input power is dissipated in the form of heat in the resistor R_e. Nonetheless, armature-circuit resistance control is often used—especially for series motors.

A third and final method of speed control involves adjustment of the applied terminal voltage. This scheme is the most desirable from the viewpoint of flexibility and high operating efficiency. But it is also the most expensive because it requires its own DC supply. It means purchasing a motor-generator set with a capacity at least equal to that of the motor to be controlled. Such expense is not generally justified except in situations where the superior performance achievable with this scheme is indispensable, as is the case in steel mill applications. Armature terminal voltage control is referred to as the Ward-Leonard system .

6.4 THREE-PHASE INDUCTION MOTOR

One distinguishing feature of the induction motor is that it is a singly excited machine. Although such machines are equipped with both a field winding and an armature winding, in normal use an energy source is connected to one winding alone, the field winding. Currents are made to flow in the armature winding by induction, which creates an ampere-conductor distribution that interacts with the field distribution to produce a net unidirectional torque. The frequency of the induced current in the conductor is affected by the speed of the rotor on which it is located; however, the relationship between the rotor speed and the frequency of the armature current is such as to yield a resulting ampere-conductor distribution that is stationary relative to the field distribution of the stator. As a result, the singly excited induction machine is capable of producing torque at any speed below synchronous speed. For this reason the induction machine is placed in the class of asynchronous machines. In contrast, synchronous machines are electromechanical energy-conversion devices in which a net torque can be produced at only one speed of the rotor. The distinguishing characteristic of the synchronous machine is that it is a doubly excited device except when it is being used as a reluctance motor.

The salient construction features of the three-phase induction motor are described in Sec.5.3 . Because the induction machine is singly excited, it is necessary that both the magnetizing current and the power component of the current flow in the same lines. Moreover, because of the presence of an air gap in the magnetic circuit of the induction machine, an appreciable amount of magnetizing current is needed to establish the flux per pole demanded by the applied voltage. Usually, the value of the magnetizing current for three-phase induction motors lies between 25 and 40% of the rated current. Consequently, the induction motor is found to operate at a low power factor at light loads and at less than unity power factor in the vicinity of rated output.

The primary functions of a controller are to furnish proper starting, stopping and reversing without damage or inconvenience to the motor, other connected loads, or the power system. However, the controller fulfills other useful purposes as well, especially the following:

(1) It limits the starting torque. Some connected shaft loads may be damaged if excessive torque is applied upon starting. For example, fan blades can be sheared off or gears having excessive backlash can be stripped. The controller supplies reduced voltage at the start and as the speed picks up the voltage is increased in steps to its full value.

(2) It limits the starting current. Most motors above 2.38 kW cannot be started directly across the three-phase line because of the excessive starting current that flows. Recall that at unity slip the current is limited only by the leakage impedance, which is usually quite a small quantity, especially in the larger motor sizes. A large starting current can be annoying because it causes light to flicker and may even cause other connected motors to stall. Reduced-voltage starting readily eliminates these annoy-

ances.

(3) It provides overload protection. All general-purpose motors are designed to deliver full-load power continuously without overheating. However, if for some reason the motor is made to deliver, say, 150% of its rated output continuously, it will proceed to accommodate the demand and burn itself up in the process. The horsepower rating of the motor is based on the allowable temperature rise that can be tolerated by the insulation used for the field and armature windings. The losses produce the heat that raises the temperature. As long as these losses do not exceed the rated values there is no danger to the motor, but if they are allowed to become excessive, damage will result. There is nothing inherent in the motor that will keep the temperature rise within safe limits. Accordingly, it is also the function of the controller to provide this protection. Overload protection is achieved by the use of an appropriate time-delay relay which is sensitive to the heat produced by the motor line currents.

(4) It furnishes undervoltage protection. Operation at reduced voltage can be harmful to the motor, especially when the load demands rated power. If the line voltage falls below some preset limit, the motor is automatically disconnected from the three-phase lie source by the controller.

6.5 INDUCTION MOTOR TORQUE-SPEED CHARACTERISTICS

The variation of torque with speed (or slip) is an important characteristic of the three-phase induction motor. The general shape of the curve can be identified in terms of the basic torque equation Eq. (6.12) and knowledge of the performance computation procedure.

$$T = 0.177 p\Phi(Z_2 K_{W2} I_2)\cos \psi \qquad (6.12)$$

where p—number of poles;

Z_2—total number of conductors of the armature winding;

K_{W2}—armature winding factor;

I_2—armature winding current per phase.

When the motor operates at a very small slip, as at no-load, the rotor current is practically zero so that only that amount of torque is developed which is needed to supply the rotational losses. As the slip is allowed to increase from nearly zero to about 10%, Eq. (6.13) shows that the rotor current increases almost linearly.

$$\overline{I}_2 = \frac{s\overline{E}_2}{r_2 + jsx_2} \qquad (6.13)$$

This is because the j part of the impedance, sx_2, is small compared to r_2. Furthermore, it can be shown that the space-displacement angle ψ in Eq. (6.12) is identical to the rotor power-factor angle θ_2. That is

$$\psi = \theta_2 = \tan^{-1}\frac{sx_2}{r_2} \qquad (6.14)$$

Therefore, for values of s from zero to 10 per cent, ψ varies over a range of about 0 to 15°. This means that the $\cos\psi$ remains practically invariant over the specified slip range, so the torque increases almost linearly in this region. Of course the quantity Φ in Eq. (6.12) is essentially fixed since the applied voltage is constant.

As the slip is allowed to increase still further, the current continues to increase but much less rapidly than at first. The reason lies in the increasing importance of the sx_2 term of the rotor impedance. In addition, the space angle ψ now begins to increase at a rapid rate which makes the $\cos\psi$ diminish more rapidly than the current increases. Since the torque equation now involves two opposing factors, it is entirely reasonable to expect that a point is reached beyond which further increases in slip culminate in decreased developed torque. In other words, the rapidly decreasing $\cos\psi$ factor predominates over the slightly increasing I_2 factor in Eq. (6.12). As ψ increases, the field pattern for producing torque becomes less and less favorable because more and more conductors that produce negative torque are included beneath a given pole flux. Accordingly, the composite torque-speed curve takes on a shape similar to that shown in Fig.6.9.

The starting torque is the torque developed when s is unity, i.e., the speed n is zero. Fig.6.9 indicates that for the case illustrated the starting torque is somewhat in excess of rated torque, which is fairly typical of such machines. The starting torque is computed in

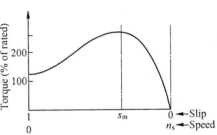

Fig. 6. 9 Typical torque-speed curve of a three-phase induction motor

the same manner as torque is computed for any value of slip. Here it merely requires using $s = 1$. Thus the magnitude of the rotor current at standstill is

$$I_2' = \frac{U_1}{\sqrt{(r_1 + r_2')^2 + (x_1 + x_2')^2}} \qquad (6.15)$$

The corresponding gap power is then

$$P_g = qI_2'^2 r_2' = \frac{qU_1^2 r_2'}{(r_1 + r_2')^2 + (x_1 + x_2')^2} \qquad (6.16)$$

where q—number of phases of the armature winding.

It is interesting to note that higher starting torques result from increased rotor copper losses at standstill.

At unity slip the input impedance is very low so that large starting currents flow. Eq.(6.15) makes this apparent. In the interest of limiting this excessive starting current, motors whose ratings exceed 2.38 kW are usually started at reduced voltage by means of line starters. Of course, starting with reduced voltage also means a reduction in the starting torque. In fact if 50% of the rated voltage is used upon starting, then clearly by Eq. (6.16) it follows that the starting torque is only one-quarter of its full-voltage value.

Another important torque quantity of the three-phase induction motor is the maximum developed torque. This quantity is so important that it is frequently the starting point in the design of the induction motor. The maximum (or breakdown) torque is a measure of the reserve capacity of the machine. It frequently has a value of 200 to 300% of rated torque. It permits the motor to operate through momentary peak loads. However, the maximum torque cannot be delivered continuously because the excessive currents that flow would destroy the insulation.

Since the developed torque is directly proportional to the gap power, it follows that the torque is a maximum when P_g is a maximum. Also, P_g is a maximum when there is a maximum transfer of power to the equivalent circuit resistor r_2'/s. Applying the maximum-power-transfer theorem to the appropriate equivalent circuit leads to the result that

$$\frac{r_2'}{s_m} = \sqrt{r_1^2 + (x_1 + x_2')^2} \qquad (6.17)$$

That is, maximum power is transferred to the gap power resistor r_2'/s when this resistor is equal to the impedance looking back into the source. Accordingly, the slip s_m at which the maximum torque is developed is

$$s_m = \frac{r_2'}{\sqrt{r_1^2 + (x_1 + x_2')^2}} \qquad (6.18)$$

Note that the slip at which the maximum torque occurs may be increased by using a larger rotor resistance. Some induction motors are in fact designed so that the maximum torque is available as a starting torque, i.e., $s_m = 1$.

With the slip s_m known, the corresponding rotor current can be found and then inserted into the torque equation to yield the final form for the breakdown torque. Thus

$$T_m = \frac{1}{\omega_s} qI'^2_2 \frac{r_2'}{s_m} = \frac{1}{\omega_s} \frac{qU_1^2}{2[r_1 + \sqrt{r_1^2 + (x_1 + x_2')^2}]} \quad (6.19)$$

An examination of Eq.(6.19) reveals the interesting information that the maximum torque is independent of the rotor winding resistance. Thus increasing the rotor winding resistance increases the slip at which the breakdown torque occurs but it leaves the magnitude of this torque unchanged. Fig.6.10 shows the effect of increasing the rotor resistance on a typical torque-speed curve.

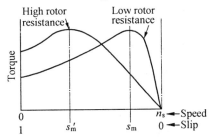

Fig.6.10 Showing the effect of increased rotor resistance on torque-speed curve

Vocabulary

1. allowable temperature rise   允许温升
2. alnico   n.   铝镍钴合金
3. asynchronous machine   异步电机
4. automobile starter motor   汽车启动机
5. backlash   n.   啮合间隙,齿隙
6. centrifugal force   离心力
7. ceramic   a.   陶瓷的
8. compound-wound   复励
9. constraint   n.   强制,约束
10. counter emf   反电势
11. counterpart   n.   对应物
12. culminate   v.   达到极值点,达到顶点
13. cumulative compound   积复励
14. demagnetization   n.   退磁,去磁

15. denominator	n.	分母
16. differential compound		差复励
17. dissipate	v.	浪费
18. doubly excited		双边励磁
19. equilibrium level		平均值
20. equivalent circuit		等效电路
21. figure of merit		品质因数,优值
22. flicker	n.	闪烁,摇曳
23. flux per pole		每极磁通
24. friction	n.	摩擦
25. in parallel with		并联
26. in series with		串联
27. in terms of		根据,在……方面
28. in the vicinity of		在……附近,在……左右
29. indispensable	a.	必需的,必不可少的
30. inherent	a.	固有的
31. insulation	n.	绝缘
32. long-shunt	n.	长复励
33. loss	n.	损耗
34. magnetization curve		磁化曲线
35. merit	n.	优点,长处,指标
36. no load		空载
37. nonetheless, none the less		仍然,依然
38. numerator	n.	分子
39. overload	n.	过载
40. permanent-magnet	n.	永磁
41. permissible	a.	允许的
42. pertinent	a.	有关的
43. power flow diagram		功率流程图
44. prefix	n. & v.	前缀,把……放在前面

45. rated torque		额定转矩
46. reaction	n.	电感
47. rheostat	n.	变阻器,电阻箱
48. series-wound		串励
49. short-shunt		短复励
50. shunt-wound		并励
51. starting current		启动电流
52. starting torque		启动转矩
53. synchronous speed		同步转速
54. theorem	n.	定理
55. turns	n.	匝数
56. undervoltage	n.	欠电压
57. Ward-Leonard system		发电机-电动机组系统
58. windage	n.	通风
59. yield	v.	产生,提供

Notes:

1. This type of DC motor has field coils which are wound of many turns of small-diameter wire and have a relatively high resistance.

这种直流电动机的励磁绕组匝数多,线径小,具有较高的电阻。

2. The compound motor is prefixed with the word cumulative in order to stress that the connections to the series field winding are such as to ensure that the series field flux aids the shunt-field flux.

为了强调所接串励绕组的串励磁通与并励磁通是相加的,在复励电动机前面加一个"积"字。

3. The electrical power input VtIL originating from the line supplies the field power needed to establish the flux field as well as the armature-circuit copper loss needed to maintain the flow of I_a.

来自电网的电功率 VtIL 提供了用于建立磁场的磁场能量以及用于维持电枢电流 I_a 的电枢电路铜损耗。

4. In fact this excess serves as an accelerating torque, which then proceeds to increase the speed to that level which corresponds to the equilibrium value of armature current.

事实上,这个差值是作为加速转矩,使转速升高至与之相平衡的电枢电流相对应。

5. As a matter of fact the applied load torque causes the motor to assume that value of speed which yields a current sufficient to produce a developed torque to overcome the applied shaft torque and the frictional torque.

事实上,外加负载转矩使电动机在某转速下运行,此时电机的电流所产生的转矩用于克服外加的负载转矩和摩擦转矩。

6. The extent to which the speed increases depends upon how large the armature circuit resistance drop is in comparison to the terminal voltage.

转速增加的趋势取决于电枢电阻压降与端电压相比有多大。

7. However, because of the weakened flux field the permissible torque that can be delivered at the higher speed is correspondingly reduced, in order to prevent excessive armature current.

然而,由于弱磁,高速时电动机(发出)的允许转矩要相应减小,这是为了防止电枢电流过大。

8. However, the relationship between the rotor speed and the frequency of the armature current is such as to yield a resulting ampere-conductor distribution that is stationary relative to the field distribution of the stator.

然而,转子转速与转子电流频率之间的关系导致载流导体(磁场)分布与定子磁场是相对静止的。

9. Moreover, because of the presence of an air gap in the magnetic circuit of the induction machine, an appreciable amount of magnetizing current is needed to establish the flux per pole demanded by the applied voltage.

此外,由于感应电机磁路中有气隙,外加电压要产生一定的励磁电流来建立所需的每极磁通。

10. When the motor operates at a very small slip, as at no-load, the rotor current is practically zero so that only that amount of torque is developed which is needed to supply the rotational losses.

当电动机在转差较小的状态下运行,如空载时,转子电流几乎为零,这样(电动机)发出的转矩仅用于提供旋转损耗(即空载损耗)。

11. Since the torque equation now involves two opposing factors, it is entirely reasonable to expect that a point is reached beyond which further increases in slip culminate in decreased developed torque.

现在,由于转矩方程式中包含两个对立的系数,完全有理由得到这样一点,在该点当转差率继续增加并超过临界值时,所产生的转矩会减小。

12. That is, maximum power is transferred to the gap power resistor r'_2/s when this resistor is equal to the impedance looking back into the source.

也就是说,当电阻 r'_2/s 与反过来看进电源的阻抗值相等时,最大功率被传到气隙功率(电磁功率)电阻 r'_2/s 上。

7

Electrical Machine Control Systems

The previous chapters have dealt primarily with the types and characteristics of electrical machines. This chapter provides an overview of several power control systems which are used with electrical machines.

7.1 CONTROL SYMBOLS

It is necessary to become familiar with the electrical symbols which are commonly used with machine control systems. Some common machine control symbols are shown in Fig.7.1.

7.2 MACHINE CONTROL WITH SWITCHES

An important type of electrical machine control is the switch. Many types of switches are used to control electrical machines. The function of a switch is to turn a circuit on or off; however, many more complex switch functions can be performed.

7.2.1 Toggle switches

Among the simplest type of switches are toggle switches. The sym-

Electrical Machine Control Systems 121

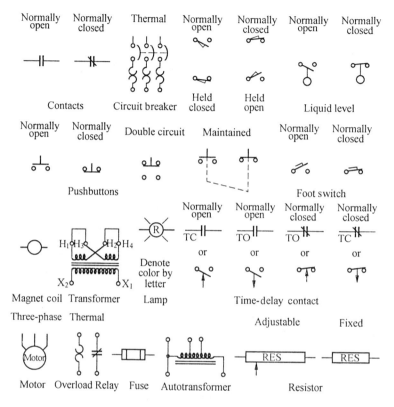

Fig. 7.1 Common machine control symbols

bols for several kinds of toggle switches are shown in Fig. 7.2. Notice the symbols that are used for various types of toggle switches.

7.2.2 Pushbutton switches

Pushbutton switches are commonly used for machine control. Many machine control applications use pushbuttons as a means of starting, stopping, or reversing a motor. Pushbuttons are manually operated to close or open a machine control circuit. There are several types of pushbuttons used for the control of machines. Pushbuttons are usually mounted in enclosures called motor control stations.

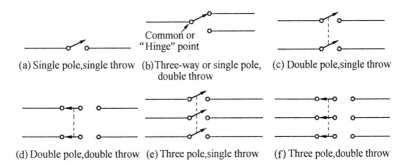

Fig.7.2 Toggle switches

Ordinarily, pushbuttons are either the normally closed (NC) or normally open (NO) types. However, there are a few modifications. A normally closed pushbutton is closed until it is depressed manually and will open a circuit when it is depressed. The normally open pushbutton is open until it is manually depressed and, then, once it is depressed, it will close a circuit. The "start" pushbutton of a motor control station is of NO type, while the "stop" switches of NC type.

7.2.3 Rotary switches

Another common type of switch is the rotary switch. Many different switching combinations can be wired by using a rotary switch. The shaft of a rotary switch is attached to sets of moving contacts. These moving contacts touch different sets of stationary contacts which are mounted on ceramic segments when the rotary shaft is turned to different positions. The shaft can lock into place in any of several positions. Rotary switches are usually controlled by manually turning the rotary shaft clockwise or counterclockwise. A knob is normally fastened to the end of the rotary shaft to permit easier turning of the rotary shaft.

7.2.4 Limit switches

Limit switches are merely on/off switches that use mechanical movement to cause a change in the operation of the electrical control circuit of a machine. The electrical current developed as a result of the mechanical movement is used to limit movement of the machine or to make some change in its operational sequence. Limit switches are often used in sequencing, routing, sorting, or counting operations in industry. Often, they are used in conjunction with hydraulic or pneumatic controls, electrical relays, or other motor-operated machinery such as drill presses, lathes, or conveyor systems.

In its most basic form, a limit switch converts mechanical motion into an electrical control current. Notice the cam, which is an external part that is usually mounted on a machine. The cam applies force to an actuator of the limit switch. The actuator is the part of the limit switch that causes the internal NO or NC contacts to change state. The actuator operates due to either linear or rotary motion of the cam, which applies force to the limit switch. The other terms associated with limit switches are pretravel and overtravel. Pretravel is the distance that the actuator must move to change the normally open or normally closed state of the limit-switch contacts. Overtravel is the distance the actuator moves beyond the point where the contacts change state. Both pretravel and overtravel settings are important in machine setups where limit switches are used.

7.2.5 Temperature switches

Temperature switches are common types of control devices. The control element of a temperature switch contains a specific amount of liquid. The liquid increase in volume when temperature increases. Thus changes in temperature can be used to change the position of a set of contacts within the temperature-switch enclosure. Temperature switches may be adjusted throughout a range of temperature settings.

7.2.6 Pressure switches

Another type of electrical control device is called a pressure switch. A pressure switch has a set of electrical contacts which change states due to a variation in the pressure of air, hydraulic fluid, water, or some other medium. Some pressure switches are diaphragm operated and rely on the intake or expelling of a medium such as air. This action takes place in a diaphragm assembly within the pressure-switch enclosure. Another type of pressure switch uses a piston mechanism to initiate the action of opening or closing the switch contacts. In this way, the movement of a piston is controlled by the pressure of a medium (air, water, etc).

7.2.7 Foot switches

A foot switch is a switch that is controlled by a foot pedal. This type of switch is used for applications where a machine operator has to use both hands during the operation of the machine. The foot switch provides an additional control position for the operation of a machine for such times as when the hands cannot be used.

7.3 CONTROL EQUIPMENT FOR ELECTRICAL MACHINES

Several types of electromechanical equipment are used for the control of electrical machines. The selection of control equipment affects the efficiency of the system and the performance of the machinery. It is very important to use the proper type of equipment for each machine control application. This section will discuss some types of equipment used for motor control.

7.3.1 Motor Starting Control

A motor starting device is a type of machine control used to accelerate a motor from a "stopped" condition to its normal operating speed.

There are many variations in motor starter design, the simplest being a manually operated on/off switch connected in series with one or more power lines. This type of starter is used only for smaller motors which do not draw an excessive amount of current.

One type of motor starter is the magnetic starter which relies on electromagnetism to open or close the power source circuit of the motor. Often, motor starters and other control equipment are grouped together for the control of adjacent machines. Such groupings of starters and associated control equipment are called power control centers. Control centers provide easier access to the power system since they are more compact and the control equipment is not scattered throughout a large area.

Several types of motor starters are used for control of electrical machines. The functions of starters vary in complexity; however, they usually perform one or more of the following functions: ① on and off control, ②acceleration, ③ overload protection, or ④ reversing direction of rotation.

Some starters control a motor by being connected directly across the power input lines. Other starters reduce the level of input voltage that is applied to the motor when it is started so as to reduce the value of the starting current. Ordinarily, motor overload protection is contained in the same enclosure as the starter.

A typical electrical motor contactor circuit is illustrated in Fig.7.3. A contactor is a control element of several types of motor starters that actuates a machine. Pressing the start pushbutton switch in Fig.7.3 completes a low-current path to the contactor coil. The contactor coil produces a magnetic field that attracts the armature. Mechanical movement of the armature then completes an electrical path between the power line and the motor through a set of contact points. When this action takes place, the motor starts its operational cycle.

126 *English in Electric Automation*

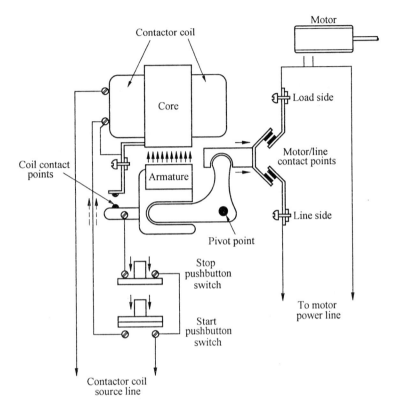

Fig.7.3 Motor contactor circuit

The coil contact points on the left side of the armature are pulled together by the same armature action. As a result, release of the start button at this time will not deenergize the contactor coil. A path to the coil source is now completed through the stop pushbutton switch and the coil contact points on the armature. The motor therefore continues to operate as long as electric power is applied. The contact used for this function is called a holding contact.

Stopping the operation of a contactor-controlled motor is achieved by pushing the stop button. This action opens the contactor coil power source, which deenergizes the coil and causes the armature to drop out of position. The contactor points in series with the motor also break contact, which deenergizes the power to the motor. This path then becomes incomplete and motor operation stops immediately.

The relay action of a motor contactor is designed to have a latching characteristic that holds it into operation once it is energized. This condition is a necessity in motor control applications. In addition to this, contactors may also be used to actuate a series of operations in a particular sequence. A circuit diagram and brief explanation of the operation of a motor contactor are provided in Fig.7.4. ① Press start pushbutton. Circuit is completed when the normally open pushbutton (PB) is momentarily closed. Current flows from voltage source, through normally closed stop PB, through start PB, through the contactor coil, to the other side of the voltage source. This energizes the coil and causes all contacts to close.

② Contacts close. Motor will start since AC voltage is applied through the contacts directly to the motor. The holding contact causes the current path through the coil to be complete after the start PB is released.

③ Motor will run.

④ Press stop pushbutton. The current path is opened by momentarily opening the normally closed stop PB. The coil deenergizes, causing the contacts to open.

⑤ Motor will stop.

7.3.2 Relays

Relays are widely used control devices. They have an electromagnet which contains a stationary core. Mounted close to one end of the core is a movable piece of magnetic material called the armature. When the coil is activated electrically, it produces a magnetic field around the metal core. The armature is then attracted toward the core. When the coil is deenergized, the armature is returned to its original position by spring action. Fig.7.5 shows a simplified diagram of a relay used to control a mo-

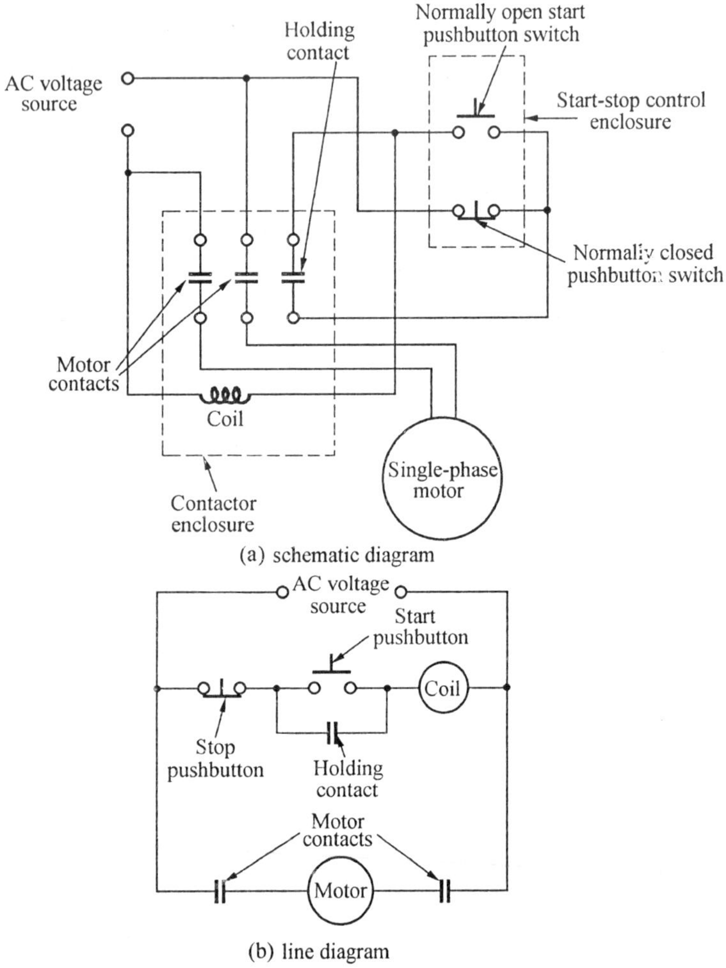

Fig.7.4 Circuit diagram of a motor contactor circuit

tor.

The armature of a relay is generally designed so that electrical contact points respond to its movement. Activation of the relay coil causes the contact points to "make" or "break" according to the design of the relay.

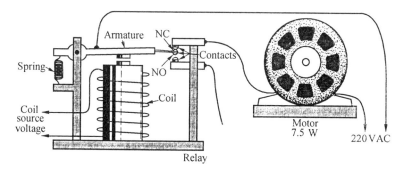

Fig. 7.5 Simplified diagram of the construction of a relay that is used to control a motor

A relay is considered to be an electromagnetic switching mechanism. There are many special-purpose relays and switch combinations used for electrical machine control.

Relays use a small amount of current to create an electromagnetic field that is strong enough to attract the armature. When the armature is attracted it either opens or closes the contacts. The contacts, then, either turn on or turn off circuits that are using large amounts of current. The minimum current that flows through the relay coil in order to create a magnetic field strong enough to attract the armature is known as the pick up current. The current through the relay coil that allows the magnetic field to become weak enough to release the armature is known as the dropout current.

There are two types of contacts used in conjunction with most relays: normally open and normally closed. The normally open contacts remain open when the relay coil is deenergized and closes when the relay is energized. The normally closed contacts remain closed when the relay is deenergized and open when the coil is energized.

7.3.3 Solenoids

A solenoid, shown in Fig. 7.6, is an electromagnetic coil with a movable core that is constructed of a magnetic material. The core, or plunger, is sometimes attached to an external spring. This spring causes the plunger to remain in a fixed position until moved by the electromagnetic field that is created by current through the coil. This external spring also causes the core or plunger to return to its original position when the coil is deenergized.

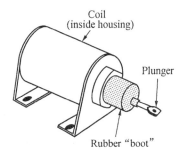

Fig.7.6 Solenoid

Solenoids are used for a variety of control applications. Many gas and fuel-oil furnaces use solenoid valves to turn the fuel supply on or off automatically upon demand. Most dishwashers use one or more solenoids to control the flow of water.

7.3.4 Special-Purpose Relays

There are many special-purpose relays used for electrical machine control. General-purpose relays are the type used for low-power applications. They are relatively inexpensive and small in size. Many small general-purpose relays are mounted in octal-base (8-pin) plug-in sockets. Latching relays are another type of relay which have a latching mechanism which holds the contacts in position after the power has been removed from the coil. Solid-state relays are electrically operated and used where improved reliability or a rapid rate of operation is necessary. Electromagnetic relays will wear out after prolonged use and have to be replaced periodically. Solid-state relays have a longer life expectancy and are not sensitive to shock, vibration, dust, moisture, or corrosion. Timing relays are used to turn a load device on or off after a specific period of time. One popular type is a pneumatic timing relay. The operation of a pneumatic timing relay is dependent on the movement of air within a chamber. Air movement is controlled by an adjustable orifice that regulates the rate of air movement through the chamber. The airflow rate determines the rate of movement of a diaphragm or piston assembly. This assembly is connected to the contacts of the relays. Therefore, the orifice adjustment controls the airflow rate, which determines the time from the activation of the relay until a load connected to it is turned on or off. There are other types of timing relays, such as solid-state, thermal, oil-filled, dashpot, and motor-driven timers. Timing relays are useful for sequencing operations where a time delay is required between operations. A typical application is as follows: ① a start pushbutton is pressed; ② a timing relay is activated; ③ after a 10 s time delay, a motor is turned on.

7.4 MOTOR STARTING SYSTEMS

Motor starting, particularly for large motors, plays an important role in the efficient operation of electrical machinery. Several different systems are used to start electric motors. The motor starting equipment that is used is placed between the electrical power source and the motor. Electric motors draw a larger current from the power source during starting than during normal operation. Motor starting equipment is often used to reduce starting currents to a level that can be handled by the electrical power system.

7.4.1 Full-voltage starting

One method of starting electric motors is called full-voltage starting. This method is the least expensive and the simplest to install. Since full power supply voltage is applied to the motor initially, maximum starting torque and minimum acceleration time result. However, the electrical power system must be able to handle the starting current drawn by the motor.

Full-voltage starting is illustrated by the diagram of Fig.7.7. In this

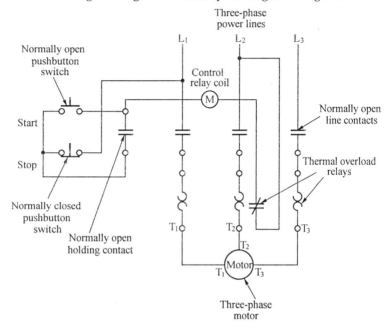

Fig.7.7 Full-voltage starting circuit for a three-phase motor

motor control circuit, a start-stop pushbutton station is used to control a three-phase motor. When the normally open start pushbutton is pressed, current flows through the relay coil (M), causing the normally open contacts to close. The line contacts allow full voltage to be applied to the motor when they are closed. When the start pushbutton is released, the relay coil remains energized due to the holding contact. This contact provides a current path from L_1 through the normally closed stop pushbutton, through the holding contact, through the coil (M), through a thermal overload relay, and back to L_2. When the stop pushbutton is pressed, this circuit is opened causing the coil to be deenergized.

7.4.2 Primary-resistance starting

Another motor starting method is called primary resistance starting. This method uses large resistors in series with the power lines to reduce the motor starting current. Often, the resistance connected into the power lines is reduced in steps until full voltage is applied to the motor. Thus starting current is reduced according to the value of the series resistance in the power lines since starting torque is reduced according to the magnitude of current flow.

Fig.7.8 shows the primary-resistance starting method used to control a three-phase motor. When the start pushbutton is pressed, coils (S) and (TR) are energized. Initially, the start contacts (S) will close, applying voltage through the primary resistors to the motor. These resistors reduce the value of starting current. Once the time-delay period of the timing relay (TR) has elapsed, contact TR will close. The run contacts (R) will then close and apply full voltage to the motor.

7.4.3 Primary-reactor starting

Another starting method, similar to primary-resistance starting, is the primary-reactor starting method. Reactors (coils) are used in place of resistors since they consume smaller amounts of power from the AC source. Usually, this method is more appropriate for large motors that are rated at over 600 V.

7.4.4 Autotransformer starting

Autotransformer starting is another method used to start electric motors. This method employs one or more autotransformers to control the voltage that is applied to a motor. The autotransformers used are ordinarily tapped to provide a range of starting-current control. When the motor has accelerated to near its normal operating speed, the autotransformer

134　English in Electric Automation

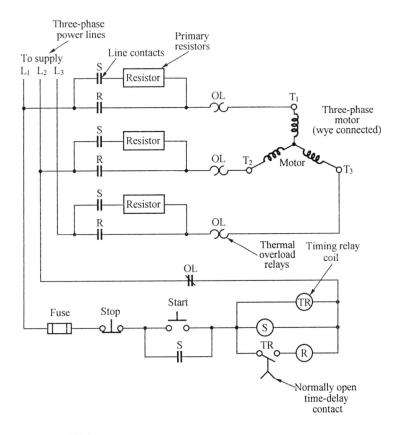

Fig.7.8　Primary-resistance starter circuit

windings are removed from the circuit. A major disadvantage of this method is the expense of the autotransformers.

　　An autotransformer starting circuit is shown in Fig.7.9. This is an expensive type of control that uses three autotransformers and four relays. When the start pushbutton is pressed, current flows through coils (1S), (2S), and (TR). The 1S and 2S contacts will then close. Voltage is applied through the autotransformer windings to the three-phase motor. One normally closed and one normally open contact are controlled by timing relay TR. When the specified time period has elapsed, the normally

Electrical Machine Control Systems   135

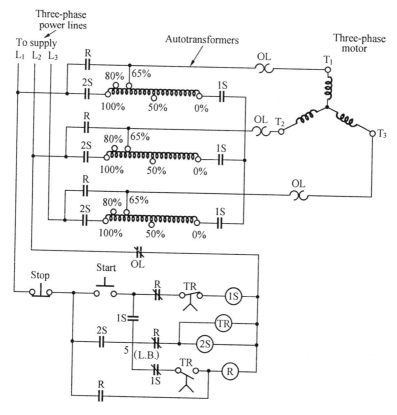

Fig.7.9 Autotransformer starter circuit with a three-phase motor

closed TR contact will open and the normally open TR contact will close. Coil (R) then energizes, causing the normally open R contacts to close and apply full voltage to the motor. Normally closed R contacts are connected in series with coils (1S), (2S), and (TR) to open their circuits when coil (R) is energized. When the stop pushbutton is pressed, the current to coil (R) is interrupted, thus opening the power-line connections to the motor.

Notice that the 65% taps of the autotransformer are used in Fig. 7.9. There are also taps for 50%, 80%, and 100%, to provide more flexibility in reducing the motor-starting current.

7.4.5 Wye-delta starting

It is possible to start three-phase motors more economically by using the wye-delta starting method. Since in a wye configuration, line voltage is equal to the phase voltage divided by 1.73 (or $\sqrt{3}$), it is possible to reduce the starting current by using a wye connection rather than a delta connection. This method, shown in Fig. 7.10, employs a switching arrangement which places the motor stator windings in a wye configuration during starting and a delta arrangement for running. In this way, starting current is reduced. Although starting torque is reduced, running torque is still high since full voltage appears across each winding when the motor is connected in a delta configuration.

When the start pushbutton in Fig. 7.10 is pressed, coil (S) is energized. The normally open S contacts then close. This action connects the motor windings in a wye configuration and also activates timing relay (TR) and coil (1M). The normally open 1M contacts then close to apply voltage to the wye-connected motor windings. After the time-delay period has elapsed, the TR contacts change state. Coil (S) deenergizes and coil (2M) energizes. The S contacts which hold the motor windings in a wye arrangement then open. The 2M contacts then close and cause the motor windings to be connected in a delta configuration. The motor will then continue to run with the stator windings connected in a delta arrangement.

7.4.6 DC starting systems

Since DC motors have no counterelectromotive force (CEMF) when they are not rotating, they have tremendously high starting currents. Therefore, they must use some type of control system to reduce the initial starting current, such as a series resistance. Resistance can be manually or automatically reduced until full voltage is applied. The four types of

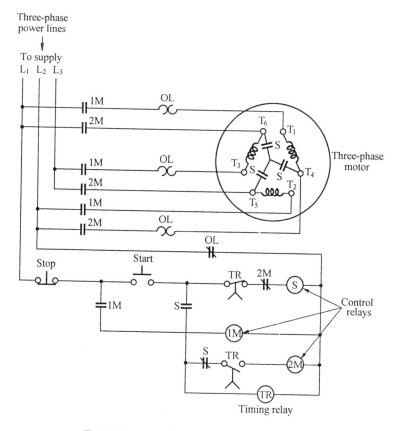

Fig.7.10 Three-phase wye-delta starting circuit

control systems commonly used with DC motors are ① current limit, ② definite time, ③ CEMF, and ④ variable voltage. The current-limit method allows the starting current to be reduced to a specified level and then advanced to the next resistance step. The definite-time method causes the motor to increase speed in timed intervals with no regard to the amount of armature current or to the speed of the motor. The CEMF method samples the amount of CEMF generated by the armature of the motor to reduce the series resistance accordingly. This method can be used effectively since CEMF is proportional to both the speed and the armature current of a DC motor. The variable-voltage method employs a variable DC power source to apply a reduced voltage to the motor initially and then gradually increase the voltage. No series resistances are needed when the variable-voltage method is used.

7.5 FORWARD AND REVERSE CONTROL

Most types of electrical motors can be made to rotate in either direction by some simple modifications of their winding connections. Ordinarily, motors require two magnetic motor contactors to accomplish forward and reverse operation. These contactors are used in conjunction with a set of three-pushbutton switches: forward, reverse, and stop. When the forward pushbutton switch is depressed, the forward contactor is energized. It is deactivated when the stop pushbutton switch is depressed. A similar procedure takes place during reverse operation.

7.5.1 DC motor reversing

Direct-current motors have their direction of rotation reversed by changing either the armature connection or the field connections to the power source. In Fig.7.11, a DC shunt motor control circuit is shown. When the forward pushbutton is pressed, coil (F) is energized, causing the F contacts to close. The armature circuit is then completed from L_1 through the lower F contact, up

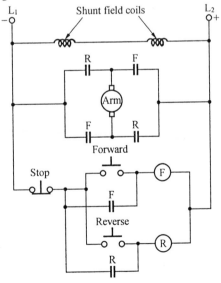

Fig.7.11 Control circuit for the forward and reverse operation of a DC shunt motor

through the armature, through the upper F contact, and back to L_2. Pressing the stop pushbutton deenergizes coil (F).

The direction of rotation of the motor is reversed when the reverse pushbutton is pressed. This is due to the change of the current direction through the armature. Pressing the reverse pushbutton energizes coil (R) and closes the R contacts. The armature current path is then from L_1 through the upper R contact, down through the armature, through the lower R contact, and back to L_2. Pressing the stop button deenergizes coil (R).

7.5.2 Single-phase induction-motor reversing

Single-phase AC induction motors that have start and run windings have their direction of rotation reversed by using the circuit in Fig.7.11. The diagram is modified by replacing the shunt field coils with the run windings and the armature with the start windings. Single-phase induction motors are reversed by changing the connections of either the start windings or the run windings but not both at the same time.

7.5.3 Three-phase induction-motor reversing

Three-phase motors have their direction of rotation reversed by simply changing the connections of any two power lines. This changes the phase sequence applied to the motor. A control circuit for three-phase induction-motor reversing is shown in Fig.7.12.

When the forward pushbutton is pressed, the forward coil will energize and close the F contacts. The three-phase voltage is applied from L_1 to T_1, L_2 to T_2, and L_3 to T_3 to cause the motor to operate. The stop pushbutton deenergizes the forward coil. When the reverse pushbutton is pressed, the reverse coil is energized and the R contacts will close. The voltage is then applied from L_1 to T_3, L_2 to T_2, and L_3 to T_1. This action reverses the L_1 and L_3 connections to the motor and causes the motor to

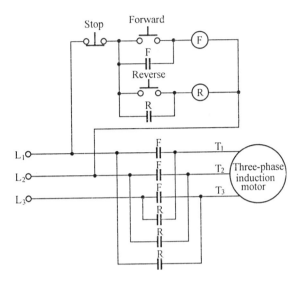

Fig.7.12 Control circuit for the forward and reverse operation of a three-phase induction motor

rotate in the reverse direction.

7.6 DYNAMIC BRAKING

When a motor is turned off, its shaft continues to rotate for a short period of time. This continued rotation is undesirable for many applications. Dynamic braking is a method used to bring a motor to a quick stop whenever power is turned off. Motors with wound armatures utilize a resistance connected across the armature as a dynamic braking method. When power is turned off, the resistance is connection across the armature. This causes the armature to act as a loaded generator, making the motor slow down immediately. This dynamic braking method is shown in Fig.7.13.

Alternating-current induction motors can be slowed down rapidly by placing a "DC" voltage across the winding of the motor. This DC voltage sets up a constant magnetic field which causes the rotor to slow down

Electrical Machine Control Systems 141

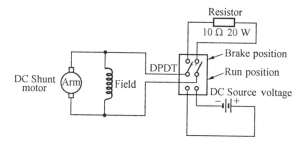

Fig.7.13 Dynamic braking circuit for a DC shunt motor

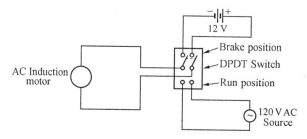

Fig.7.14 Dynamic braking circuit for a single-phase AC induction motor

rapidly. A circuit for the dynamic braking of a single-phase AC induction motor is shown in Fig.7.14.

Vocabulary

1. adjacent	a.	相邻的,邻近的
2. autotransformer	n.	自耦变压器
3. braking	n.	制动
4. cam	n.	凸轮
5. chamber	n.	室,腔
6. conveyor	n.	传送机
7. corrosion	n.	腐蚀
8. counterclockwise	n.	逆时针
9. counterelectromotive force, CEMF		反电势

10. dashpot relay　　　　　　　　　油壶式继电器
11. diaphragm　　　　　　n.　　　膜片,挡板
12. drill　　　　　　　　　n.　　　钻床
13. elapse　　　　　　　　vi.　　　过去,消逝
14. enclosure　　　　　　　n.　　　机壳
15. expel　　　　　　　　　v.　　　排出,放出
16. fasten　　　　　　　　v.　　　固定,连接
17. furnace　　　　　　　　n.　　　炉
18. fuse　　　　　　　　　n.　　　熔断器,保险丝
19. general-purpose relay　　　　　通用继电器
20. hydraulic　　　　　　　a.　　　液压传动
21. initiate　　　　　　　　v.　　　引起,促进
22. intake　　　　　　　　v.　　　吸入
23. knob　　　　　　　　　n.　　　旋钮,圆形把手
24. latching relay　　　　　　　　自锁继电器
25. lathe　　　　　　　　　n.　　　车床
26. limit switch　　　　　　　　　限位开关
27. moisture　　　　　　　n.　　　潮气,湿度
28. mount　　　　　　　　v.　　　安装
29. octal-base　　　　　　　　　　八脚的
30. orifice　　　　　　　　n.　　　孔,注孔
31. pedal　　　　　　　　　n.　　　踏板,脚蹬
32. phase sequence　　　　　　　　相序
33. piston　　　　　　　　n.　　　活塞
34. pivot　　　　　　　　　n.　　　轴,支点,旋转中心
35. plunger　　　　　　　　n.　　　可动铁心,插棒式铁心
36. pneumatic　　　　　　　a.　　　气动的
37. relay　　　　　　　　　n.　　　继电器
38. single-phase　　　　　　　　　单相
39. solenoids　　　　　　　n.　　　螺线管

40. solid-state relay   固态继电器
41. spring   *n.*   弹簧
42. tap   *n.*   抽头
43. three-phase   三相
44. timing relay   延时继电器
45. toggle   *n.*   搬扭,刀闸
46. vibration   *n.*   振动

Notes:

1. The shaft of a rotary switch is attached to sets of moving contacts. These moving contacts touch different sets of stationary contacts which are mounted on ceramic segments when the rotary shaft is turned to different positions.

旋转开关的转轴与一系列运动触点相连。当转轴被转到不同位置时,这些运动触点与装在瓷片上的一系列不同静止触点接触。

2. Limit switches are often used in sequencing, routing, sorting, or counting operations in industry. Often, they are used in conjunction with hydraulic or pneumatic controls, electrical relays, or other motor-operated machinery such as drill presses, lathes, or conveyor systems.

在工业中,限位开关常被用于顺序、行程、分类或计数操作。他们常被用于与流体或气动控制,继电器或其它诸如钻床、车床或传送带系统等电动机驱动的机械相联。

3. Pretravel is the distance that the actuator must move to change the normally open or normally closed state of the limit-switch contacts. Overtravel is the distance the actuator moves beyond the point where the contacts change state.

预行程是执行机构运动而改变限位开关触点常开或常闭状态的距离。过行程是执行机构在触点改变状态时运动的距离。

4. Control centers provide easier access to the power system since they are more compact and the control equipment is not scattered through a large area.

由于控制中心较紧凑,控制设备不是大面积分布的,使其易于接近电源系统。

5. The relay action of a motor contactor is designed to have a latching character-

istic that holds it into operation once it is energized.

电动机接触器的继电器动作被设计为具有自锁特性,即继电器一旦得电,可保持它的操作。

6. Latching relays are another type of relay which have a latching mechanism which holds the contacts in position after the power has been removed from the coil.

自锁继电器是另一种具有自锁机构的继电器,当线圈掉电时,自锁机构可保持触点的位置。

7. Air movement is controlled by an adjustable orifice that regulates the rate of air movement through the chamber.

空气的运动由一个(大小)可调的孔来控制,该孔可以控制通过腔的空气的速度。

8. Since in a wye configuration, line voltage is equal to the phase voltage divided by 1.73 (or $\sqrt{3}$), it is possible to reduce the starting current by using a wye connection rather than a delta connection.

对 Y 接法,相电压等于线电压除以 1.73,因此可采用 Y 接法减小启动电流,而不是采用△接法。

8

Control Sensors

8.1 INTRODUCTION

In feedback control systems – plant response is measured and compared with a reference input and the error is automatically employed in controlling the plant. It follows that a measurement system is an essential component in any feedback control system and forms a vital link between the plant and the controller. Measurements are needed in many engineering applications. The measurement process has to be automated, however, in control systems applications.

A typical measurement system consists of one or more sensor-transducer units and associated signal-conditioning (and modification) devices (see Fig. 8.1). Filtering to remove unwanted noise and amplification to strengthen a needed signal are considered signal conditioning. Analog-to-digital conversion (ADC), digital-to-analog conversion (DAC), modulation, and demodulation are signal modification methods. Note that signal conditioning can be considered under the general heading of signal modification. Even though data recording is an integral function in a typical data

Fig.8.1 Schematic representation of a measurement system

acquisition system, it is not a crucial function in a feedback control system. For this reason, we shall not go into details of data recording devices in this book. In a multiple measurement environment, a multiplexer could be employed prior to or following the signal-conditioning process, in order to pick one measured signal at a time from a bank of data channels for subsequent processing. In this manner, one unit of expensive processing hardware can be time-shared between several signals. Sensor-transducer devices are predominantly analog components that generate analog signals, even though direct digital transducers are becoming increasingly popular in digital control applications. When analog transducers are employed, analog-to-digital converters (ADCs) have to be used to convert analog signals into digital data for digital control. This signal modification process requires sampling of analog signals at discrete time points. Once a value is sampled, it is encoded into a digital representation such as straight binary code, a gray code, binary-coded decimal (BCD) code or American Standard Code for Information Interchange (ASCII). The changes in an analog signal due to its transient nature should not affect this process of ADC. To guarantee this, a sample-and-hold operation is required during each sampling period. For example, the value of an analog signal is detected (sampled) in the beginning of each sampling period and is assumed constant (held) throughout the entire sampling period. This is, in fact, the zero-order hold operation. The operations of multiplexing, sampling, and digitizing have to be properly synchronized under the control of an accurate timing device (a clock) for proper operation of the control system. This procedure is shown schematically in Fig.8.2.

All devices that assist in the measurement procedure can be inter-

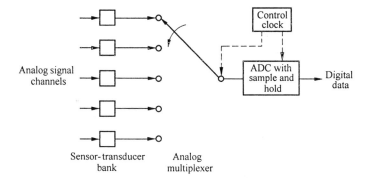

Fig. 8.2 Measurement, multiplexing, and analog-to-digital conversion

preted as components of the measurement system. Selection of available components for a particular application or design of new components should rely heavily on performance specification for these components. A great majority of instrument ratings provided by manufacturers are in the form of static parameters. In control applications, however, dynamic performance specifications are also very important.

When two or more components are interconnected, the behavior of individual components in the overall system can deviate significantly from their behavior when each component operates independently. Matching of components in a multicomponent system, particularly with respect to their impedance characteristics, should be done carefully in order to improve system performance and accuracy.

8.2 SENSORS AND TRANSDUCERS

The output variable (or response) that is being measured is termed the measurand. Examples are acceleration and velocity of a vehicle, temperature and pressure of a process plant, and current through an electric circuit. A measuring device passes through two stages while measuring a signal. First, the measurand is sensed. Then, the measured signal is transduced (or converted) into a form that is particularly suitable for transmitting, signal conditioning, processing, or driving a controller or actuator. For this reason, output of the transducer stage is often an electrical signal. The measurand is usually an analog signal, because it represents the output of a dynamic system in feedback control applications. Transducer output is discrete in direct digital transducers. This facilitates the direct interface of a transducer with a digital processor.

The sensor and transducer stages of a typical measuring device are represented schematically in Fig.8.3(a). As an example, consider the operation of a piezoelectric accelerometer (see Fig.8.3(b)). In this case, acceleration is the measurand. It is first converted into an inertia force through a mass element and is exerted on a piezoelectric crystal within which a strain (stress) is generated. This is considered the sensing stage. The stress generates a charge inside the crystal, which appears as an electric signal at the output of the accelerometer. This stress-to-charge conversion or stress-to-voltage conversion can be interpreted as the transducer stage.

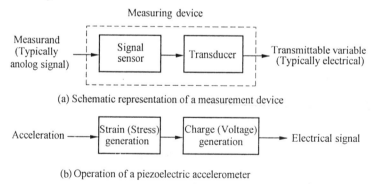

(a) Schematic representation of a measurement device

(b) Operation of a piezoelectric accelerometer

Fig.8.3

A complex measuring device can have more than one sensing stage. More often, the measurand goes through several transducer stages before it is available for control and actuating purposes. Sensor and transducer stages are functional stages, and sometimes it is not easy or even feasible to identify physical elements associated with them. Furthermore, this separation is not very important in using existing devices. Proper separation of sensor and transducer stages (physically as well as functionally) can be crucial, however, when designing new measuring instruments.

In some books, signal-conditioning devices such as electronic amplifiers are also classified as transducers. Since we are treating signal-conditioning and modification devices separately from measuring devices, this unified classification is avoided whenever possible in this book. Instead, the term transducer is used primarily in relation to measuring instruments. Following the common practice, however, the terms sensor and transducer will be used interchangeably to denote measuring instruments.

8.3 ANALOG SENSORS FOR MOTION MEASUREMENT

8.3.1 Introduction

Measurement of plant outputs, is essential for feedback control. Output measurements are also useful in performance evaluation of a process. Furthermore, in learning systems (e.g., teach-repeat operation of robotic manipulators), measurements are made and stored in the computer for subsequent use in operating the system. Input measurements are needed in feedforward control. It is evident, therefore, that the measurement subsystem is an important part of a control system.

The measurement subsystem in a control system contains sensors and transducers that detect measurands and convert them into acceptable signals—typically, voltages. These voltage signals are then appropriately modified using signal-conditioning hardware such as filters, amplifiers, demodulators, and analog-to-digital converters. Impedance matching might be necessary to connect sensors and transducers to signal-conditioning hardware.

Accuracy of sensors, transducers, and associated signal-conditioning devices is important in control system applications for two main reasons. The measurement system in a feedback control system is situated in the feedback path of the control system. Even though measurements are used to compensate for the poor performance in the open-loop system, any errors in measurements themselves will enter directly into the system and cannot be corrected if they are unknown. Furthermore, it can be shown that sensitivity of a control system to parameter changes in the measurement system is direct. This sensitivity cannot be reduced by increasing the loop gain, unlike in the case of sensitivity to the open-loop components. Accordingly, the design strategy for closed-loop (feedback) control is to make the measurements very accurate and to employ a suitable controller to reduce other types of errors.

Most sensor-transducer devices used in feedback control applications are analog components that generate analog output signals. This is the case even in real-time direct digital control systems. When analog transducers are used in digital control applications, however, some type of analog-to-digital conversion (ADC) is needed to obtain a digital representation of the measured signal. The resulting digital signal is subsequently conditioned and processed using digital means.

In the sensor stage, the signal being measured is felt as the "response of the sensor element." This is converted by the transducer into the transmitted (or measured) quantity. In this respect, the output of a measuring device can be interpreted as the "response of the transducer." In control system applications, this output is typically (and preferably) an electrical signal. Note that it is somewhat redundant to consider electrical-to-electrical sensors-transducers as measuring devices, particularly in control system studies, because electrical signals need conditioning only before they are fed into a controller or to a drive system. In this sense, electrical-to-electrical transduction should be considered a "conditioning" task rather than a "measuring" function.

8.3.2 Motion Transducers

By motion, we mean the four kinematic variables:
• Displacement (including position, distance, proximity, and size or gage)
• Velocity
• Acceleration
• Jerk

Note that each variable is the time derivative of the preceding one. Motion measurement are extremely useful in controlling mechanical responses and interactions in dynamic systems. Numerous examples can be cited of situations in which motion measurements are used for control purposes. The rotating speed of a work piece and the feed rate of a tool are measured in controlling machining operations. Displacements and speeds (both angular and translatory) at joints (revolute and prismatic) of robotic manipulators or kinematic linkages are used in controlling manipulator trajectory. In high-speed ground transit vehicles, acceleration and jerk measurements can be used for active suspension control to obtain improved ride quality. Angular speed is a crucial measurement that is used in the control of rotating machinery, such as turbines, pumps, compressors, motors, and generators in power-generating plants. Proximity sensors (to measure displacement) and accelerometers (to measure acceleration) are the two most common types of measuring devices used in machine protection systems for condition monitoring, fault detection, diagnosis, and on-line (often real-time) control of large and complex machinery. The accelerometer is often the only measuring device used in controlling dynamic test rigs. Displacement measurements are used for valve control in process applications. Plate thickness (or gage) is continuously monitored by the automatic gage control (AGC) system in steel rolling mills.

A one-to-one relationship may not always exist between a measuring device and a measured variable. For example, although strain gages are devices that measure strains (and, hence, stresses and forces), they can be adapted to measure displacements by using a suitable front-end auxiliary sensor element, such as a cantilever (or spring). Furthermore, the same measuring device may be used to measure different variables through appropriate data interpretation techniques. For example, piezoelectric accelerometers with built-in microelectronic integrated circuitry are marketed as piezoelectric velocity transducers. Resolver signals that provide angular displacements are differentiated to get angular velocities. Pulse-generating (or digital) transducers, such as optical encoders and digital tachometers, can serve as both displacement transducers and velocity transducers, depending on whether the absolute number of pulses generated is counted or the pulse rate is measured. Note that pulse rate can be measured either by counting the number of pulses during a unit interval of time or by gating a high-frequency clock signal through the pulse width. Furthermore, in principle, any force sensor can be used as an acceleration sensor, velocity sensor, or displacement sensor, depending on whether an inertia element (converting acceleration into force), a damping element (converting velocity into force), or a spring element (converting displacement into force), respectively, is used as the front-end auxiliary sensor.

We might question the need for separate transducers to measure the four kinematic variables—displacement, velocity, acceleration, and jerk—because any one variable is related to any other through simple integration or differentiation. It should be possible, in theory, to measure only one of these four variables and use either analog processing (through analog circuit hardware) or digital processing (through a dedicated processor) to obtain any of the remaining motion variables. The feasibility of this approach is highly limited, however, and it depends crucially on several factors, including the following:

(1) The nature of the measured signal (e.g., steady, highly transient, periodic, narrow-band, broad-band).

(2) The required frequency content of the processed signal (or the frequency range of interest).

(3) The signal-to-noise ratio (SNR) of the measurement.

(4) Available processing capabilities (e.g., analog or digital processing, limitations of the digital processor, and interface, such as the speed of processing, sampling rate, and buffer size).

(5) Controller requirements and the nature of the plant (e.g., time constants, delays, hardware limitations).

(6) Required accuracy in the end objective (on which processing requirements and hardware costs will depend).

For instance, differentiation of a signal (in the time domain) is often unacceptable for noisy and high-frequency narrow-band signals. In any event, costly signal-conditioning hardware might be needed for preprocessing prior to differentiating a signal. As a rule of thumb, in low-frequency applications (on the order of 1 Hz), displacement measurements generally provide good accuracies. In intermediate-frequency applications (less than 1 kHz), velocity measurement is usually favored. In measuring high-frequency motions with high noise levels, acceleration measurement is preferred. Jerk is particularly useful in ground transit (ride quality), manufacturing (forging, rolling, and similar impact-type operations), and shock isolation (delicate and sensitive equipment) applications.

Our discussion of motion transducers will be limited mainly to the following types of devices:

- Potentiometers (resistively coupled devices)
- Variable-inductance transducers (electromagnetically coupled devices)
- Eddy current transducers
- Variable-capacitance transducers

· Piezoelectric transducers

8.4 DIGITAL TRANSDUCERS

8.4.1 Introduction

Any transducer that presents information as discrete samples and that does not introduce a quantization error when the reading is represented in the digital form may be classified as a digital transducer. A digital processor plays the role of controller in a digital control system. This facilitates complex processing of measured signals and other known quantities in order to obtain control signals for the actuators that drive the plant of the control system. If the measured signals are in analog form, an analog-to-digital conversion (ADC) stage is necessary prior to digital processing. There are several other shortcomings of analog signals in comparison to digital processing. These considerations help build a case in favor of direct digital measuring devices for digital control systems.

Digital measuring devices (or digital transducers, as they are commonly known) generate discrete output signals such as pulse trains or encoded data that can be directly read by a control processor. Nevertheless, the sensor stage of digital measuring devices is usually quite similar to that of their analog counterparts. There are digital measuring devices that incorporate microprocessors to perform numerical manipulations and conditioning locally and provide output signals in either digital or analog form. These measuring systems are particularly useful when the required variable is not directly measurable but could be computed using one or more measured outputs (e. g. , power = force × speed). Although a microprocessor is an integral part of the measuring device in this case, it performs not a measuring task but, rather, a condition task. For our purposes, we shall consider the two tasks separately.

The objective of this section is to study the operation and utilization of several types of direct digital transducers. Our discussion will be limited to motion transducers. Note, however, that by using a suitable auxiliary front-end sensor, other measurands—such as force, torque, and pressure—may be converted into a motion and subsequently measured using a motion transducer. For example, altitude (or pressure) measurements in aircraft and aerospace applications are made using a pressure-sensing front end, such as a bellows or diaphragm device, in conjunction with an optical encoder to measure the resulting displacement. Motion, as manifested in physical systems, is typically continuous in time. Therefore, we cannot speak of digital motion sensors in general. Actually, it is the transducer stage that generates the discrete output signal in a digital motion measuring device. Commercially available direct digital transducers are not as numerous as analog sensors, but what is available has found extensive application.

When the output of a digital transducer is a pulse signal, a counter is used either to count the pulses or to count clock cycles over one pulse duration. The count is first represented as a digital word according to some code; then it is read by a data acquisition and control computer. If, on the other hand, the output of digital transducer is automatically available in a coded form (e.g., binary, binary-coded decimal, ASCII), it can be directly read by a computer. In the latter case, the coded signal is normally generated by a parallel set of pulse signals; the word depends on the pattern of the generated pulses.

8.4.2 Shaft Encoders

Any transducer that generates a coded reading of a measurement can be termed an encoder. Shaft encoders are digital transducers that are used for measuring angular displacements and angular velocities. Application of these devices include motion measurement in performance monitoring and control of robotic manipulators, machine tools, digital tape-transport mechanisms, servo plotters and printers, satellite mirror positioning systems, and rotating machinery such as motors, pumps, compressors, turbines, and generators. High resolution (depending on the word size of the encoder output and the number of pulses per revolution of the encoder), high accuracy (particularly due to noise immunity of digital signals and superior construction), and relative ease of adaptation in digital control systems (because transducer output is digital), with associated reduction in system cost and improvement of system reliability, are some of the relative advantages of digital transducer over their analog counterparts.

Shaft encoders can be classified into two categories, depending on the nature and the method of interpretation of the transducer output: ① incremental encoders and ② absolute encoders. The output of an incremental encoder is a pulse signal that is generated when the transducer disk rotates as a result of the motion that is being measured. By counting the pulses or by timing the pulse width using a clock signal, both angular displacement and angular velocity can be determined. Displacement, however, is obtained with respect to some reference point on the disk, as indicated by a reference pulse (index pulse) generated at that location on the disk. The index pulse count determines the number of full revolutions.

An absolute encoder (or whole-word encoder) has many pulse tracks on its transducer disk. When the disk of an absolute encoder rotates, several pulse trains—equal in number to the tracks on the disk—are generated simultaneously. At a given instant, the magnitude of each pulse signal will have one of two signal levels (i.e., a binary state), as determined by a level detector. This signal level corresponds to a binary digit (0 or 1). Hence, the set of pulse trains gives an encoded binary number at any instant. The pulse windows on the tracks can be organized into some pattern (code) so that each of these binary numbers corresponds to the angular position of the encoder disk at the time when the particular binary number is detected. Furthermore, pulse voltage can be made compatible with some form of digital logic (e.g., transistor-to-transistor logic, or TTL). Consequently, the direct digital readout of an angular position is possible, thereby expediting digital data acquisition and processing. Absolute encoders are commonly used to measure fractions of a revolution. However, complete revolutions can be measured using an additional track that generates an index pulse, as in the case of incremental encoder.

The same signal generation (and pick-off) mechanism may be used in both types of transducers. Four techniques of transducer signal generation can be identified:

(1) Optical (photosensor) method.
(2) Sliding contact (electrical conducting) method.
(3) Magnetic saturation (reluctance) method.
(4) Proximity sensor method.

For a given type of encoder (incremental or absolute), the method of signal interpretation is identical for all four types of signal generation.

In many control applications, encoders are built into the plant itself, rather than being externally fitted onto a rotation shaft. For instance, in a robot arm, the encoder might be an integral part of the joint motor and may be located within its housing. This reduces coupling errors (e.g., errors due to backlash, shaft flexibility, and resonances added by the transducer and fixtures), installation errors (e.g., eccentricity), and overall cost.

8.4.3 Digital Tachometers

Since shaft encoders are also used for measuring angular velocities, they can be considered tachometers. In classic terminology, a digital tachometer is a device that employs a toothed wheel to measure angular velocities. A schematic diagram of one such device is shown in Fig.8.4. This is a magnetic induction tachometer of the variable-reluctance type.

The teeth on the wheel are made of ferromagnetic material. The two magnetic induction (and variable-reluctance) proximity probes are placed facing the teeth radially, a quarter-pitch apart. When the toothed wheel rotates, the two probes generate output signals that are 90° out of phase. One signal leads the other in one direction of rotation and lags the other in the opposite direction of rotation. In this manner, directional readings are obtained. The speed is computed either by counting pulses over a sampling period or by timing the pulse width, as in the case of an incremental encoder.

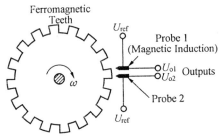

Fig. 8.4 Schematic representation of a pulse tachometer

The advantages of these digital (pulse) tachometers over optical encoders include simplicity, robustness, and low cost. The disadvantages include poor resolution (determined by the number of teeth, the speed of rotation, and the word size used for data transmission), and mechanical errors due to loading, hysteresis, and manufacturing irregularities.

8.4.4 Hall Effect Sensors

Consider a semiconductor element subject to a DC voltage U_{ref}. If a magnetic field is applied perpendicular to the direction of this voltage, a voltage U_o will be generated in the third orthogonal direction within the semiconductor element. This is known as the Hall Effect (observed by E. H. Hall in 1897). A schematic representation of a Hall effect sensor is shown in Fig. 8.5.

A Hall effect sensor may be used for motion sensing in many ways—for example, as an analog proximity sensor, a digital limit switch, or a digital shaft encoder. Since the output voltage U_o increases as the distance from the magnetic source to the semiconductor element decreases, the output signal U_o can be used as a measure of proximity. Alternatively, a certain threshold level of output voltage U_o can be used to activate a digital switch or to create a digital output, hence forming a digital limit switch.

A more practical arrangement would be to have the semiconductor element and the magnetic source fixed relative to one another

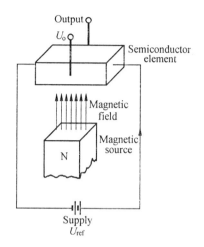

Fig. 8.5 Schematic representation of a hall effect sensor

in a single package. By moving a ferromagnetic member into the air gap between the magnetic source and the semiconductor element, the flux linkage can be altered. This changes U_o. This arrangement is suitable both as an analog proximity sensor and as a limit switch. Furthermore, if a toothed ferromagnetic wheel is used to change U_o, we have a shaft encoder or a digital tachometer (see Fig.8.6).

The longitudinal arrangement of a proximity sensor, in which the moving element approaches head-on toward the sensor, is not suitable when there is a danger of overshooting the target, since it will damage the sensor. A more desirable configuration is the lateral arrangement, in which the moving member slides by the sensing face of the sensor. The sensitivity will be lower, however, with this lateral arrangement.

The relationship between the output voltage U_o and the distance x of a Hall effect sensor measured from the moving member is nonlinear. Linear Hall effect sensors use calibration to linearize their output.

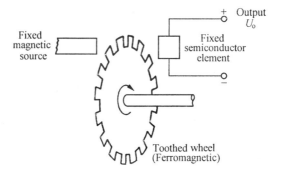

Fig.8.6 Schematic representation of a hall effect shaft encoder or digital tachometer

Vocabulary

1. absolute encoder   绝对编码器
2. accelerometer   n.   加速度测量仪
3. actuator   n.   执行机构
4. analog-to-digital
   conversion, ADC   模数转换器
5. angular   a.   角的
6. auxiliary   a.   辅助的
7. as a rule of thumb   根据经验
8. bellows   n.   膜盒
9. binary-coded decimal, BCD   BCD 码,二-十进制编码
10. calibration   n.   校准;标定;刻度
11. cantilever   n.   悬臂
12. closed-loop   n.   闭环
13. crystal   a. & n.   晶体的;水晶,晶体
14. demodulation   n.   解调
15. derivative   n.   导数
16. diaphragm   n.   膜片
17. differentiation   n.   微分

18. digital-to-analog conversion, DAC　　　数模转换器
19. discrete　　　*a.*　　　离散的
20. displacement　　　*n.*　　　位移
21. eddy　　　*n.*　　　涡流
22. encoder　　　*n.*　　　编码器
23. error　　　*n.*　　　误差，偏差
24. expedite　　　*v.*　　　加速
25. feedback　　　*n.*　　　反馈
26. feedforward　　　*n.*　　　前馈
27. forging　　　*n.*　　　锻造
28. hysteresis　　　*n.*　　　磁滞
29. immunity　　　*n.*　　　抗扰性
30. impedance　　　*n.*　　　阻抗
31. increment encoder　　　　　　增量编码器
32. inertia　　　*n.*　　　惯性
33. integration　　　*n.*　　　积分
34. interface　　　*n.*　　　接口
35. jerk　　　*n.*　　　振动，冲击
36. kinematic　　　*a.*　　　运动的，运动学的
37. longitudinal　　　*a.*　　　经度的；纵向的
38. manipulations　　　*n.*　　　操作；控制；处理
39. manipulator　　　*n.*　　　机械手，操作器
40. measurand　　　*n.*　　　被测量，被测对象
41. modulation　　　*n.*　　　调制
42. multiplexer　　　*n.*　　　多路转换器
43. offset　　　*n.*　　　偏心
44. open-loop　　　*n.*　　　开环
45. orthogonal　　　*a.*　　　垂直的，正交的
46. perpendicular　　　*n.*　　　垂直的，正交的

47. photosensor	n.	光电传感器
48. piezoelectric	a.	压电的
49. plant	n.	装置,设备
50. potentiometer	n.	电位器
51. predominant	a.	主要的,突出的
52. prismatic	a.	棱形的
53. proximity	n.	距离,接近度
54. quantization	n.	量化
55. radial	a.	径向的,辐射状的
56. redundant	a.	多余的,重复的
57. representation	n.	代表,表示
58. resolver	n.	解算器
59. resonance	n.	共振
60. revolute	a.	旋转的,转动的
61. rig	n.	设备
62. robustness	n.	鲁棒性
63. rolling	n.	轧制
64. sampling period		采样周期
65. signal-to-noise ratio, SNR		信噪比
66. strategy	n.	策略
67. subsequently	ad.	其后
68. tachometer	n.	测速仪
69. terminology	n.	术语,专门名词
70. threshold	n.	门;界限;阈值
71. thumb	n.	拇指
72. trajectory	a.	轨迹
73. transducer	n.	传感器
74. transient	a.	瞬态的
75. transistor-to-transistor logic, TTL		晶体管-晶体管逻辑

76. transit　　　　　　　$v.$　　　运输

77. translatory　　　　　$a.$　　　平移的

Notes:

1. In feedback control systems, plant response is measured and compared with a reference input and the error is automatically employed in controlling the plant.

在反馈控制系统中,测量设备的响应,并将其与参考输入相比较,所得偏差被自动用于控制该设备。

2. In a multiple measurement environment, a multiplexer could be employed prior to or following the signal-conditioning process, in order to pick one measured signal at a time from a bank of data channels for subsequent processing.

在多测量环境中,在信号调整之前或之后,可采用多路转换开关,在某一时刻从一组数据通道中选择一个被测信号用于后续处理。

3. The operations of multiplexing, sampling, and digitizing have to be properly synchronized under the control of an accurate timing device (a clock) for proper operation of the control system.

为使控制系统正确运行,多路转换、采样以及数字处理操作在一个精确的定时器件(时钟)控制下应完全同步。

4. Matching of components in a multicomponent system, particularly with respect to their impedance characteristics, should be done carefully in order to improve system performance and accuracy.

在多元件系统中,为提高系统的性能和精度,元件的匹配,尤其对其阻抗特性,应仔细处理。

5. It is first converted into an inertia force through a mass element and is exerted on a piezoelectric crystal within which a strain (stress) is generated.

加速度首先通过质量元件转变为惯性力,然后被施加在压电式晶体上,在晶体内产生压力。

6. Sensor and transducer stages are functional stages, and sometimes it is not easy or even feasible to identify physical elements associated with them.

传感器和变换器级为功能级,有时不易或无法区分与其相关的物理原理。

7. Even though measurements are used to compensate for the poor performance in the open-loop system, any errors in measurements themselves will enter directly into the system and cannot be corrected if they are unknown.

尽管在开环系统中测量可用于补偿不良特性,但测量本身的误差会直接进入系统,若误差未知,则无法校正。

8. Note that it is somewhat redundant to consider electrical-to-electrical sensors-transducers as measuring devices, particularly in control system studies, because electrical signals need conditioning only before they are fed into a controller or to a drive system.

注意认为电信号至电信号的传感器为测量器件有些多余,尤其在控制系统的学习中,这是由于电信号仅在被送入控制器或驱动系统之前才需调整。

9. Displacements and speeds (both angular and translatory) at joints (revolute and prismatic) of robotic manipulators or kinematic linkages are used in controlling manipulator trajectory.

机器人操纵臂或连动装置关节(旋转和棱形运动)的(角和平移)位移和速度用于控制其轨迹。

10. Proximity sensors (to measure displacement) and accelerometers (to measure acceleration) are the two most common types of measuring devices used in machine protection systems for condition monitoring, fault detection, diagnosis, and on-line (often real-time) control of large and complex machinery.

接近传感器(测位移)和加速度计(测加速度)是两种最普通的用在机械保护系统中进行大型复杂机械的状态监测、故障检测、诊断以及在线(常为实时)控制的测量器件。

11. Pulse-generating (or digital) transducers, such as optical encoders and digital tachometers, can serve as both displacement transducers and velocity transducers, depending on whether the absolute number of pulses generated is counted or the pulse rate is measured.

脉冲发生(或数字)变换器(传感器),如光学编码器和数字转速计,能用作位移传感器,也能用作速度传感器,这取决于所产生的绝对脉冲数被计数还是测量脉冲的速度。

12. Furthermore, in principle, any force sensor can be used as an acceleration sensor, velocity sensor, or displacement sensor, depending on whether an inertia element (converting acceleration into force), a damping element (converting velocity into

force), or a spring element (converting displacement into force), respectively, is used as the front-end auxiliary sensor.

此外,原则上任何压力传感器皆可作为加速度传感器、速度传感器或位移传感器,这取决于所采用的前端辅助传感器是惯性元件(把加速度转变为力)、阻尼元件(把速度转变为力)还是弹性元件(把位移转变为力)。

13. Any transducer that presents information as discrete samples and that does not introduce a quantization error when the reading is represented in the digital form may be classified as a digital transducer.

任何传感器,当其产生的信息为离散采样值,并且以数字形式读取不会产生量化误差时,都可以认为是数字传感器。

14. High resolution (depending on the word size of the encoder output and the number of pulses per revolution of the encoder), high accuracy (particularly due to noise immunity of digital signals and superior construction), and relative ease of adaptation in digital control systems (because transducer output is digital), with associated reduction in system cost and improvement of system reliability, are some of the relative advantages of digital transducer over their analog counterparts.

与相对应的模拟传感器相比,数字传感器的优点为分辨率高(取决于编码器输出字的大小以及编码器每转的脉冲数),精度高(尤其取决于数字信号及上级结构的抗扰性),适用于数字控制系统(因为传感器的输出是数字的),可降低系统成本,提高系统可靠性。

15. The longitudinal arrangement of a proximity sensor, in which the moving element approaches head-on toward the sensor, is not suitable when there is a danger of overshooting the target, since it will damage the sensor.

运动元件与接近传感器的正面靠近,当接近传感器存在与目标过近的危险时,由于会损坏传感器,则(此时)传感器的纵向安装是不合适的。

PART 3
COMPUTER CONTROL TECHNIQUES

9

Introduction of Computernets

Each of the past three centuries has been dominated by a single technology. The 18th Century was the time of the great mechanical systems accompanying the Industry Revolution. The 19th Century was the age of the steam engine. During the 20th Century, the key technology has been information gathering, processing, and distribution. Among other developments, we have seen the installation of worldwide telephone networks, the invention of radio and television, the birth and unprecedented growth of the computer industry, and the launching of communication satellites.

Due to rapid technological progress, these areas are rapidly converging, and the differences between collecting, transporting, storing, and processing information are quickly disappearing. Organizations with hundreds of offices spread over a wide geographical area routinely expect to be able to examine the current status of even their most remote outpost at the push of a button. As our ability to gather, process, and distribute information grows, the demand for even more sophisticated information processing grows even faster.

Although the computer industry is young compared to other industries (e.g., automobiles and air transportation), computers have made spectacular progress in a short time. During the first two decades of their existence, computer systems were highly centralized, usually within a single large room. Not infrequently, this room had glass walls, through which visitors could gawk at the great electronic wonder inside. A medium-size company or university might have had one or two computers, while large institutions had at most a few dozen. The idea that within 20 years equally powerful computers smaller than postage stamps would be mass produced by the millions was pure science fiction.

The merging of computers and communications has had a profound influence on the way computer systems are organized. The concept of the "computer center" as a room with a large computer to which users bring their work for processing is now totally obsolete. The old model of a single computer serving all of the organization's computational needs has been replaced by one in which a large number of separate but interconnected computers do the job. These systems are called computer networks. The design and organization of these networks are the subjects of this chapter.

We will use the term "computer network" to mean an interconnected collection of autonomous computers. Two computers are said to be interconnected if they are able to exchange information. The connection need not be via a copper wire, fiber optics, microwaves, and communication satellites can also be used. By requiring the computers to be autonomous, we wish to exclude from our definition systems in which there is a clear master/slave relation, if one computer can forcibly start, stop, or control another one, the computers are not autonomous. A system with one control unit and many slaves is not a network; nor is a large computer with remote printers and terminals.

There is considerable confusion in the literature between a computer network and a distributed system. The key distinction is that in a distributed system, the existence of multiple autonomous computers is transparent (i.e., not visible) to the user. He can type a command to run a program, and it runs. It is up to the operating system to select the best processor, find and transport all the input files to that processor, and put the results in the appropriate place.

In other words, the user of a distributed system is not aware that there are multiple processors; it looks like virtual uniprocessor. Allocation of jobs to the processors and files to disks, movement of files between where they are stored and where they are needed, and all other system functions must be automatic.

With a network, users must explicitly log onto one machine, explicitly submit jobs remotely, explicitly move files around and generally handle all the network management personally. With a distributed system, nothing has to be done explicitly; it is all automatically done by the system without the users' knowledge.

In effect, a distributed system is a software system built on top of a network. The software gives it a high degree of cohesiveness and transparency. Thus the distinction between a network and distributed system lies with the software (especially the operating system), rather than with the hardware.

Nevertheless, there is considerable overlap between the two subjects. For example, both distributed systems and computer networks need to move files around. The difference lies in who invokes the movement, the system or the user.

9.1 USES OF COMPUTER NETWORKS

Before we start to examine the technical issues in detail, it is worth devoting some time to pointing out why people are interested in computer networks and what they can be used for.

9.1.1 Networks for Companies

Many organizations have a substantial number of computers in operation, often located far apart. For example, a company with many factories may have a computer at each location to keep track of inventories, monitor productivity, and do the local payroll. Initially, each of these computers may have worked in isolation from the others, but at some point, management may have decided to connect them to be able to extract and correlate information about the entire company.

Put in slightly more general form, the issue here is resource sharing, and the goal is to make all programs, equipment, and especially data available to anyone on the network without regard to the physical location of the resource and the user. In other words, the mere fact that a user happens to be 1 000 km away from his data should not prevent him from using the data as though they were local. This goal may be summarized by saying that it is an attempt to end the "tyranny of geography."

A second goal is to provide high reliability by having alternative sources of supply. For example, all files could be replicated on two or three machines, so if one of them is unavailable (due to a hardware failure), the other copies could be used. In addition, the presence of multiple CPUs means that if one goes down, the others may be able to take over its work, although at reduced performance. For military, banking, air traffic control, nuclear reactor safety, and many other applications, the ability to continue operating in the face of hardware problems is of utmost importance.

Another goal is saving money. Small computers have a much better price/performance ratio than large ones. Mainframes (room-size computers) are roughly a factor of ten faster than personal computers, one per user, with data kept on one or more shared file server machines. In this model, the users are called clients, and the whole arrangement is called the client-server model. It is illustrated in Fig.9.1.

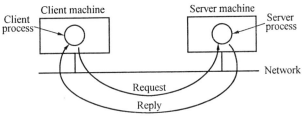

Fig.9.1 The client-server model

In the client-server model, communication generally takes the form of a request message from the client to the server asking for some work to be done. The server then does the work and sends back the reply. Usually, there are many clients using a small number og servers.

Another networking goal is scalability, the ability to increase system performance gradually as the workload grows just by adding more processors. With centralized mainframes, when the system is full, it must be replaced by a larger one, usually at great expense and even greater disruption to the users. With the client-server model, new clients and new servers can be added as needed.

Yet another goal of setting up a computer network has little to do with technology at all. Computer network can provide a powerful communication medium among widely separated employees. Using a network, it is easy for two or more people who live far apart to write a report together. When one worker makes a change to an on-line document, the others can see the change immediately, instead of waiting several days for a letter. Such a speedup makes cooperation among far-flung groups of people easy where it previously had been impossible. In the long run, the use of networks to enhance human-to-human communication will probably prove more important than technical goals such as improved reliability.

9.1.2 Networks for People

The motivations given above for building computer networks are all essentially economic and technological in nature. If sufficiently large and powerful mainframes were available at acceptable prices, most companies would simply choose to keep all their data on them and give employees terminals connected to them. In the 1970s and early 1980s, most companies operated this way. Computer networks only became popular when networks of personal computers offered a huge price/performance advantage over mainframes.

Starting in the 1990s, computer networks began to start delivering services to private individuals at home. These services and the motivations for using them are quite different than the "corporate efficiency" mode described in the previous section. Below we will sketch three of the more exciting ones that are starting to happen:

(1) Access to remote information.
(2) Person-to-person communication.
(3) Interactive entertainment.

Access to remote information will come in many forms. One area in which it is already happening is access to financial institutions. Many people pay their bills, manage their bank accounts, and handle their investments electronically. Home shopping is also becoming popular, with the ability to inspect the on-line catalogs of thousands of companies. Some of these catalogs will soon provide the ability to get an instant video on any product by just clicking on the product's name.

Newspapers will go on-line and be personalized. It will be possible to tell the newspaper that you want everything about corrupt politicians, big fires, scandals involving celebrities, and epidemics, but no football, thank you. At night while you sleep, the newspaper will be downloaded to your computer's disk or printed on your laser printer. On a small scale, this service already exists. The next step beyond newspapers (plus magazines and scientific journals) is the on-line digital library. Depending on the cost, size, and weight of book-sized notebook computers, printed books may become obsolete. Skeptics should take note of the effect the printing press had on the medieval illuminated manuscript.

Another application that falls in this category is access to information systems like the current world Wide Web, which contains information about the arts, business, cooking, government, health, history, hobbies recreation, science, sports, travel, and too many other topics to even mention.

All of the above applications involve interactions between a person and a remote database. The second broad category of network use will be person-to-person interactions, basically the 21st Century's answer to the 19th Century's telephone. Electronic mail or email is already widely used by millions of people and will soon routinely contain audio and video as well as text. Smell in messages will take a bit longer to perfect.

Real-time email will allow remote users to communicate with no delay, possibly seeing and hearing each other as well. This technology makes it possible to have virtual meetings, called videoconference, among far-flung people. It is sometimes said that transportation and communication are having a race, and whichever wins will make the other obsolete. Virtual meetings could be used for remote school, getting medical opinions from distant specialists, and numerous other applications.

Worldwide newsgroups, with discussions on every conceivable topic are already commonplace among a select group of people, and this will grow to include the population at large. These discussions, in which one person posts a message and all the other subscribers to the newsgroup can read it, run the gamut from humorous to impassioned.

Our third category is entertainment, which is a huge and growing industry. The killer application here (the one that may drive all the rest) is video on demand. A decade or so hence, it may be possible to select any movie or television program ever made, in any country, and have it displayed on your screen instantly. New films may become interactive, where the user is occasionally prompted for the story direction (should MacBeth murder Duncan or just bide his time?) with alternative scenarios provided for all cases. Live television may also become interactive, with the audience participating in quiz shows, choosing among contestants, and so on.

On the other hand, maybe the killer application will not be video on demand. Maybe it will be game playing. Already we have multiperson real-time simulation games, like hide-and-seek in a virtual dungeon, and flight simulators with the players on one team trying to shoot down the players on the opposing team. If done with goggles and 3-dimensional real-time, photographic-quality moving images, we have a kind of worldwide shared virtual reality.

In short, the ability to merge information, communication, and entertainment will surely give rise to a massive new industry based on computer networking.

9.1.3 Social Issues

The widespread introduction of networking will introduce new social, ethical, political problems (Loudon, 1995). Let us just briefly mention a few of them; a thorough study would require a full book, at least. A popular feature of many networks are newsgroups or bulletin boards where people can exchange messages with like-minded individuals. As long as the subjects are restricted to technical topics or hobbies like gardening, not too many problems will arise.

The trouble comes when newsgroups are set up on topics that people actually care about, like politics, or religion. Views posted to such groups may be deeply offensive to some people. Furthermore, messages need not be limited to text. High-resolution color photographs and even short video clips can now easily be transmitted over computer networks. Some people takes a live-and -let-live view, but others feel that posting certain material (e.g., child pornography) is simply unacceptable. Thus the debate rages.

People have sued network operators, claiming that they are responsible for the contents of what they carry, just as newspapers and magazines are. The inevitable response is that a network is like a telephone company or the post office and cannot be expected to police what its users say. Stronger yet, having network operators censor messages would probably cause them to delete everything with even the slightest possibility of their being sued, and thus violate their users' rights to free speech. It is probably safe to say that this debate will go on for a while.

Another fun area is employee rights versus employer rights. Many people read and write email at work. Some employee messages, including messages sent from a home terminal after work. Not all employees agree with this.

Even if employers have power over employees, does this relation also govern universities and students? How about high schools and students? In 1994, Carnegie-Mellon University decided to turn off the incoming message stream for several newsgroups dealing with sex because the university felt the material was inappropriate for minors (i.e., those few students under 18). The fallout from this event will take years to settle.

Computer networks offer the potential for sending anonymous messages. In some situations, this capability may be desirable. For example, it provides a way for students, soldiers, employees and citizens to blow the whistle on illegal behavior on the part of professors, officers, superiors, and politicians without fear of reprisals. On the other hand, in the

United States and most other democracies, the law specifically permits an accused person the right to confront and challenge his accuser in court. Anonymous accusations cannot be used as evidence.

In short, computer networks, like the printing press 500 years ago, allow ordinary citizens to distribute their views in different ways and to different audiences than were previously possible. This new-found freedom brings with it many unsolved social, political, and moral issues. The solution to these problems is left as an exercise for the reader.

9.2 NETWORK HARDWARE

It is now time to turn our attention from the applications and social aspects of networking to the technical issues involved in network design. There is no generally accepted taxonomy into which all computer networks fit, but two dimensions stand out as important: transmission technology and scale. We will now examine each of these in turn.

Broadly speaking, there are two types of transmission technology:

(1) Broadcast networks.

(2) Point-to-point networks.

Broadcast networks have a single communication channel that is shared by all the machines on the network. Short messages, called packets in certain contexts, sent by any machine are received by all the others. An address field within the packet specifies for whom it is intended. Upon receiving a packet, a machine checks the address field. If the packet is intended for itself, it is just ignored.

As an analogy, consider someone standing at the end of a corridor with many rooms off it and shouting "Watson, come here. I want you." Although the packet may actually be received (heard) by many people, only Watson responds. The others just ignore it. Another example is an airport announcement asking all flight 644 passengers to report to gate 12.

Broadcast systems generally also allow the possibility of addressing a packet to all destinations by using a special code in the address field. When a packet with this code is transmitted, it is received and processed by every machine on the network. This mode of operation is called broadcasting. Some broadcast systems also support transmission to a subset of the machines, something known as multicasting. One possible scheme is to reserve one bit to indicate multicasting. The remaining $n - 1$ address bits can hold a group number. Each machine can "subscribe" to any or all of the groups. When a packet is sent to a certain group, it is delivered to all machines subscribing to that group.

In contrast, point-to-point networks consist of many connections between individual pairs of machines. To go from the source to the destination, a packet on this type of network may have to first visit one or more intermediate machines. Often multiple routes of different lengths are possible, so routing algorithms play an important role in point-to-point networks. As a general rule (although there are many exceptions), smaller, geographically localized networks tend to use broadcasting, whereas larger networks usually are point-to-point.

An alternative criterion for classifying networks is their scale. In Fig.9.2

Interprocessor distance	Processors located in same	Example
0.1 m	Circuit board	Data flow machine
1 m	System	Multicomputer
10 m	Room	Local area network
100 m	Building	
1 km	Campus	
10 km	City	Metropolitan area network
100 km	Country	Wide area network
1 000 km	Continent	
10 000 km	Planet	The internet

Fig.9.2 Classification of interconnected processors by scale

we give a classification of multiple processor systems arranged by their physical size. At the top are data flow machines, highly parallel computers with many functional units all working on the same program. Next come the multicomputers, systems that communicate by sending messages over very short, very fast buses. Beyond the multicomputers are the true networks, computers that communicate by exchanging messages over longer cables. These can be divided into local, metropolitan, and wide area networks. Finally, the connection of two or more networks is called an internetwork. Distance is important as a classification metric because different techniques are used at different scales. Here we will be concerned with only the true networks and their interconnection. Below we give a brief introduction to the subject of network hardware.

9.2.1 Local Area Networks

Local area networks, generally called LANs, are privately-owned networks within a single building or campus of up to a few kilometers in size. They are widely used to connect personal computers and workstations in company offices and factories to share resources (e.g., printers) and exchange information. LANs are distinguished from other kinds of networks by three characteristics: ① their size, ② their transmission technology, and ③ their topology.

LANs are restricted in size, which means that the worst-case transmission time is bounded and known in advance. Knowing this bound makes it possible to use certain kinds of designs that would not otherwise be possible. It also simplifies network management.

LANs often use a transmission technology consisting of a single cable to which all the machines are attached, like the telephone company party lines once used in rural areas. Traditional LANs run at speeds of 10 to 100 Mbps, have low delay (tens of microseconds), and make very few errors. Newer LANs may operate at higher speeds, up to hundreds of megabits/sec. We will adhere to tradition and measure line speeds in megabits/sec (Mbps), not megabytes/sec (MB/sec). A megabit is 1 000 000 bits, not 1 048 576 (220) bits.

Various topologies are possible for broadcast LANs. Fig. 9.3 shows two of them. In a bus (i.e., a linear cable) network, at any instant one

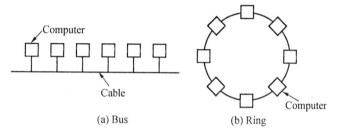

(a) Bus   (b) Ring

Fig. 9.3 Two broadcast networks

machine is the master and is allowed to transmit. All other machines are required to refrain from sending. An arbitration mechanism is needed to resolve conflicts when two or more machines want to transmit simultaneously. The arbitration mechanism may be centralized or distributed. IEEE 802.3, popularly called Ethernet, for example, is a bus-based broadcast network with decentralized control operating at 10 or 100 Mbps. Computers on an Ethernet can transmit whenever they want to; if two or more packets collide, each computer just waits a random time and tries again later.

A second type of broadcast system is the ring. In a ring, each bit propagates around on its own, not waiting for the rest of the packet to which it belongs. Typically, each bit circumnavigates the entire ring in the time it takes to transmit a few bits, often before the complete packet has even been transmitted. Like all other broadcast systems, some rule is needed for arbitrating simultaneous accesses to the ring. Various methods are in use and will be discussed later. IEEE 802.5 (the IBM token ring), is a popular ring-based LAN operating at 4 and 16 Mbps.

Broadcast networks can be further divided into static and dynamic, depending on how the channel is allocated. A typical static allocation would be to divide up time into discrete intervals and run a round robin algorithm, allowing each machine to broadcast only when its time slot comes up. Static allocation wastes channel capacity when a machine has nothing to say during its allocated slot. So most systems attempt to allocate the channel dynamically (i.e., on demand).

Dynamic allocation methods for a common channel are either centralized or decentralized. In the centralized channel allocation method, there is a single entity, for example a bus arbitration unit, which determines who goes next. It might do this by accepting requests and making a decision according to some internal algorithm. In the decentralized channel allocation method, there is no central entity; each machine must decide for itself whether or not to transmit. You might think that this always leads to chaos, but it does not. Later we will study many algorithms designed to bring order out of the potential chaos.

The other kind of LAN is built using point-to-point lines. Individual lines connect a specific machine with another specific machine. Such a LAN is really a miniature wide area network. We will look at these later.

9.2.2 Metropolitan Area Networks

A metropolitan area network, or MAN (plural: MANs, not MEN) is basically a bigger version of a LAN and normally uses similar technology. It might cover a group of nearby corporate offices or a city and might be either private or public. A MAN can support both data and voice, and might even be related to the local cable television network. A MAN just has one or two cables and does not contain switching elements, which shunt packets over one of several potential output lines. Not having to switch simplifies the design.

The main reason for even distinguishing MANs as a special category is that a standard has been adopted for them, and this standard is now being implemented. It is called DQDB (Distributed Queue Dual Bus) or for people who prefer numbers to letters, 802.6 (the number of the IEEE standard that defines it). DQDB consists of two unidirectional buses (cables) to which all the computers are connected, as shown in Fig.9.4. Each bus has a head-end, a device that initiates transmission activity. Traffic that is destined for a computer to the right of the sender uses the upper bus. Traffic to the left uses the lower one.

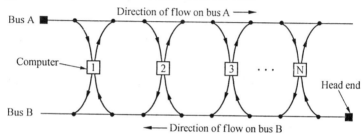

Fig.9.4　Architecture of the DQDB metropolitan area network

A key aspect of a MAN is that there is a broadcast medium (for 802.6, two cables) to which all the computers are attached. This greatly simplifies the design compared to other kinds of networks.

9.2.3　Wide Area Networks

A wide area network, or WAN, spans a large geographical area, often a country or continent. It contains a collection of machines intended for running user (i.e., application) programs. We will follow traditional usage and call these machines hosts. The term end system is sometimes also used in the literature. The hosts are connected by a communication subnet, or just subnet for short. The job of the subnet is to carry messages from host to host, just as the telephone system carries words from speaker to listener. By separating the pure communication aspects of the network (the subnet) from the application aspects (the hosts), the complete network design is greatly simplified.

In most wide area networks, the subnet consists of two distinct components: transmission lines and switching elements. Transmission lines (also called circuits, channels, or trunks) move bits between machines.

The switching elements are specialized computers used to connect two or more transmission lined. When data arrive on an incoming line, the switching element must choose an outgoing line to forward them on. Unfortunately, there is no standard terminology used to name these computers. They are variously called packet switching nodes, intermediate systems, and data switching exchanges, among other things. As a generic term for the switching computers, will use exists here. In this model, shown in Fig. 9.5, each host is generally connected to a LAN on a router. The collection of communication lines and routers (but not the hosts) form the subnet.

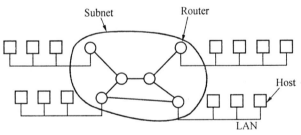

Fig.9.5 Relation between hosts and the subnet

An aside about the term "subnet" is worth making. Originally, its only meaning was the collection of routers and communication lines that moved packets from the source host to the destination host. However, some years later, it also acquired a second meaning in conjunction with network addressing. Hence the term has a certain ambiguity about it. Unfortunately, no widely-used alternative exists for its initial meaning, so with some hesitation we will use it in both senses. From the context, it will always be clear which is meant.

In most WANs, the network contains numerous cables or telephone lines, each one connecting a pair of routers. If two routers that do not share a cable nevertheless wish to communicate, they must do this indirectly, via other routers. When a packet is sent from one router to another via one or more intermediate routers, the packet is received at each intermediate router in its entirety, stored there until the required output line is free, and then forwarded. A subnet using this principle is called a point-to-point, store-and-forward, or packet-switched subnet. Nearly all wide area networks (except those using satellites) have store-and-forward subnets. When the packets are small and all the same size, they are often called cells.

When a point-to-point subnet is used, an important design issue is what the router interconnection topology should look like. Fig.9.6 shows

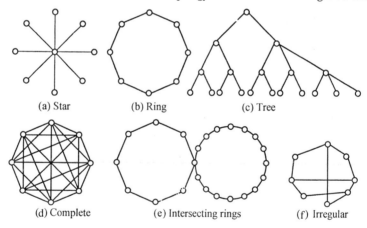

Fig.9.6 Some possible topologies for a point-to-point subnet

several possible topologies. Local networks that were designed as such usually have a symmetric topology. In contrast, wide area networks typically have irregular topologies.

A second possibility for a WAN is a satellite or ground radio system. Each router has an antenna through which it can send and receive. All routers can hear the output from the satellite, and in some cases they can also hear the upward transmissions of their fellow routers to the satellite as well. Sometimes the routers are connected to a substantial point-to-point subnet, with only some of them having a satellite antenna. Satellite networks are inherently broadcast and are most useful when the broadcast property is important.

9.2.4 Wireless Networks

Mobile computers, such as notebook computers and personal digital assistants (PDAs), are the fastest-growing segment of the computer industry. Many of the owners of these computers have desktop machines on LANs and WANs back at the office and want to be connected to their home base even when away from home or a route. Since having a wired connection is impossible in cars and airplanes, there is a lot of interest in wireless networks. On this section we will briefly introduce this topic.

Actually, digital wireless communication is not a new idea. As early as 1901, the Italian physicist Guglielmo Marconi demonstrated a ship-to-shore wireless telegraph using Morse Code (dots and dashes are binary, after all). Modern digital wireless systems have better performance, but the basic idea is the same.

Wireless networks have many uses. A common one is the portable office. People on the road often want to use their portable electronic equipment to send and receive telephone calls, faxes, and electronic mail, read remote files, login on remote machines, and so on, and do this from anywhere on land, sea, or air.

Wireless networks are of great value to fleets of trucks, taxis, buses, and repairpersons for keeping in contact with home. Another use is for rescue workers at disaster sites (fires, floods, earthquakes, etc.) where the telephone system has been destroyed. Computers there can send messages, keep records, and so on.

Finally, wireless networks are important to the military. If you have to be able fight a war anywhere on earth on short notice, counting on using the local networking infrastructure is probably not a good idea. It is better to bring your own.

Although wireless networking and mobile computing are often related, they are not identical, as Fig. 9.7 shows. Portable computers are sometimes wired. For example, if a traveler plugs a portable computer into the telephone jack in a hotel, we have mobility without a wireless network. Another example is someone carrying a portable computer along as he inspects a train for technical problems. Here a long cord can trail along behind (vacuum cleaner model).

Wireless	Mobile	Applications
No	No	Stationary workstations in offices
No	Yes	Using a portable in a hotel; train maintenance
Yes	No	LANs in older, unwired buildings
Yes	Yes	Portable office; PDA for store inventory

Fig.9.7 Combinations of wireless networks and mobile computing

On the other hand, some wireless computers are not portable. An important example here is a company that owns an older building that does not have network cabling installed and wants to connect its computers. Installing a wireless LAN may require little more than buying a small box with some electronics and setting up some antennas. This solution may be cheaper than wiring the building.

Although wireless LANs are easy to install, they also have some disadvantages. Typically they have a capacity of 1 to 2 Mbps, which is much slower than wired LANs. The error rates are often much higher, too, and the transmissions from different computers can interfere with one another.

But of course, there are also the true mobile, wireless applications, ranging from the portable office to people walking around a store with a

PDA doing inventory. At many busy airports, car rental return clerks work out in the parking lot with wireless portable computers. They type in the license plate number of returning cars, and their portable, which has a built-in printer, calls the main computer, gets the rental information, and prints out the bill on the spot.

Wireless networks come in many forms. Some universities are already installing antennas all over campus to allow students to sit under the trees and consult the library's card catalog. Here the computers communicate directly with the wireless LAN in digital form. Another possibility is using a cellular (i.e., portable) telephone with a traditional analog modem. Direct digital cellar service, called CDPD (Cellular Digital Packet Data) is becoming available in many cities.

Finally, it is possible to have different combinations of wired and wireless networking. For example, in Fig.9.8(a), we depict an airplane

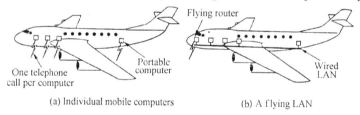

(a) Individual mobile computers   (b) A flying LAN

Fig.9.8

with a number of people using modems and seat-back telephones to call the office. Each call is independent of the other ones. A much more efficient option, however, is the flying LAN of Fig.9.8(b). Here each seat comes equipped with an Ethernet connector into which passengers can plug their computers. A single router on the aircraft maintains a radio link with some router on the ground, changing routers as it flies along. This configuration is just a traditional LAN, except that its connection to the outside world happens to be a radio link instead of a hardwired line.

While many people believe that wireless portable computers are the wave of the future, at least one dissenting voice has been heard. Bob Metcalfe, the inventor of Ethernet, has written: "Mobile wireless computers are like mobile pipeless bathrooms—portapotties. They will be common on vehicles, and at construction sites, and rock concerts. My advice is to wire up your home and stay there." Will most people follow Metcalfe's advice? Time will tell.

9.2.5 Internetworks

Many networks exist in the world, often with different hardware and software. People connected to one network often want to communicate with people attached to a different one. This desire requires connecting together different, and frequently incompatible networks, sometimes by using machines called gateways to make the connection and provide the necessary translation, both in terms of hardware and software. A collection of interconnected networks is called an internetwork or just internet.

A common form of internet is a collection of LANs connected by a WAN. In fact, if we were to replace the label "subnet" in Fig.9.5 by "WAN," nothing else in the figure would have to change. The only real distinction between a subnet and a WAN in this case is whether or not hosts are present. If it contains both routers and hosts with their own users, it is a WAN.

To avoid confusion, please note that the word "internet" will always be used in a generic sense. In contrast, the Internet (note uppercase I) means a specific worldwide internet that is widely used to connect universities, government offices, companies, and of late, private individuals.

Subnets, networks, and internetworks are often confused. Subnet makes the most sense in the context of a wide area network, where it refers to the collection of routers and communication lines owned by the network operator, for example, companies like America Online and CompuServe. As an analogy, the telephone system consists of telephone switching offices connected to each other by high-speed lines, and to houses and businesses by low-speed lines. These lines and equipment, owned and managed by the telephone company, form the subnet of the telephone system. The telephones themselves (the hosts in this analogy) are not part of the subnet. The combination of a subnet and its hosts forms a network. In the case of a LAN, the cable and the hosts form the network. There really is no subnet.

An internetwork is formed when distinct networks are connected together. In our view, connecting a LAN and a WAN or connecting two LANs forms an internetwork, but there is little agreement in the industry over terminology in this area.

9.3 NETWORK SOFTWARE

The first computer networks were designed with the hardware as the main concern and the software as an afterthought. This strategy no longer works. Network software is now highly structured. In the following sections we examine the software structuring technique in some detail. The method described here forms the keystone of the entire book and will occur repeatedly later on.

9.3.1 Protocol Hierarchies

To reduce their design complexity, most networks are organized as a series of layers or levels, each one built upon the one below it. The number of layers, the name of each layer, the contents of each layer, and the function of each layer differ from network to network. However, in all networks, the purpose of each layer is to offer certain services to the higher layers, shielding those layers from the details of how the offered services are actually implemented.

Layer n on one machine carries on a conversation with layer n on another machine, The rules and conventions used in this conversation are collectively known as the layer n protocol. Basically, a protocol is an agreement between the communicating parties on how communication is to proceed. As an analogy, when a woman is introduced to a man, she may choose to stick out her hand. He, in turn, may decide either to shake it or kiss it, depending, for example, on whether she is an American lawyer at a business meeting or a European princess at a formal ball. Violating the protocol will make communication more difficult, if not impossible.

A five-layer network is illustrated in Fig.9.9. The entities comprising the corresponding layers on different machines are called peers. In other words, it is the peers that communicate using the protocol.

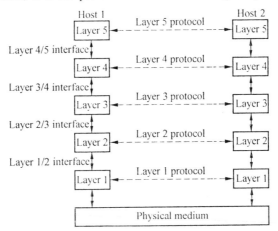

Fig.9.9 Layers, protocols, and interfaces

In reality, no data are directly transferred from layer n on one machine to layer n on another machine. Instead, each layer passes data and control information to the layer immediately below it, until the lowest layer is reached. Below layer 1 is the physical medium through which actual communication occurs. In Fig.9.9, virtual communication is shown by dotted lines and physical communication by solid lines.

Between each pair of adjacent layers there is an interface. The interface defines which primitive operations and services the lower layer offers to the upper one. When network designers decide how many layers to include in a network and what each one should do, one of the most important considerations is defining clean interfaces between the layers. Doing so, in turn, requires that each layer perform a specific collection of well-understood functions. In addition to minimizing the amount of information that must be passed between layers, clean-cut interfaces also make it simpler to replace the implementation of one layer with a completely different implementation (e.g., all the telephone lines are replaced by satellite channels), because all that is required of the new implementation is that it offers exactly the same set of services to its upstairs neighbor as the old implementation did.

A set of layers and protocols is called a network architecture. The specification of an architecture must contain enough information to allow an implementer to write the program or build the hardware for each layer so that it will correctly obey the appropriate protocol. Neither the details of the implementation nor the specification of the interfaces are part of the architecture because these are hidden away inside the machines and not visible from the outside. It is not even necessary that the interfaces on all machines in a network be the same, provided that each machine can correctly use all the protocols. A list of protocols used by a certain system, one protocol per layer, is called a protocol stack. The subjects of network architectures, protocol stacks, and the protocols themselves are the principal topics of this book.

An analogy may help explain the idea of multilayer communication. Imagine two philosophers (peer processes in layer 3), ones of whom speaks Urdu and English and one of whom speaks Chinese and French. Since they have no common language, they each engage a translator (peer processes at layer 2), each of whom in turn contacts a secretary (peer processes in layer 1). Philosopher 1 wishes to convey his affection for oryctolagus cuniculus to his peer. To do so, he passes a message (in English) across the 2/3 interface, to his translator, saying "I like rabbits," as illustrated in Fig.9.10. The translators have agreed on a neutral lan-

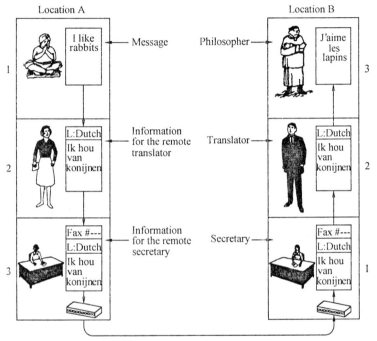

Fig.9.10 The philosopher-translator-secretary architecture

guage. Dutch, so the message is converted to "Ik hou van konijnen." The choice of language is the layer 2 protocol and is up to the layer 2 peer processes.

The translator then gives the message to a secretary for transmission, by, for example, fax (the layer 1 protocol). When the message arrives, it is translated into French and passed across the 2/3 interface to philosopher 2. Note that each protocol is completely independent of the other ones as long as the interfaces are not changed. The translators can switch from Dutch to say, Finnish, at will, provided that they both agree, and neither changes his interface with either layer 1 or layer 3. Similarly the secretaries can switch from fax to email, or telephone without disturbing (or even informing) the other layers. Each process may add some information intended only for its peer. This information is not passed upward to the layer above.

Now consider a more technical example: how to provide communication to the top layer of the five-layer network in Fig.9.11. A message,

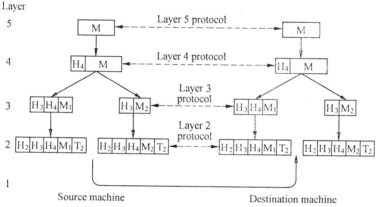

Fig.9.11 Example information flow supporting virtual communication in layer 5

M, is produced by an application process running in layer 5 and given to layer 4 for transmission. Layer 4 puts a header in front of the message to identify the message and passes the result to layer 3. The header include control information, such as sequence numbers, to allow layer 4 on the destination machine to deliver messages in the right order if the lower layers do not maintain sequence. In some layers, headers also contain sizes, times, and other control fields.

In many networks, there is no limit to the size of messages transmitted in the layer 4 protocol, but there is nearly always a limit imposed by the layer 3 protocol. Consequently, layer 3 must break up the incoming messages into smaller units, packers, prepending a layer 3 header to each packet. In this example, M is split into two parts, M_1 and M_2.

Layer 3 decides which of the outgoing lines to use and passes the packets to layer 2. Layer 2 adds not only a header to each piece, but also a trailer, and gives the resulting unit to layer 1 for physical transmission. At the receiving machine the message moves upward, from layer to layer, with headers being stripped off as it progresses. None of the headers for layers below n are passed up to layer n.

The important thing to understand about Fig.9.11 is the relation between the virtual and actual communication and the difference between protocols and interfaces. The peer processes in layer 4, for example, conceptually think of their communication as being "horizontal," using the layer 4 protocol. Each one is likely to have a procedure called something like "Send To Other Side" and "Get From Other Side," even though these procedures actually communicate with lower layers across the 3/4 interface, not with the other side.

The peer process abstraction is crucial to all network design. Using it, the unmanageable task of designing the complete network can be broken into several smaller, manageable, design problems, namely the design of the individual layers.

Although Sec.9.3 is called"Network Software", it is worth pointing out that the lower layers of a protocol hierarchy are frequently implemented in hardware or firmware. Nevertheless, complex protocol algorithms are involved, even if they are embedded (in whole or in part) in hardware.

9.3.2 Design Issues for the Layers

Some of the key design issues that occur in computer networking are present in several layers. Below, we will briefly mention some of the more important one.

Every layer needs a mechanism for identifying senders and receivers. Since a network normally has many computers, some of which have multiple processes, a means is needed for a process on one machine to specify with whom it wants to talk. As a consequence of having multiple destinations, some form of addressing is needed in order to specify a specific destination.

Another set of design decisions concerns the rules for data transfer. In some systems, data only travel in one direction (simplex communication). In others they can travel in either direction, but not simultaneously (half-duplex communication). In still others they travel in both directions at once (full-duplex communication). The protocol must also determine how many logical channels the connection corresponds to, and what their priorities are. Many networks provide at least two logical channels per connection, one for normal data and one for urgent data.

Error control is an important issue because physical communication circuits are not perfect. Many error-detecting and error-correcting codes are known, but both ends of the connection must agree on which one is being used. In addition, the receiver must have some way of telling the sender which messages have been correctly received and which have not.

Not all communication channels preserve the order of messages sent on them. To deal with a possible loss of sequencing, the protocol must make explicit provision for the receiver to allow the pieces to be put back together properly. An obvious solution is to number the pieces, but this solution still leaves open the question of what should be done with pieces that arrive out of order.

An issue that occurs at every level is how to keep a fast sender from swamping a slow receiver with data. Various solutions have been proposed and will be discussed later. Some of them involve some kind of feedback from the receiver to the sender, either directly or indirectly, about the receiver's current situation. Others limit the sender to an agreed upon transmission rate.

Another problem that must be solved at several levels is the inability of all processes to accept arbitrarily long messages. This property leads to mechanisms for disassembling, transmitting, and then reassembling messages. A related issue is what to do when processes insist upon transmitting data in units that are so small that sending each one separately is inefficient. Here the solution is to gather together several small messages heading toward a common destination into a single large message and dismember the large message at the other side.

When it is inconvenient or expensive to set up a separate connection for each pair of communicating processes, the underlying layer may decide to use the same connection for multiple, unrelated conversations. As long as this multiplexing and demultiplexing is done transparently, it can be used by any layer. Multiplexing is needed in the physical layer, for example, where all the traffic for all connections has to be sent over at most a few physical circuits.

When there are multiple paths between source and destination, a route must be chosen. Sometimes this decision must be split over two or more layers. For example, to send data from London to Rome, a high-level decision might have to be made to go via France or Germany based on their respective privacy laws, and a low-level decision might have to be made to choose one of the many available circuits based on the current traffic load.

9.3.3 Interfaces and services

The function of each layer is to provide services to the layer above it. In this section we will look at precisely what service is in more detail, but first we will give some terminology.

The active elements in each layer are often called entities. An entity can be a software entity (such as a process), or a hardware entity (such as an intelligent I/O chip). Entities in the same layer on different machines are called peer entities. The entities in layer n implement a service used by $n + 1$. In this case layer n is called the service provider and layer $n + 1$ is called the service user. Layer n may use the services of layer $n - 1$ in order to provide its service. It may offer several classes of service, for example, fast, expensive communication and slow, cheap communication.

Services are available at SAPs (Service Access Points). The layer n SAPs are the places where layer $n + 1$ can access the services offered. Each SAP has an address that uniquely identifies it. To make this point clearer, the SAPs in the telephone system are the sockets into which modular telephones can be plugged, and the SAP addresses are the telephone numbers of these sockets. To send a letter, you must know the address's SAP address.

In order for two layers to exchange information, there has to be an a-greed upon set of rules about the interface. At a typical interface, the layer $n + 1$ entity passes an IDU (Interface Data Unit) to the layer entity through the SAP as shown in Fig. 9.12. The IDU consists of an SDU

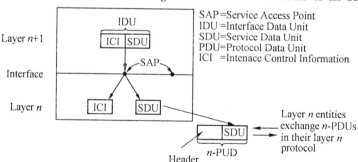

Fig.9.12 Relation between layers at an interface

(Service Data Unit) and some control information. The SDU is the information passed across the network to the peer entity and then up to layer $n + 1$. The control information is need to help the lower layer do its job (e. g., the number of bytes in the SDU) but is not part of the data itself.

In order to transfer the SDU, the layer n entity may have to fragment it into several pieces, each of which is given a header and sent as a separate PDU (Protocol Data Unit) such as a packet.

The PDU headers are used by the peer entities to carry out their peer protocol. They identify which PDUs contain control information, provide sequence numbers and counts, and so on.

9.3.4 Connection-Oriented and Connectionless Service

Layers can offer two different types of service to the layers above them: connection-oriented and connectionless. In this section we will look at these two types and examine the differences between them.

Connection-Oriented service is modeled after the telephone system. To talk someone, you pick up the phone, dial the number, talk, and then hang up. Similarly, to use a connection-oriented network service, the service user first establishes a connection, uses the connection, and releases the connection. The essential aspect of a connection is that it acts like a tube: the sender pushes objects (bits) in at one end, and the receiver takes them out in the same order at the other end.

In contrast, connectionless service is modeled after the postal system. Each message (letter) carries the full destination address, and each one is routed through the system independent of all the others. Normally, when two messages are sent to the same destination, the first one sent will be the first one to arrive. However, it is possible that the first one sent can be delayed so that the second one arrives first. With a connection-oriented service this is impossible.

Each service can be characterized by a quality of service. Some services are reliable in the sense that they never lose data. Usually, a reliable service is implemented by having the receiver acknowledge the receipt of each message, so the sender is sure that it arrived. The acknowledgment process introduces overhead and delays, which are often worth it but are sometimes undesirable.

A typical situation in which a reliable connection-oriented service is appropriate is file transfer. The owner of the file wants to be sure that all the bits arrive correctly and in the same order they were sent. Very few file transfer customers would prefer a service that occasionally scrambles or loses a few bits, even if it is much faster.

Reliable connection-oriented service has two minor variations: message sequences and byte streams. In the former, the message boundaries are preserved. When two 1 KB messages are sent, they arrive as two distinct 1 KB message, never as one 2 KB message. (Note: KB means kilobytes.) In the latter, the connection is simply a stream of bytes, with no message boundaries. When 2 K bytes arrive at the receiver, there is no way to tell if they were sent as one 2 KB message, two 1 KB, or 2 048 1-byte messages. If the pages of a book are sent over a network to a phototypesetter as separate message, it might be important to preserve the message boundaries. On the other hand, with a terminal logging into a remote timesharing system, a byte stream from the terminal to the computer is all that is needed.

As mentioned above, for some applications, the delays introduced by acknowledgments are unacceptable. One such application is digitized voice traffic. It is preferable for telephone users to hear a bit of noise on the line or a garbled word from time to time than to introduce a delay to wait for acknowledgments. Similarly, when transmitting a video film, having a few pixels wrong is no problem, but having the film jerk along as the flow stops to correct errors is very irritating.

Not all applications require connection. For example, as electronic mail becomes more common, can electronic junk mail be far behind? The electronic junk mail sender probably does not want to go to the trouble of setting up and later tearing down a connection just to send one item. Nor is 100 percent reliable delivery essential, especially if it costs more. All that is needed is a way to send a single message that has a high probability of arrival, but no guarantee. Unreliable (meaning not acknowledged) connectionless service is often called datagram service, in analogy with telegram service, which also does not provide an acknowledgment back to the sender.

In other situations, the convenience of not having to establish a connection to send one short message is desired, but reliability is essential. The acknowledged datagram service can be provided for these applications. It is like sending a registered letter and requesting a return receipt. When the receipt comes back, the sender is absolutely sure that the letter was delivered to the intended party and not lost along the way.

Still another service is the request-reply service. In this service the sender transmits a single datagram containing a request; the reply contains the answer. For example, a query to the local library asking where Uighur is spoken falls into this category. Request-reply is commonly used to implement communication in the client-server model: the client issues a request and the server responds to it. Fig.9.13 summarizes the types of services discussed above.

	Service	Example
Connection-oriented	Reliable message stream	Sequence of pages
	Reliable byte stream	Remote login
	Unreliable connection	Digitized voice
Connection-less	Unreliable datagram	Electronic junk mail
	Acknowledged datagram	Registered mail
	Request-reply	Database query

Fig.9.13 Six different types of service

9.3.5 Service Primitives

A service is formally specified by a set of primitives (operations) available to a user or other entity to access the service. These primitives tell the service to perform some action or report on an action taken by a peer entity. One way to classify the service primitives is to divide them into four classes as shown in Fig.9.14.

Primitive	Meaning
Request	An entity wants the service to do some work
Indication	An entity is to be informed about an event
Response	An entity wants to respond to an event
Confirm	The response to an earlier request has come back

Fig.9.14 Four classes of service of primitives

To illustrate the uses of the primitives, consider how a connection is established and released. The initiating entity does a "CONNECT. request" which results in a packet being sent. The receiver then gets a "CONNECT. Indication" announcing that an entity somewhere wants to set up a connection to it. The entity getting the "CONNECT. indication" then uses the "CONNECT. respond" primitive to tell whether it wants to accept or reject the proposed connection. Either way, the entity issuing the initial "CONNECT. request" finds out what happened via a "CONNECT. confirm" primitive.

Primitives can have parameters, and most of them do. The parameters to a "CONNECT. request" might specify the machine to connect to, the type of service desired, and the maximum message size to be used on the connection. The parameters to a "CONNECT. indication" might contain the caller's identity, the type of service desired, and the proposed maximum message size. If the calls entity did not agree to the proposed maximum message size, it could make a counterproposal in the confirm. The details of this negotiation are part of the protocol. For example, in the case of two conflicting proposals about maximum message size, the protocol might specify that the smaller value is always chosen.

As an aside on terminology, we will carefully avoid the terms "open a connection" and "close a connection" because to electrical engineers, an "open circuit" is one with a gap or break in it. Electricity can only flow over "closed circuits." Computer scientists would never agree to having information flow over a closed circuit. To keep both camps pacified, we will use the terms "establish a connection" and "release a connection."

Services can be either confirmed or unconfirmed. In a confirmed service, there is a request, an indication, a response, and a confirm. In an unconfirmed service, there is just a request and an indication. CONNECT is always a confirmed service, because the remote peer must agree to establish a connection. Data transfer, on the other hand, can be either confirmed or unconfirmed, depending on whether or not the sender needs an acknowledgment. Both kinds of services are used in networks.

To make the concept of a service more concrete, let us consider as an example a simple connection-oriented service with eight service primitives as follows:

(1) CONNECT. request-Request a connection to be established.
(2) CONNECT. indication-Signal the called party.
(3) CONNECT. response-Used by the caller to accept/reject calls.
(4) CONNECT. confirm-Tell the caller whether the call was accepted.
(5) DATA. request-Request that a data be sent.
(6) DATA. indication-Signal the arrival of data.
(7) DISCONNECT. request-Request that a connection be released.
(8) DISCONNECT. indication-Signal the peer about the request.

In this example, CONNECT is a confirmed service (an explicit response is required), whereas DISCONNECT is unconfirmed (no response).

It may be helpful to make an analogy with the telephone system to see how these primitives are used. For this analogy, consider the steps required to call Aunt Millie on the telephone and invite her to your house for tea.

(1) CONNECT.request-Dial Aunt Millie's phone number.
(2) CONNECT.indication-Her phone rings.
(3) CONNECT.response-She picks up the phone.
(4) CONNECT.confirm-You hear the ringing stop.
(5) DATA.request-You invite her to tea.
(6) DATA.indication-She hears your invitation.
(7) DATA.request-She says she would be delighted to come.
(8) DATA.indication-You hear her acceptance.
(9) DISCONNECT.request-You hang up the phone.
(10) DISCONNECT.indication-She hears it and hangs up too.

Fig.9.15 shows this same sequence of steps as a series of service primitives, including the final confirmation of disconnection. Each step involves an interaction between two layers on one of the computers. Each request or response causes an indication or confirm at the other side a little later. In this example, the service users (you and Aunt Millie) are in layer $n + 1$ and the service provider (the telephone system) is in layer n. The numbers near the tail end of each arrow refer to the eight service primitives discussed in this section.

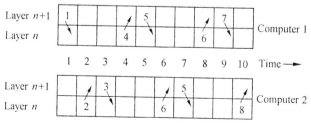

Fig.9.15 How a computer would invite its Aunt Mille to tea

9.3.6 The Relationship of Service to Protocols

Services and protocols are distinct concepts, although they are frequently confused. This distinction is so important, however, that we emphasize it again here. A service is a set of primitives (operations) that a layer provides to the layer above it. The service defines what operations the layer is prepared to perform on behalf of its users, but it says nothing at all about how these operations are implemented. A service relates to an interface between two layers, with the lower layer being the service provider and the upper layer being the service user.

A protocol, in contrast, is a set of rules governing the format and meaning of the frames, packets, or messages that are exchanged by the peer entities within a layer. Entities use protocols in order to implement their service definitions. They are free to change their protocols at will, provided they do not change the service visible to their users. In this way, the service and the protocol are completely decoupled.

An analogy with programming languages is worth making. A service is like an abstract data type or an object in an object-oriented language. It defines operations that can be performed on an object but does not specify how these operations are implemented. A protocol relates to the implementation of the service and as such is not visible to the user of the service.

Many old protocols did not distinguish the service from the protocol. In effect, a typical layer might have had a service primitive SEND PACKET with the user providing a pointer to a fully assembled packet. This arrangement meant that all changes to the protocol were immediately visible to the users. Most network designers now regard such a design as a serious blunder.

9.4 EXAMPLE NETWORKS

Numerous networks are currently operating around the world. Some of these are public networks run by common carries or PTTs, others are 4 research networks, yet others are cooperative networks run by their users, and still others are commercial or corporate networks. In the following sections we will take a look at a few current and historical networks to get an idea of what they are (or were) like and how they differ from one another.

Networks differ in their history, administration, facilities offered, technical design, and user communities. The history and administration can vary from a network carefully planned by a single organization with a well-defined goal, to an ad hoc collection of machines that have been connected to one another over the years without any master plan or center administration at all. The facilities available range from arbitrary process-to-process communication to electronic mail, file transfer, remote login, and remote execution. The technical designs can differ in the transmission media used, the naming and routing algorithms employed, the number and contents of the layers present, and the protocols used. Finally, the user community can vary from a single corporation to all the academic computer scientists in the industrialized world.

In the following sections we will look at a few examples. These are the popular commercial LAN networking package, Novell NetWare, the worldwide Internet (including its predecessors, the ARPANET and NSFNET), and the first gigabit networks.

9.4.1 Novell Net Ware

The most popular network system in the PC world is Novell NetWare. It was designed to be used by companies downsizing from a mainframe to a network of PCs. In such systems, each user has a desktop PC functioning as a client. In addition, some number of powerful PCs operate as servers, providing file services, database services, and other services to a collection of clients. In other words, Novell NetWare is based on the client-server model.

NetWare uses a proprietary protocol stack illustrated in Fig.9.16. It is based in the old Xerox Network System, XNS but with various modifications. Novell NetWare predates OSI and is not based on it. If anything, it looks more like TCP/IP than like OSI.

Layer			
Application	SAP	File server	...
Transpor	NCP		SPX
Network	IPX		
Data link	Ethernet	Token ring	ARCnet
Physical	Ethernet	Token ring	ARCnet

Fig.9.16 The Novell NetWare reference model

The physical and data link layers can be chosen from among various industry standards, including Ethernet, IBM token ring, and ARCnet. The network layer runs an unreliable connectionless internetwork protocol called IPX. It passes packets transparently from source to destination, even if the source and destination are on different networks. IPX is functionally similar to IP, except that it uses 10 byte addresses instead of 4 byte addresses.

Above IPX comes a connection-oriented transport protocol called NCP (Network Core Protocol). NCP also provides various other services besides user data transport and is really the heart of NetWare. A second protocol, SPX, is also available, but provide only transport. TCP is another option. Application can choose any of them. The file system uses NCP and Lotus Notes uses SPX, for example. The session and presentation layers do not exist. Various application protocols are present in the application layer.

As in TCP/IP, the key to the entire architecture is the internet datagram packet on top of which everything else is built. The format of an IPX packet is shown in Fig. 9.17. The checksum field is rarely used, since

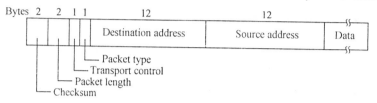

Fig.9.17 A Novell NetWare IPX packet

the underlying data link layer also provides a checksum. The Packet length field tells how long the entire packet is, header plus data. The Transport control field counts how many networks the packet has traversed. When this exceeds a maximum, the packet is discarded. The Packet type field is used to mark various control packets. The two addresses each contain a 32 bit network number, a 48 bit machine number (the 802 LAN address), and 16 bit local address (socket) on that machine. Finally, we have the data, which occupy the rest of the packet, with the maximum size being determined by the underlying network.

About a once a minute, each server broadcasts a packet giving its address and telling what services it offer. These broadcasts use the SAP (Service Advertising Protocol) protocol. The packets are seen and collected by special agent processes running on the router machines. The agents use the information contained in them to construct databases of which servers are running where.

When a client machine is booted, it broadcasts a request asking where the nearest server is. The agent on local router machine sees this request, looks in its database of servers, and matches up the request with the best server. The choice of server to use is then sent back to the client. The client can now establish an NCP connection with the server. Using this connection, the client and server negotiate the maximum packet size. From this point on, the clinician can access the file system and other services using this connection. It can also query the server's database to look for other (more distant) servers.

9.4.2 The ARPANET

Let us now switch gears from LANs to WANs. In the mid-1960s, at the height of the Cold War, the DoD wanted a command and control network that could survive a nuclear war. Traditional circuit-switched telephone networks were considered too vulnerable, since the loss of one line or switch would certainly terminate all conversations using them and might even partition the network. To solve this problem, DoD turned to its research arm, ARPA (later DARPA, now ARPA again), the (periodically Defense) Advanced Research Projects Agency.

ARPA was created in response to the Soviet Union's launching Sputnik in 1957 and had the mission of advancing technology that might be useful to military. ARPA had no scientists or laboratories, in fact, it had nothing more than an office and a small (by Pentagon standards) budget. It did its work by issuing grants and contracts to universities and companies whose ideas looked promising to it.

Several early grants went to universities for investigating the then-radical idea of packet switching, something that had been suggested by Paul Baran in a series of RAND Corporation reports published in the early 1960s. After some discussions with various experts, ARPA decided that the network the DoD needed should be a packet-switched network, consisting of a subnet and host computers.

The subnet would consist of minicomputers called IMPs (Interface Message Processors) connected by transmission lines. For high reliability, each IMP would be connected to at least two other IMPs. The subnet was to be a datagram subnet, so if some lines and IMPs were destroyed, messages would automatically rerouted along alternative paths.

Each node of the net work was to consist of an IMP and a host, in the same room, connected by a short wire. A host could send messages of up to 8 063 bits to its IMP, which would then break these up into packets of at most 1 008 bits and forward them independently toward the destination. Each packet was received in its entirety before being forward, so the subnet was the first electronic store-and-forward packet-switching network.

ARPA then put out a tender for building the subnet. Twelve companies bid for it. After evaluating all the proposals, ARPA selected BBN, a consulting firm in Cambridge, Massachusetts, and in December 1968, awarded it a contract to build the subnet and write the subnet software. BBN chose to use specially modified Honeywell DDP-316 minicomputers with 12K 16 bit words of core memory as the IMPs. The IMPs did not have disks, since moving parts were considered unreliable. The IMPs were interconnected by 56 kbps lines leased from telephone companies.

The software was split into two parts: subnet and host. The subnet software consisted of the IMP end of the host-IMP connection, the IMP-IMP protocol, and a source IMP to destination IMP protocol designed to improve reliability. The original ARPANET design is shown in Fig.9.18.

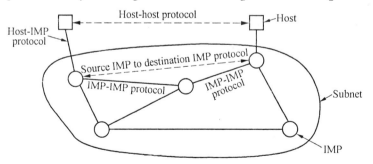

Fig.9.18 The original ARPANET design

Outside the subnet, software was also needed, namely, the host end of the host—IMP connection, the host-host protocol, and the application software. It soon became clear that BBN felt that when it had accepted a message on a host-IMP wire and placed it on the host-IMP wire at the destination, its job was done.

To deal with problem of host software, Larry Roberts of ARPA convened a meeting of network researchers, mostly graduate students, at Snowbird, Utah, in the summer of 1969. The graduate students expected some network exert to explain the design of the network and its software to them and then to assign each of them the job of writing part of it. They were astounded when there was no network expert and no grand design. They had to figure out what to do on their own.

Nevertheless, somehow an experimental network went on the air in December 1969 with four nodes, at UCLA, UCSB, SRI, and the University of Utah. These four were chosen because all had a large number of ARPA contracts, and all had different and completely incompatible host computers (just to make it more fun). The network grew quickly as more IMPs were delivered and installed; it soon spanned the United States, Fig.9.19 shows how rapidly the ARPANET grew in the first 3 years.

Later the IMP software was changed to allow terminals to connect directly to a special IMP, called a TIP (Terminal Interface Processor), without having to go through a host. Subsequent changes included having multiple hosts per IMP (to save money), hosts talking to multiple IMPs (to protect against IMP failures), and hosts and IMPs separated by a large distance (to accommodate hosts far from the subnet).

In addition to helping the fledging ARPANET grow, ARPA also funded research on satellite networks and mobile packet radio networks. In one famous demonstration, a truck driving around in California used the packet radio network to send messages to SRI, which were then forwarded over the ARPANET to the East Coast, where they were shipped to University College in London over the satellite network. This allowed a

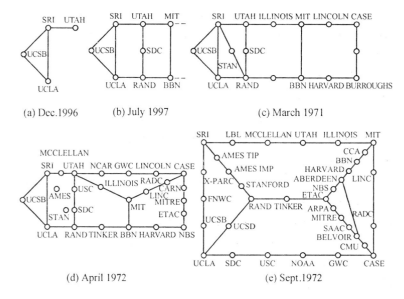

Fig.9.19 Growth of the ARPNET

researcher in the truck to use a computer in London while driving around in California.

This experiment also demonstrated that the existing ARPANET protocols were not suitable for running over multiple network. This observation led to more research on protocols, culminating with the invention of the TCP/IP model and protocols (Cerfand Kahn, 1974). TCP/IP was specifically designed to handle communication over internetworks, something becoming increasingly important as more and more networks were being hooked up to the ARPANET.

To encourage adoption of these new protocols, ARPA awarded several contracts to BBN and the University of California at Berkeley to integrate them into Berkeley UNIX. Researchers at Berkeley developed a convenient program interface to the network (sockets) and wrote many application, utility, and management programs to make networking easier.

The timing was perfect. Many universities had just acquired a second or third VAX computer and a LAN to connect them, but they had no networking software. When 4.2BSD came along, with TCP/IP, sockets, and many network utilities, the complete package was adopted immediately. Furthermore, with TCP/IP, it was easy for the LANs to connect to the ARPANET, and many did.

By 1983, the ARPANET was stable and successful, with over 200 IMPs and hundreds of hosts. At this point, ARPA turned the management of the network over to the Defense Communications Agency (DCA), to run it as an operational network. The first thing DCA did was to separate the military portion (about 160 IMPs, of which 110 in the United States and 50 abroad) into a separate subnet, MILNET, with stringent gateways between MILNET and the remaining research subnet.

During the 1980s, additional networks, especially LANs, were connected to the ARPANET. As the scale increased, finding hosts became increasingly expensive, so DNS (Domain Naming System) was created to organize machines into domains and map host names onto IP address. Since then, DNS has become a generalized, distributed database system for storing a variety of information related to naming.

By 1990, the ARPANET had been overtaken by newer networks that it itself had spawned, so it was shot down and dismantled, but it lives on in the hearts and minds of network researchers everywhere. MILNET continues to operate, however.

9.4.3 NSFNET

By the late 1970s, NSF (the U.S. National Science Foundation) saw the enormous impact the ARPANET was having on university research, allowing scientist across the country to share data and collaborate on research projects. However, to get on the ARPANET, a university had to have a research contract with the DoD, which many did not have. This lack of universal access prompted NSF to set up a virtual network.

CSNET, centered around a single machine at BBN that supported dial-up lines and had connections to ARPANET and other networks. Using CSNET, academic researchers could call up and leave email for other people to pick up later. It was simple, but it worked.

By 1984 NSF began designing a high-speed successor to the ARPANET that would be open to all university research groups. To have something concrete to start with, NSF decided to build a backbone network to connect its six supercomputer centers, in San Diego, Boulder, Champaign, Pittsburgh, Ithaca, and Princeton. Each supercomputer was given a little brother, consisting of a LSI-11 microcomputer called a fuzzball. The fuzzballs were connected with 56 kbps leased lines and formed the subnet, the same hardware technology as the ARPANET used. The software technology was different however: the fuzzballs spoke TCP/IP right from the start, making it the first TCP/IP WAN.

NSF also funded some (eventually about 20) regional networks that connected to the backbone to allow users at thousands of universities, research labs, libraries, and museums to access any of the supercomputers and to communicate with one another. The complete network, including the backbone and the regional networks, was called NSFNET. It connected to the ARPANET through a link between backbone is illustrated in Fig.9.20.

NSFNET was an instantaneous success and was overloaded from the word go. NSF immediately began planning its successor and awarded a contract to the Michigan-based MERIT consortium to run it. Fiber optic channels at 448 kbps were leased from MCI to provide the version 2 backbone. IBM RS6000s were used as routers. This, too, was soon overwhelmed, and by 1990, the second backbone was upgraded to 1.5 Mbps.

As growth continued, NSF realized that the government could not continue financing networking forever. Furthermore, commercial organizations wanted to join but were forbidden by NSF's charter from using net-

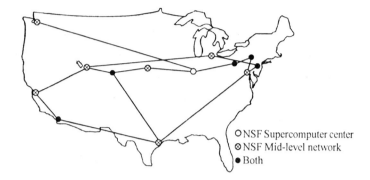

Fig.9.20 The NSFNET backbone in 1988

works NSF paid for. Consequently, NSF encouraged MERIT, MCI, and IBM to form a nonprofit corporation, ANS (Advanced Networks and Services) as a step along the road to commercialization. In 1990, ANS took over NSFNET and upgraded the 1.5 Mbps links to 45 Mbps to form ANSNET.

In December 1991, the U.S. congress passed a bill authorizing NREN, the National Research and Educational Network, the research successor to NSFNET, only running at gigabits speeds. The goal was a national network running at 3 Gbps before the millennium. This network is to act as a prototype for the much-discussed information superhighway.

By 1995, the NSFNET backbone was no longer needed to interconnect the NSF regional networks because numerous companies were running commercial IP networks, When ANSNET was sold to America Online in 1995, the NSF regional networks had to go out and buy commercial IP service to interconnect.

To ease the transition and make sure every regional network could communicate with every other regional network, NSF awarded contracts to four different network operators to establish a NAP (Network Access Point). These operators were PackBell (San Francisco), Ameritech (Chicago), MFS(Washington, DC), and Sprint (New York City, where for NAP purposes, Pennsauken, N. J. counts as New York City). Every network operator that wanted to provide backbone service to the NSF regional networks had to connect to all the NAPs, this arrangement meant that a packet originating on any regional network had a choice of backbone carriers to get from its NAP to the destination's NAP. Consequently, the backbone carriers were forced to compete for the regional networks' business on the basis of service and price, which was the idea, of course. In addition to the NSF NAPs, various government NAPs (e.g., FIX-E, FIX-W, MAE-East and MAE-West) and commercial NAPs (e.g., CIX) have also been created, so the concept of a single default backbone was replaced by a commercially-driven competitive infrastructure.

Other countries and regions are also building networks comparable to NSFNET. In Europe, for example, EBONE is an IP backbone for research organizations and EuropaNET is a more commercially oriented network. Both connect numerous cities in Europe with 2 Mbps lines. Upgrades to 34 Mbps are in progress, Each country in Europe has one or more national networks, which are roughly comparable to the NSF regional networks.

9.4.4 The Internet

The number of networks, machines, and users connected to the ARPANET grew rapidly after TCP/IP became the only official protocol on Jan. 1, 1983. When NSFNET and the ARPANET were interconnected, the growth became exponential. Many regional networks joined up, and connections were made to networks in Canada, Europe, and the Pacific.

Sometime in the mid-1980s, people began viewing the collection of networks as an internet, and later as the Internet, although there was no official dedication with some politician breaking a bottle of champagne over a fuzzball.

Growth continued exponentially, and by 1990 the Internet had grown to 3 000 networks and 200 000 computers. In 1992, the one millionth host was attached. By 1995, there were multiple backbones, hundreds of mid-level (i.e., regional) networks, tens of thousands of LANs, millions of hosts, and tens of millions of users. The size doubles approximately every year (Paxson, 1994).

Much of the growth comes from connecting existing networks to the Internet. In the past these have included SPAN, NASA's space physics network, HEPNET, a high energy physics network, BITNET, IBM's mainframes network, EARN, a European academic network now widely used in Eastern Europe, and many others. Numerous transatlantic links are in use, running from 64 kbps to 2 Mbps.

The glue that holds the Internet together is the TCP/IP makes universal service possible and can be compared to the telephone system or the adoption of standard gauge by the railroads in the 19th Century.

What does it actually mean to be on the Internet? Our definition is that a machine is on the Internet if it runs the TCP/IP protocol stack, has an IP address, and has the ability to send and receive electronic mail is not enough, since email is gatewayed to many networks outside the Internet. However, the issue is clouded somewhat by the fact that many personal computers have the ability to call up an Internet service provider using a modem, be assigned a temporary IP address, and send IP packets to other Internet hosts. It makes sense to regard such machines as being on the Internet for as long as they are connected to the service provider's router.

With exponential growth, the old informal way of running the Internet no longer works. In January 1992, the Internet Society was set up, to promote the use of the Internet and perhaps eventually take over managing it.

Traditionally, the Internet had four main applications, as follows:

(1) Email. The ability to compose, send, and receive electronic

mail has been around since the early days of the ARPANET and is enormously popular. Many people get dozens of messages a day and consider it their primary way of interacting with the outside world, far outdistancing the telephone and snail mail. Email programs are available on virtually every kind of computer these days.

(2) News. Newsgroups are specialized forums in which users with a common interest can exchange messages. Thousands of newsgroups exist, on technical and non-technical topics, including computers, science, recreation, and politics. Each newsgroup has its own etiquette, style, and customs, and woe be to anyone violating them.

(3) Remote login. Using the telnet, Rlogin, or other programs, users anywhere on the Internet can log into any other machine on which they have an account.

(4) File transfer. Using the FTP program, it is possible to copy files from one machine on the Internet to another. Bast numbers of articles, databases, and other information are available this way.

Up until the early 1990s, the Internet was largely populated by academic, government, and industrial researchers. One new application, the WWW (World Wide Web) changed all that and brought millions of new, nonacademic users to the net. This application, invented by CERN physicist Tim Berners-Lee, did not change any of the underlying facilities but made them easier to use. Together with the Mosaic viewer, written at the National Center for Supercomputer Applications, the WWW made it possible for a site to set up a number of pages of information containing text, pictures, sound, and even video, with embedded links to other pages. By clicking on a link, the user is suddenly transported to the page pointed to by that link. For example, many companies have a home page with entries pointing to other pages for product information, price lists, sales, technical support, communication with employees, stockholder information, and much more.

Numerous other kinds of pages have come into existence in a very short time, including maps, stock market tables, library card catalogs, recorded radio programs, and even a page pointing to the complete text of many books whose copyrights have expired (Mark Twain, Charles Dickens, etc.). Many people also have personal homes pages.

In the first year after Mosaic was released, the number or WWW servers grew from 100 ~ 7 000. Enormous growth will undoubtedly continue for years to come, and will probably be the force driving the technology and use of the Internert into the next millenium.

9.4.5 Gigabit Testbeds

The Internet backbones operate at megabit speeds, so for people who want to push the technological envelope, the next step is gigabit networking. With each increase in network bandwidth, new applications become possible, and gigabit networks are no exception. In this section we will first say a few words about gigabit applications, mention two of them, and then list some example gigabit testbeds that have been built.

Gigabit networks provide better bandwidth than megabit networks, but not always much better delay. For example, sending a 1 KB packet from New York to San Francisco at 1 Mbps takes 1 msec to pump the bits out and 20 msec for the transcontinental delay, for a total of 21 msec. A 1 Gbps network can reduce this to 20.000 1 msec. While the bits go out faster, the transcontinental delay remains the same, since the speed of light in optical fiber (or copper wire) is about 200 000 km/s, independent of the data rate. Thus for wide area applications in which low delay is critical, going to higher speeds may not help much. Fortunately, for some applications, bandwidth is what counts, and these are the applications for which gigabit networks will make a big difference.

One application is telemedicine. Many peoples think that a way to reduce medical costs is to reintroduce family doctors and family clinics on a large scale, so everyone has convenient access to first line medical care. When a serious medical problem occurs, the family doctor can order lab tests and medical imaging, such as X-rays, CAT scans, and MRI scans. The test results and images can then be sent electronically to a specialist who then makes the diagnoses.

Doctors are generally unwilling to make diagnoses from computer images unless the quality of the transmitted image is as good as the original image. This requirement means images will probably need 4K * 4K pixels, with 8 bits per pixel (black and while images) or 24 bits per pixel (color images). Since many tests require up to 100 images (e.g., different cross section of the organ in question), a single series for one patient can generate 40 gigabits. Moving images (e.g., a beating heart) generate even more data. Compression can help some but doctors are leary of it because the most efficient algorithms reduce image quality. Furthermore, all the images must be stored for years but may need to be retrieved at a moment's notice in the event of a medical emergency. Hospitals do not want to become computer centers, so off-site storage combined with high-bandwidth electronic retrieval is essential.

Another gigabit application is the virtual meeting. Each meeting room contains a spherical camera and ones or more people. The bit streams from each of the cameras are combined electronically to give the illusion that everyone is in the same room. Each person sees this image using virtual reality goggles. In this way meetings can happen without travel, but again, the data rates required are stupendous.

Staring in 1989, ARPA and NSF jointly agreed to finance a number of university-industry gigabit testbeds, later as part of the NREN project. In some of these, the data rate in each direction was 622 Mbps, so only by counting the data going in both directions do you get a gigabit. This kind of gigabit is sometimes called a "government gigabit." (Some cynics call it a gigabit after taxes.) Below we will briefly mention the first five projects. They have done their job and been shut down, but deserve some credit as pioneers, in the same way the ARPANET does.

(1) Aurora was a testbed linking four sites in the Northeast: M.I.T., the University of Pennsylvania, IBM's T.J. Watson Lab, and Bellcore (Motristown. N.J.) at 622 Mbps using fiber optics provided by MCI, Bell Atlantic, and NYNEX. Aurora was largely designed to help debug Bellcore's Sunshine switch and IBM's (proprietary) plaNET switch using parallel networks. Research issues included switching technology, gigabit protocols, routing, network control, distributed virtual memory, and collaboration using videoconferencing.

(2) Blanca was originally a research project called XUNET involving AT&T Bell Labs, Berkeley, and the University of Wisconsin. In 1990 it added some new sites (LBL, Cray Research, and the University of Illinois) and acquired NSF/ARPA funding. Some of it ran at 622 Mbps, but other parts ran at lower speeds. Blanca was the only nationwide testbed; the rest were regional. Consequently, much of the research was concerned with the effects of speed-of-light delay. The interest here was in protocols, especially network control protocols, host interfaces, and gigabit applications such as medial imaging, meteorological modeling, and radio astronomy.

(3) CASA was aimed at doing research on supercomputer applications, especially those in which part of the problem ran best on one kind of supercomputer (e.g., a Cray vector supercomputer) and part ran best on a different kind of supercomputer (e.g., a parallel supercomputer). The applications investigated included geology (analyzing Lansat images), climate modeling, and understanding chemical reactions. It operated in California and New Mexico and connected Los Alamos, Cal Tech, JPL, and the San Diego Supercomputer Center.

(4) Nectar differed from the three testbeds given above in that it was an experimental gigabit MAN running from CMU to the Pittsburgh Super-

computer Center. The designers were interested in applications involving chemical process flowsheeting and operations research, as well as the tools for debugging them.

(5) VISTAnet was a small gigabit testbed operated in Research Triangle Park, North Carolina, and connecting the University of North Carolina, North Carolina State University, and MCNC. The interest here was in a prototype for a public switched gigabit network with switches having hundreds of gigabit lines, meaning that the switches had to be capable of processing terabits/sec. The scientific research focused on using 3D images to plan radiation therapy for cancer patients, with the oncologist being able to vary the beam parameters and instantaneously see the radiation dosages being delivered to the tumor and surrounding tissue.

Vocabulary

1. algorithm	n.	算法
2. ambiguity	n.	模棱两可
3. antenna	n.	天线
4. arbitration	n.	仲裁,公断
5. autonomous	adj.	匿名的
6. capacity	n.	容量
7. chao	adj.	混乱
8. checksum	n.	检查和
9. circumnavigate	v.	绕过
10. client-server		客户服务器
11. client-server model		客户服务器模型
12. corridor	n.	通道,走廊
13. decouple	v.	解耦,去除干扰
14. depict	v.	描述
15. distributed system		分布式系统
16. dungen	n.	地牢
17. electronic mail		电子邮件

18. entity   n.   实体
19. etiquette   n.   规则
20. exponential   n.   指数
21. fallout   n.   余波,附带结果
22. forward   v.   转发
23. full-duplex   全双工
24. gamut   n.   全体,整体
25. goggles   n.   护目镜,潜水镜
26. half-duplex   半双工
27. hierarchy   n.   阶梯,等级
28. host   n.   主机
29. infrastructure   n.   基础,底层结构
30. interactive   adj.   交互式
31. Interface Data Unit   接口数据单元
32. inventory   n.   存货(清单)
33. killer   adj.   迷人的
34. newsgroup   n.   新闻组
35. object-oriented   面向对象的
36. outgoing   外出的,离开的
37. pointer   n.   指针
38. primitive   n.   操作,原型
39. process   n.   进程
40. propagation   v.   传播,宣传
41. protocol   n.   协议
42. Protocol Data Unit   协议数据单元
43. remote database   远程数据库
44. remote login   远程登录
45. remote terminal   终端
46. reprisal   v.   报复
47. router   n.   路由器

48. Service Data Unit   服务数据单元
49. simultaneous   adv. 同时的
50. static allocation   静态分配
51. subnet   n.   子网
52. taxonomy   n.   分类学,分类
53. telemedicine   n.   远程医疗
54. terminology   n.   术语
55. testbed   n.   测试平台
56. therapy   v.   治疗
57. token   n.   令牌
58. topology   n.   拓扑学
59. videoconference   n.   可视会议
60. virtual reality   虚拟现实
61. worldwide shared   全球共享的
62. wide area network   广域网

Notes:

1. Due to rapid technological progress, these areas are rapidly converging, and the differences between collecting, transporting, storing, and processing information are quickly disappearing.

由于技术的快速进步,这些领域正在快速融合。信息的收集、传送、存储和处理之间的区别正在迅速消失。

2. The old model of a single computer serving all of the organization's computational needs has been replaced by one in which a large number of separate but interconnected computers do the job.

为组织内部所有的计算需求提供服务的旧的单机模式已经被另一个模式替换,在这个模式中,由许多独立的但又相互联系在一起的计算机完成工作任务。

3. Stronger yet, having network operators censor messages would probably cause them to delete everything with even the slightest possibility of their being sued, and

thus violate their users' rights to free speech.
尽管他们很强大而且他们被起诉的可能性很小,让网络操作员检查信息可能会造成他们删除所有内容,因此会破坏他们用户自由言论的权利。

4. This desire requires connecting together different, and frequently incompatible networks, sometimes by using machines called gateways to make the connection and provide the necessary translation, both in terms of hardware and software.
这个需求要求连接不同的而且通常是不兼容的网络,有时通过采用称为网关的机器进行连接并提供硬件和软件方面的必要转换。

5. The specification of an architecture must contain enough information to allow an implementer to write the program or build the hardware for each layer so that it will correctly obey the appropriate protocol.
结构的规范必须包含足够的信息,允许使用者为每一层写程序或建立硬件以便于正确地遵守特有的协议。

6. In order to transfer the SDU, the layer n entity may have to fragment it into several pieces, each of which is given a header and sent as a separate PDU (Protocol Data Unit) such as a packet.
为了传送服务数据单元(SDU),第 n 层实体可能需要把它分成几个部分,每一部分都分配一个头,而且作为像包一样的独立协议数据单元被发送。

7. A host could send messages of up to 8 063 bits to its IMP, which would then break these up into packets of at most 1 008 bits and forward them independently toward the destination.
主机发送 8 063 位的信息到它的接口信息处理器(IMP),该处理器把接到的信息分为最大为 1 008 位的包,并独立地把它们转发到目的地。

8. The glue that holds the Internet together is the TCP/IP makes universal service possible and can be compared to the telephone system or the adoption of standard gauge by the railroads in the 19th Century.
把互联网粘结在一起的是 TCP/IP 使通用的服务成为可能,这可以和电话系统或 19 世纪铁路中的标准轨距的采用相比较。

9. Together with the Mosaic viewer, written at the National Center for Supercomputer Applications, the WWW made it possible for a site to set up a number of pages of information containing text, pictures, sound, and even video, with embedded links to other pages.
借助于在国家中心为超级计算机应用所开发的 Mosaic 浏览器,WWW 使网站建立包含文本、图形、声音,甚至影像的网页成为可能,这些网页带有其他网页的嵌入链接。

10. The scientific research focused on using 3D images to plan radiation therapy for cancer patients, with the oncologist being able to vary the beam parameters and instantaneously see the radiation dosages being delivered to the tumor and surrounding tissue.

科学研究集中采用三维图像为癌症患者提供放射治疗,肿瘤医生可以变换射线束的参数并立即观察到发送到肿瘤和周围组织的放射剂量。

10

Introduction of Programmable Controllers

From a simple heritage, these remarkable systems have evolved to not only replace electromechanical devices, but to solve an ever-increasing array of control problems in both process and nonprocess industries. By all indications, these microprocessor powered giants will continue to break new ground in the automated factory into the 1990s.

10.1 HISTORY

In the 1960s, electromechanical devices were the order of the day as far as control was concerned. These devices, commonly known as relays, were being used by the thousands to control many sequential-type manufacturing processes and stand-alone machines. Many of these relays were in use in the transportation industry, more specifically, the automotive industry. These relays used hundreds of wires and their interconnections to effect a control solution. The performance of a relay was basically reliable—at least as a single device. But the common applications for relay panels called for 300 to 500 or more relays, and the reliability and maintenance issues associated with supporting these panels became a very great challenge. Cost became another issue, for in spite of the low cost of the relay itself, the installed cost of the panel could be quite high. The total cost including purchased parts, wiring, and installation labor, could range from $ 30 ~ $ 50 per relay. To make matters worse, the constantly changing needs of a process called for recurring modifications of a control panel. With relays, this was a costly prospect, as it was accomplished by a major rewiring effort on the panel. In addition, these changes were sometimes poorly documented, causing a second-shift maintenance nightmare months later. In light of this, it was not uncommon to discard an entire control panel in favor of a new one with the appropriate components wired in a manner suited for the new process. Add to this the unpredictable, and potentially high, cost of maintaining these systems as on high-volume motor vehicle production lines, and it became clear that something was needed to improve the control process - to make it more reliable, easier to troubleshoot, and more adaptable to changing control needs.

That something, in the late 1960s, was the first programmable controller. This first 'revolutionary' system was developed as a specific response to the needs of the major automotive manufacturers in the United States. These early controllers, or programmable logic controllers (PLC), represented the first systems that ① could be used on the factory floor, ② could have there 'logic' changed without extensive rewiring or component changes, and ③ were easy to diagnose and repair when problems occurred.

It is interesting to observe the progress that has been made in the past 15 years in the programmable controller area. The pioneer products of the late 1960s must have been confusing and frightening to a great number of people. For example, what happened to the hardwired and electromechanical devices that maintenance personnel were used to repairing with hand tools? They were replaced with 'computers' disguised as electronics designed to replace relays. Even the programming tools were designed to appear as relay equivalent presentations. We have the opportunity now to examine the promise, in retrospect, that the programmable controller brought to manufacturing.

10.2 BASIC CONCEPTS

All programmable controllers consist of the basic functional blocks shown in Fig.10.1. We'll examine each block to understand the relationship to the control system. First we look at the center, as it is the heart (or at least the brain) of the system. It consists of a microprocessor, logic memory for the storage of the actual control logic, storage or variable memory for use with data that will ordinarily change as a function of the control program execution, and a power supply to provide electrical power for the processor and memory. Next comes the I/O block. This function takes the control level signals for the CPU and converts them to voltage and current levels suitable for connection with factory grade sensors and actuators. The I/O type can range from digital (discrete or on /

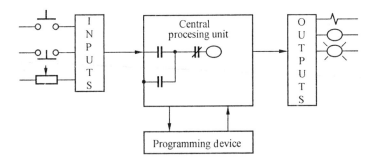

Fig.10.1 Diagram of basic programmable controller functions blocks

off), analog (continuously variable), or a variety of special purpose 'smart' I/O which are dedicated to a certain application task. The programmer is shown here, but it is normally used only to initially configure and program a system and is not required for the system to operate. It is also used in troubleshooting a system, and can prove to be a valuable tool in pinpointing the exact cause of a problem. The field devices shown here represent the various sensors and actuators connected to the I/O. These are the arms, legs, eyes, and ears of the system, including pushbuttons, limit switches, proximity switches, photosensors, thermocouples, RTDs, position sensing devices, and bar code reader as input; and pilot lights, display devices, motor starters, DC and AC drives, solenoids, and printers as outputs.

No single attempt could cover its rapidly changing scope, but three basic characteristics can be examined to give classify an industrial control device as a programmable controller.

(1) Its basic internal operation is to solve logic from the beginning of memory to some specified point, such as end of memory or end of program. Once the end is reached, the operation begins again at the beginning of memory. This scanning process continues from the time power is supplied to the time it is removed.

(2) The programming logic is a form of a relay ladder diagram. Normally open, normally closed contacts, and relay coils are used within a format utilizing a left and a right vertical rail. Power flow (symbolic positive electron flow) is used to determine which coils or outputs are energized or deenergized.

(3) The machine is designed for the industrial environment from its basic concept; this protection is not added at a later date. The industrial environment includes unreliable AC power, high temperatures (0 to 60 degree Celsius), extremes of humidity, vibrations, RF noise, and other similar parameters.

10.3 GENERAL APPLICATION AREAS

The programmable controller is used in a wide variety of control applications today, many of which were not economically possible just a few years ago. This is true for two general reasons: ① their cost effectiveness (that is, the cost per I/O point) has improved dramatically with the falling prices of microprocessors and related components, and ② the ability of the controller to solve complex computation and communication tasks has made it possible to use it where a dedicated computer was previously used.

Applications for programmable controllers can be categorized in a number of different ways, including general and industrial application categories. But it is important to understand the framework in which controllers are presently understood and used so that the full scope of present and future evolution can be examined. It is through the power of applications that controllers can be seen in their full light. Industrial applications include many in both discrete manufacturing and process industries. Automotive industry applications, the genesis of the programmable controller, continue to provide the largest base of opportunity. Other industries, such as food processing and utilities, provide current development opportunities.

There are five general application areas in which programmable controllers are used. A typical installation will use one or more of these integrated to form a complete solution to the control system problem. The five general areas are explained briefly below.

10.3.1 Sequence Control

This is the largest and most common application for programmable controllers today, and is the closest to traditional relay control in its 'sequential' nature. Because of the very general nature of this category, it is sometimes difficult to understand the breadth of power that it brings to so many applications. From an applications standpoint, sequence control is found on individual machines or machine lines, on conveyor and packaging machinery, and even on modern elevator control systems.

10.3.2 Motion Control

This is the integration of linear or rotary motion control in the programmable controller. This could be a single or multiple axis drive system control, and can be used with servo, stepper, or multiple axis drive system control, and can be used with servo, stepper, or hydraulic drives. In early systems, a stand-alone servo drive would be connected to the programmable controller with a series of individual conductors to discrete inputs and outputs. Newer systems integrate this functionality directly into the I/O racks through the use of special I/O boards dedicated to motion control. This eliminates the need to interface the two devices together with discrete I/O. Programmable controller motion control applications include an unending variety of machinery; metal cutting (grinders), metal forming (press brake), assembly machines, and multiple axes of motion can be coordinated for both discrete part and process industry applications. Examples of these would include Cartesian robots, and many web related processes that is, film, rubber, and nonwoven textile systems.

10.3.3 Process Control

This is the ability of the programmable controller to control a number of physical parameters such as temperature, pressure, velocity, and flow. This involves the use of analog (continuously variable) I/O to achieve a closed-loop control system. The use of Proportion-Integral-Derivative (PID), software always allow the programmable controller to replace the function of stand-alone loop controllers. Another alternative is to integrate the loop controllers with the programmable controller, retaining the best features of each. Typical examples of applications include plastic injection molding machines, extrusion process machines, heat treat furnaces, and many other batch-type control applications.

10.3.4 Data Management

The ability to collect, analyze, and manipulate data has only become possible with programmable controllers in the last few years. With the advanced instruction sets and expanded variable memory capacities of the newer programmable controllers, it is now possible for the system to act as a data concentrator, collecting data about the machine or process it is controlling. This data can then be sent via a communication function to another intelligent device for analysis or report generation. Any comments that are made about the importance and growing use of data management are probably understatements considering the leap-frog technical solution capabilities it brings to a wide range of applications. Data management is frequently found on large materials handling systems, in unmanned flexible manufacturing cells, and in many process industry applications, that is, paper, primary metals, and food processing.

10.3.5 Communications

This is the ability for the programmable controller to have a "window" to other programmable controllers and intelligent devices. One of the most active development areas in today's industrial control area and much Local Area Network (LAN) activity is currently driven by the MAP communications standard. The Manufacturing Automation Protocol (MAP), an activity initiated by General Motors, is intended to connect multi-vendor intelligent devices, including programmable controllers, into a coherent, efficient control network. In addition, higher performance control-oriented networks, sometimes referred to as subnets, offer the ability to tie together a small number of programmable controllers to form an 'island of automation.' Communications are most often used with a factory host computer, for the purpose of collecting process data and configuring the controllers for a certain production sequence. The majority of communica-

Introduction of Programmable Controllers 231

tion networks involving programmable controllers today are in the automotive industry. These are used in the production of a variety of engines, transmissions, and in assembly and paint operations. It is clear, however, that other industries will be catching up in the use of factory communications, most notably perhaps the aircraft, chemical, and heavy equipment industries.

As mentioned earlier, these applications may be found alone, or in combination on a variety of apparatus. Let's examine two hypothetical cases, the first a simple sequencing application, and the second a machine which integrates all five application categories.

A stretch-wrap is a machine which automatically wraps plastic film or other material around and unitizes quantities of material (bags, boxes) in the most optimum way on a pallet for shipping. It normally involves sections of a powered conveyor and an operating area for the product layers to be placed together and wrapped. The programmable controller is used to sequence the operation of the stretch-wrap machine, sensing the presence of a pallet, and using actuators and sensors to move that pallet automatically to its proper place in the machine. Stretch-wrap patterns are 'remembered' by the controller, and alternating wraps are staggered to improve the transportability of the loaded pallet. When a pallet is complete, it is sequenced by the controller to the exit conveyor section, to be loaded on a truck.

Plastic injection molding machines produce millions of items used in daily life. A programmable controller can be used here in a combination of the application areas listed above. Sequence control is used to arrange the various actions needed to load, unload, and execute the molding process. Motion control is used to control the velocity and position of the ram, which provides the force required to perform the actual molding process. Process control is used to control the temperature and pressure of the molding cavity. Data on the number and quality of parts produced is collected and concentrated using data management functions, and this data summary is made available to a communications network, for integration into a plant-wide network of molding machine controllers and factory host computers. Fig.10.2 shows a typical plastic injection molding machine.

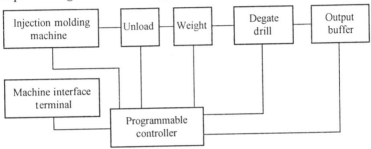

Fig.10.2 Diagram of plastic injection molding machine

As you can see from this introduction, applications for programmable controllers are extremely diverse and varied. This diversity will continue to increase in the future as cost-effectiveness and creativity combine to form an unbeatable team for automation productivity.

10.4 OPERATING ENVIRONMENT CONSIDERATIONS

One of the primary differences between programmable controllers and their general purpose computer cousins is the environment in which they can operate. A factory can provide some very unfriendly, sometimes hostile, conditions. All manner of dirt, grime, shock, vibration, temperature and humidity extremes, and electromagnetic field interference are present for the life of a typical programmable controller application. Couple this with an unreliable source of power, and you have the makings of a very difficult design challenge, for both the programmable controller and the installation process. We will examine briefly the various areas of concern for the programmable controller environment.

Dirt. This is just plain day-to-day factory dirt, and can be counted on for causing problems in many electrical installations of all types. All programmable controllers are enclosed to one degree or another, but the insurance here is to mount the controller in a good quality cabinet, NEMA 12 or NEMA 4, and keep it closed as much as possible. The National Electrical Manufacturers Association (NEMA) defines standards for cabinet design for a variety of environments, including oil-and water-tight. And while a commonsense cabinet protection may seem obvious, on two- and three-shift operations the cabinet doors may be left open for extended periods, especially during production pressured maintenance efforts. Most controllers can withstand an astonishing amount of abuse, but it makes practical sense to protect them as much as possible.

Shock and Vibration. Most controllers are designed and tested to substantial limits for shock and vibration. In turn, many applications deliver substantial levels of shock and vibration. Most designs will work well in the average factory environment, but if your installation calls for above-average expected levels of shock and vibration, you should consult the manufacturer for his test limits and experience. If these are not suitable for your application, you should inquire about the availability of special mounting techniques to reduce the shock and vibration impact. Special applications that may require vibration considerations include some non-traditional application areas such as mining, marine, and railroads.

Temperature Extremes. The industrial standard ambient operating temperature at the time of this writing is $0° \sim 60°$ (degree) Celsius. Again, this is quite suitable for the majority of factory installation, but there are conditions that can cause trouble. At the high end, the internal temperature of a closed, nonventilated control cabinet can exceed $60°$ Celsius in summer peaks, but may not cause a problem since the controllers have the traditional design tolerance band. If you experience erratic operation of the controller during extremely hot periods, supplemental cooling may be required. The low end of the temperature range can cause similar concerns. Normally the ambient heat generated from the operating controller will provide sufficient warmth for reliable operations. However, if low temperatures are suspected as the reason for erratic operations, supplemental heat may be required. This is especially true if the controller will be 'cold started', since the advantage of self-generated ambient heat will not be consistently available. As a point of interest, some programmable controller manufactures are seeing an increase in the call for lower temperature ratings for their controllers. This is especially true for those that operate on 24 V DC. Some installations are being made in remote areas, where heat and AC line power are considered luxuries. Included here are remote oil pumping stations and railroad track switching applications.

Humidity. The standard here is 5% ~ 95% relative humidity (RH) noncondensing. Note the "noncondensing," as this suggests that the controller will not survive in conditions where moisture would collect on an extended basis. This is quite understandable and normally does not cause any design or operational problems with a good cabinet choice.

Interference. This can be an elusive culprit, but can be dealt with for most applications. Without proper design, electrical interference will wreak havoc on an otherwise sound programmable controller installation. Unpredictable, and sometimes dangerous, I/O or logic status changes can occur in heavy interference environments. Some controllers, because of their designs, will fare better in this environment than others. A few guidelines will improve the chances for a successful application. Good cabinet design choice along with avoidance of any known interference source in the physical placement will help. In the wiring of the controller power and I/O, segregation of 115 V and low voltage (i.e., 24 V AC/DC) will minimize induction coupling. In extreme situations, external filtering may be required although optically coupled I/O and power supply designs will normally provide adequate protection.

Power. Nothing is so unreliable as the power supply in a typical factory environment. Fluctuations in voltage and availability are common. The quality of line service can be improved by using conditioning equipment such as isolation transformers and line conditioners. Highly cortical applications may warrant an uninterruptible power supply (UPS), which provides clean power and battery backup during power failures. Most installations will not require this extreme action, since the power that supplies the controller also supplies the rest of the manufacturing grosses. In that case it is important to understand, and design for, the orderly shutdown and automatic power-up sequence of the controller. Some applications will call for a manual restart after power failure for safety reasons.

10.5 DEDICATED MICROPROCESSOR BASED SYSTEM —A CONTRAST

One of the premises on which the programmable controller is based is the idea that it is a general purpose control product, capable of being configured, modified, and tailored to the application by the original equipment manufacturer (OEM) of user that purchased the controller. The hardware and software of such a system is such that it can be supported by a normal maintenance electrician.

There is a category of control product that is much more narrow and optimized for a particular control task. It uses a sometimes unique design, customized for the particular application by the manufacturer. The system is normally programmed in a programming language not familiar to the average control engineer and maintenance electrician (Assembly), which makes the support of the system difficult. The advantages of such a system are its cost-effectiveness for the given purpose, and sometimes its efficiency of execution. For example, certain automatic testing systems employ dedicated microprocessor based systems, sometimes in conjunction with a programmable controller. In this case the microprocessor system is used to collect large amounts of process data at high speeds, and the programmable controller executes the proper coordination with the rest of the manufacturing process. Another example of an application where dedicated controls are sometimes used is high-speed packaging where a general purpose system does not provide the throughput needs.

The distinction between the programmable controller and the microprocessor-based system is beginning to blur as controllers continue to gain data processing and communication control attributes while the microprocessor-based system takes on discrete I/O. This trend, combined with the desire of factory personnel to 'standardize' on a hardware and software vendor(s), will make the dedicated system unattractive in all but the most demanding applications.

10.6 PERSONAL COMPUTER IMPLICATIONS

Relative newcomers to the industrial control arena, personal computers are finding more and more tasks suitable for their application. Most of the current uses of personal computers are related to program development and documentation of programmable controllers and dedicated microprocessor-based systems. Recent design enhancements have been made by certain manufactures to allow the computer to survive in a more hostile environment that was previously conceivable. Improvements in operating temperature limits and filters to prevent foreign materials from being drawn into the system, are allowing a much higher level of 'industrialization' than the office-grade product would allow. This trend is system design will allow a higher level of system product to evolve with much greater computing power, coupled with a greatly enhanced and intelligent I/O system. The result will be an inherently distributed and intelligent system, allowing system control ad communications improvements not considered attainable before, The favorable by-product of all this activity will be an increase in productivity, with attractive payback and improved corporate profitability.

There are two types of personal computer installations currently finding their way into industrial control applications. One is the portable device, industrialized to survive on most factory floors, at least for short periods of time. It is used for loading programs into the programmable controller memory, and for on-line monitoring and troubleshooting. It is also normally used for program development and documentation in an offline mode. The second personal computer installation type is a larger, more powerful system than the portable device. It will have more memory, both semiconductor and disk storage. These systems use a real-time multitasking operating system, and are permanently installed in a standard control cabinet using no fans for cooling. They are modular in design, allowing custom configurations and easy maintenance. They are used as data concentrators in flexible manufacturing systems at the cell or zone level. They are also used as system directors, planning work scheduling in the cell along with the tools and materials required for a given sequence of operations. Fig. 10.3 illustrates a typical hierarchical control scheme, showing the relationship of these 'cell controller' computers to programmable controllers and other intelligent devices.

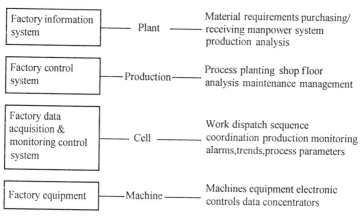

Fig. 10.3 Diagram of cell automation hierarchy

10.7 FACTORY AUTOMATION AND PROGRAMMABLE CONTROLLERS

Programmable controllers play a fundamental role in factory automation efforts. Their breadth of application capabilities allow firms to use the product of one or two manufacturers in a wide array of process and non-process areas. There are several levels of evolution involved in factory automation advances in most plants. Most firms will be interested in modernizing existing facilities because the construction of entirely new facilities will not be economically feasible. In many instances, the first stage of automation involves small contiguous production areas, concentrating on improving productivity in that area alone. It is not uncommon to fund automation efforts through the savings of reduced in-process inventory alone. These small contiguous areas have come to be called "islands of automation." Programmable controllers are used here to operate machinery within the island, including stand-alone machine tools, dedicated machinery (i. e., packing machinery), and material handling equipment for both within the island and to bring items in and out of the area.

The normal extension of this type of automation is to tie multiple islands together, both physically with bulk or unit handling systems, and through the data communication links of a proprietary or standard local area network. This control network, linking programmable controllers and other factory automation control products, allows real-time flexible execution of the optimum production process. Fig. 10.4 shows a factory automation system including programmable controllers, numerical controllers, robot and vision systems, and communication networks.

Introduction of Programmable Controllers   239

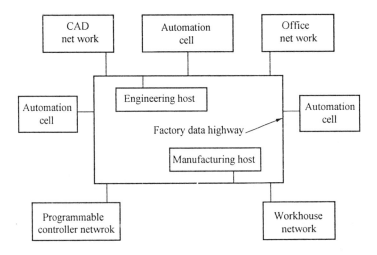

Fig.10.4 Diagram of factory automation system

Vocabulary

1. actuator   n.   执行器
2. bar code reader   条码阅读器
3. by-product   副产品
4. call for   需要
5. contiguous   adj.   临近的
6. culprit   n.   犯罪者
7. electromechanical   adj.   机电的
8. elusive   adj.   难以捉摸的
9. filter   n.   滤波
10. fluctuation   n.   升降波动,不规则的变化
11. hardwired   adv.   硬接线的
12. havoc   n.   大破坏
13. high-volume   adv.   大容量
14. humidity   n.   湿度
15. induction coupling   感应耦合

16. inference	v.	干扰
17. injection molding		注模
18. instruction set		指令集
19. interconnection	n.	相互连接
20. isolation transformer	n.	隔离变压器
21. limit switch		限位开关
22. Local Area Network		局域网
23. maintenance	v.	维护
24. Manufacturing Automation Protocol		加工自动化协议
25. multiple axis drive		多轴驱动
26. photosensor	n.	光感应器
27. pilot light		信号灯
28. proximity switch		接近开关
29. pushbutton	n.	按钮
30. relay	n.	继电器
31. relay panel		继电器盘
32. reliability	n.	可靠性
33. RF noise		射频干扰
34. scan	v.	扫描
35. shock	v.	冲击
36. solenoid	n.	线圈
37. stand-alone	adj.	独立的
38. stepper	n.	步进电机
39. subnet	n.	子网
40. thermocouple	n.	热电偶
41. troubleshoot	v.	排除故障
42. uninterruptible power supply		不间断电源
43. vendor	n.	生产厂商
44. vibration	n.	震动
45. water-tight		防水

46. wreak　　　　　　　　　　v.　　　发泄,报复

Notes:

1. These devices, commonly known as relays, were being used by the thousands to control many sequential-type manufacturing processes and stand-alone machines.
这些通常称为继电器的设备被数以千计的人用来控制许多顺序制造过程和单独机器。

2. But the common applications for relay panels called for 300 to 500 or more relays, and the reliability and maintenance issues associated with supporting these panels became a very great challenge.
但是,继电器柜的常规应用需要 300 到 500 或更多继电器,可靠性和支持这些柜的维护问题成为一个很大的挑战。

3. This first "revolutionary" system was developed as a specific response to the needs of the major automotive manufacturers in the United States.
这个受次"革命性"的系统按照美国汽车制造业的特定要求开发出来的。

4. From an applications standpoint, sequence control is found on individual machines or machine lines, on conveyor and packaging machinery, and even on modern elevator control systems.
从应用的角度看,顺序控制建立在单台机器或生产线上、传送带和包装机器上、甚至在现代电梯控制系统中。

5. With the advanced instruction sets and expanded variable memory capacities of the newer programmable controllers, it is now possible for the system to act as a data concentrator, collecting data about the machine or process it is controlling.
由于新的可编程控制器采用高级指令集,扩展了变量存储器的容量,这个系统现在可以作为数据集中器用来收集被控制机器或过程的数据。

6. The Manufacturing Automation Protocol (MAP), an activity initiated by General Motors, is intended to connect multi-vendor intelligent devices, including programmable controllers, into a coherent, efficient control network.
由通用汽车公司提出的制造自动化协议(MAP)用来连接多个供应商的智能设备,组成一个连贯的有效的控制网络。这些智能设备包括可编程控制器。

11

Foundation of PLC

11.1 THE CENTRAL PROCESSING UNIT

Although referred to as the brain of the system, the Central Processing Unit in a normal installation is the unsung hero, buried in a control cabinet, all but forgotten.

11.1.1 Basic Functionality

In a programmable controller system, the central processing unit (CPU) provides both the heart and the brain required for successful and timely control execution. It rapidly and efficiently scans all of the system inputs, examines and solves the application logic, and updates all of the system outputs. In addition, it also gives itself a checkup each scan to ensure that its structure is still intact. In this chapter we will examine the central processing unit as it relates to the entire system. Included will be the various functional blocks in the CPU, typical scan techniques, I/O interface and memory uses, power supplies, and system diagnostics.

11.1.2 Typical Function Block Interactions

In practice, the central processing unit can vary in its architecture, but consists of the basic building block structure illustrated in Fig.11.1.

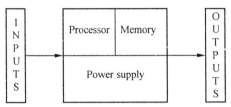

Fig.11.1 CPU block diagram

The processor section consists of one or more microprocessors and their associated circuitry. While it is true that some of the older generation programmable controllers were designed without the luxury of using microprocessors, most modern systems use either a single microprocessor such as the 8086 or Z-80, or multiple microprocessors such as the AMD 2903, used in a bit slice architecture. This multi-tasking approach is used in the multiple microprocessor system to break the control system tasks into many small components which can be executed in parallel. The result of this approach is to achieve execution speeds that are orders of magnitude faster than their single-tasking counterparts. In addition to efficiently processing direct I/O control information and being programmable, the real advantage that microprocessor-based systems have over their hardwired relay counterparts is the ability to acquire and manipulate numerical data easily. It is this attribute that makes programmable controllers the powerhouses that they are today in solving tough factory automation problems. The factory of tomorrow will run efficiently only if quality information about process needs and status of the process equipment are known on a real-times basis. This can and will come about only if the unit level controllers, including programmable controllers, are empowered with the ability to collect, analyze, concentrate, and deliver data about the process. As the market continues to exhibit this demand, manufactures are likely to continue to outfit their controllers with more and more variable memory, and enhanced instruction sets to perform these tasks.

The memory segment shown in Fig.11.1 refers to the programmable controller's active storage medium. This can be either volatile or nonvolatile in design, and can be configured and used in a variety of ways for both executive program storage, with which the system executes its instructions, and application program storage, for the actual control program.

The power supply shown here is used for providing sufficient electrical current for the various semiconductors and other power-consuming devices on one or more of the CPU circuit boards. It can be arranged in a number of different physical ways. It may be located in the same chassis in which the CPU boards are located, or can be mounted in a stand-alone fashion, connected externally to the CPU chassis. Depending on the particular manufacturer's configuration, it may also provide power for some of the I/O functions, as well as the CPU.

11.1.3 Scan Techniques

By definition and design, the programmable controller is dedicated to the continuous, repetitive task of examining the system inputs, solving the current control logic, and updating the system outputs. This task is referred to as scanning (sometimes called sweeping), and is accomplished in slightly different ways in each manufacturer's programmable controller. Since many of the variations are not material to the basic functionality of the system, we will only examine the basic varieties.

Fig.11.2 shows the functional operation of a typical scan mechanism. You'll notice that the I/O servicing is at the end of the scan cycle, and is also an integral part of the scan timing. This type of scan is referred to as synchronous scan and is used with very fast machines that can update all of the I/O without lengthening the scan time materially. A typical scan time in a modern programmable controller ranges from 10 ~ 100 ms (milliseconds). Most controllers have a

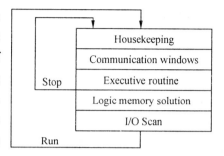

Fig.11.2 Scan sequence diagram

mechanism, watchdog timer, to measure the scan length each cycle and initiate a critical alarm if the scan time exceeds a certain preset length, normally 150 ~ 200 ms. Referring to Fig. 11.1 again, the synchronous scan contains four other actives in addition to the I/O scan. Housekeeping refers to a small number of routine chores performed by the programmable controller to ensure that its internal structure is still healthy and functioning properly. Next comes the communications windows to allow structured communications to other devices in the system, or externally. Included in this group would be the programming device, special microprocessor-based communications modules to allow ultimate communication of the programmable controller system to another intelligent device. Next in line comes the executive routine, in which the actual base intelligence of the system is used to interpret the current control program. This interpretation is then used in the next step to solve the current control logic program. The last step of this basic scan process is to integrate the currently interpreted control logic program with the most current input statuses from the I/O scan, and to update the output statuses with the current results.

The primary variation of this basic scanning technique comes from architectures that service and update I/O with a separate processor, asynchronous to the main logic solution scan. This alternative is common in systems where serial communication is used to control and update racks of remotely mounted I/O. It is also used where all of the I/O is serial, and run in multiple channels, to suit a particular system configuration need. This parallel asynchronous scanning technique has the advantage that it allows extensive flexibility in configuring a programmable controller system for a particular application need. It has the disadvantage that while the basic scan rate maybe fast enough to suit an application, the I/O scan(s) actually be longer than the primary CPU scan. This can cause problems in a fast acting system in that the logic solution can occur with relatively "old" input data from the remote I/O channel. While this is at times bothersome, the more dramatic case involves a peculiarity of some programmable controllers in that they may allow input and output data to be updated on separate time bases, providing the possibility of "bad" logic solutions and unpredictable machine actions.

As part of the basic CPU structure, a number of error checking procedures are used to maintain a high level of integrity in the communications between itself and its subsystems. This can involve both the internal subsystems, such as the memory, and the so-called external subsystems, for example the I/O system. The more common error-checking schemes are outlined bellow. The first and most common is parity. This is used on many communication link subsystems to detect errors by examining the number of "ones" in each byte of information received, and comparing the total number in any one byte to a predetermined choice of even or odd parity. This corresponds to the total of ones in the byte summing to an even or odd number. This has the disadvantage of being able to detect a single-bit error, that is where a zero or one has changed state during some operation; but cannot detect two single but opposing bit changes in a byte of memory that cancel each other out and still result in the correct parity. Checksum, the second most commonly used method for error checking, involves the examination of a block of memory for errors as compared to an individual word as done in parity checking. The procedure involves the adding of a single word of memory to a block that is unique to that block. Common varieties of the checksum are the Cyclic Redundancy Check (CRC) and the Longitudinal Redundancy Check (LRC). The checksum advantage over the parity check is that it more efficiently uses memory. The third error checking method that we will consider is Error Detection and Correction (EDC). It is used in the more sophisticated programmable controllers provided by a few manufacturers today. In essence it involves a number of complex error correcting codes implemented in the hardware. The Error Detecting and Correcting method has the added advantage that it can sense and correct single-bit error, while only sensing double bit errors

11.1.4 I/O Control

Today's modern programmable controller includes a sophisticated method to control the CPU's execution of the Input/Output chain. This is referred to as I/O control, or sometimes Bus control. This is actually handled in different ways, depending on the type and style of controller involved. In the small programmable controller, the I/O servicing is performed as an integral part of the primary microprocessor used to control all of the major functions. In medium and large-sized systems, it is common to include a microprocessor board or subsystem to handle the execution of the I/O updating. This is especially important in the systems that update I/O separately, or synchronously from the main scan.

Regardless of the way it is achieved, the I/O control, or updating, is performed for the same reasons. For a successful scan sequence, an accurate execution of the signal level communication to the physical Input and Output modules is required. It is then, and only then, that any changes in the I/O status can be physically updated to actuators or from the sensors.

11.1.5 Memory-uses and Structure

Fig. 11.1 shows how the programmable controller memory relates to the other functional block in the CPU. It is memory, along with a microprocessor to exercise it, that separates today's programmable controller from its predecessor. Current advances in memory allows both the rapid creation and efficient editing of control programs used to run the manufacturing processes. Different types of memory are used in a variety of programmable controllers for different application or design reasons. Let's examine some of them in detail.

There are two basic memory categories used by programmable controllers, or for that matter, any microprocessor-based system. They are volatile and nonvolatile. Volatile means that the contents of the memory have no means to remain intact without an external power source connected to maintain the data integrity. Nonvolatile means that by the very design of the memory, a means exists by which the contents of the memory remain intact without an external power supply.

The segments of memory in a programmable controller system are straightforward.

Application Memory. Also called logic memory, it is the section of memory used to store the actual control program that the controller uses to control the manufacturing process. This control program is usually created by the system user.

Data Table Memory. This term collectively refers to the variable (register) memory, and the input/output status or image tables. The variable memory contains timer and counter values, along with any data used in mathematical calculations performed by the application program. The I/O image tables contain, as the name suggests, a representation of the actual input/output point status, either on or off.

Executive. Also called firmware (or just firmware), this section of

Foundation of PLC 249

memory contains the base intelligence of the system. The executive program supervises the basic chores of the programmable controller system including communications with subsystems, control program interpretation and execution, CPU diagnostics, and other housekeeping tasks included in every scan.

Scratch Pad. This is a temporary memory area used by the system to store the step-by-step and interim results obtained through some calculations. In some systems, the scratch pad memory contains the programmable controller statistics, such as memory size, amount used, and any active diagnostic flags set. Various segments of the programmable controller use different memory types to accomplish different design or application purposes. Below, we shall examine a sample of memory types, and contrast their use in programmable controllers.

Read Only Memory (ROM). This memory was one of the first commercially variable nonvolatile memory types used in microprocessor-based systems. ROM get its name from the fact that the memory can be read from (information extracted), but cannot be written into (information placed in). A number of manufacturers of programmable controllers use ROM memory to store the executive programs. This is because it normally to store the executive programs. This is because it normally requires no adjustment or editing once the system is shipped from the manufacturer. ROM is rarely, if ever, used as application memory, and cannot be used as data table or scratch pad memory because it cannot be updated with data from the operation of the programmable controller execution.

Random Access Memory (RAM). This is a volatile memory, but has the advantage over ROM of being capable of being written to as well as read from. It is for this reason that it is sometimes called read/write memory. Any location within the memory can be accessible. Because it is volatile, the memory contents will be lost if power is lost. With a properly designed battery backup system, RAM can retain its current contents during extended power outages. Most RAM today is of the Complementary Metallic Oxide Semiconductor (CMOS) type, and uses very little power. It is this combination that makes RAM the memory of choice formats of today's programmable controller systems, especially for use in the application, data table, and portions of some scratch pad memories. RAM's volatile design is offset by its high speed and low cost.

Programmable Read Only Memory (PROM). PROM is a type of ROM that is programmable with commercially available equipment. Once programmed, however, it cannot be altered and hence is nonvolatile. It would therefore be generally unsuitable for use as application or data table memory. In some programmable controllers, PROM is used as application memory, but has a RAM memory used for the portions of the program that might change later. It could, however, be used as executive program storage memory.

Erasable Programmable Read Only Memory (EPROM). This is a category of PROM memory that can be erased after initial programming and reprogrammed for another use. The erasing process is performed with the use of ultraviolet light applied the lens window in the top of the PROM integrated circuit package. EPROM is sometimes used as executive and scratch pad memories, and can be used as application memory with a complementing RAM memory to act as operational memory. Many times a machine builder will design a machine control program and set the completed, debugged results into EPROM. This provides the end user with a nonvolatile system that the machine builder is sure will not easily change. It would in be appropriate to use EPROM if multiple changes are required at the user's silt after installation of the machine.

Electrically Alterable Read Only Memory (EAROM). This category of ROM memory is actually quite similar to PROM, but is electrically erasable using voltage applied to the integrated circuit instead of ultraviolet light. While a useful form of nonvolatile memory, the EAROM requires RAM as backup when used as application memory.

Electrically Erasable Programmable Read Only Memory (EEPROM). This remarkable nonvolatile memory combines the attributes or E-PROM with the speed and flexibility of RAM. EEPROM can be programmed and reprogrammed with the standard programming device supplied with most programmable controllers. Because of this fact, it's being used in some of the newer programmable controllers as application memory. It could also be used as scratch pad and data table memory, and even as executive memory if precautions are taken to prevent accidental erasure. EEPROM has a slight delay involved in the reprogramming process, and has a finite reprogramming life. In spites of these minor drawbacks, EEPROM has many outstanding benefits.

Core. Core memory is a relatively mature memory technology that is nonvolatile by design. It was one of the few memories commercially available for the first programmable controllers. It works by using a tiny toroidal ferrite coil which is energized to store each bit of information. An electrical pulse is used to "set" each coil to a zero or a one. Although core was a good functional solution for its day, the speed and cost improvements of the newer semiconductor memories have attracted most of the manufacturers of programmable controllers today. There are still a few controllers today that offer core memory as an alternate to RAM.

Programmable controller memory is formatted into bits, bytes, and words of memory. A bit is a single storage element for either a zero or a one. A byte consists of eight bits, and a word (normally) consists of 16 bits, or two bytes. Some systems still use a word length of eight bits, but most have adopted a 16 bit word, even though they may use an 8 bit microprocessor.

Depending on the specific design of the programmable controller, it will have a stated memory capacity. This is an indication, although not the only one, of the capability and power of the system. Medium and large controllers are normally expandable from one memory size to their maximum size. Small controllers are normally fixed in their memory size. Size of the memory capacity must be examined relative to the word size (8 bit or 16 bit) and utilization. While it is clear that twice the information can be stored in a 16 bit word than in an 8 bit word, it may not be immediately clear that some controllers utilize memory more efficiently than others. For example, a normally open contact and its associated reference address (e.g. Input 1), may use in 8 bit byte each for storage. Combined, they consume one 16 bit word. Some controllers may use more memory than this for these instructions or others. In a large program, these inefficiencies can build on each other to cause a poor utilization of the system memory. A careful analysis of the various programmable controller models is required to assess utilization efficiency. Normal practice calls for an additional 20% ~ 40% of memory size to be specified to allow for modifications and later expansion. This analysis, combined with knowledge of the application needs, will allow for an intelligent choice of programmable controller.

The memory of a programmable controller is organized in what is called a memory map. This segments, through a process known as partitioning, the memory into functional units. All manufacturers use a slightly different technique in designing their controller's memory map. Some have variable partitions while others are fixed. All, however, are designed to segment the following functional areas:

Executive program(s)
Scratch pad
Input/Output image tables
Data tables
Application program

We will now elaborate, in overview fashion, on each of the memory map segments. As noted earlier, some controllers offer the user the flexibility (sometimes considered a constraint) of being able to vary the partitions within the memory map. This, in essence, allows the user or system builder to customize the sizes of the application, data table, and other memory segments to suit the particular application. Other controllers offer a preconfigured system, making assumptions about appropriate sizes for the various memory segments and their associated partitions. This eliminates the need for the user to deal with this sometimes confusing operation. As the architecture of programmable controllers continues to evolve, it is likely that the variable partition method will gain favorable momentum. This is likely because it accommodates a wider variety of operating systems and application programs since it can be tailored more effectively. This more flexible future may include the ability to utilize a standard hardware from many manufacturers with special application software to accomplish an industry specific solution.

Executive. This is the basic intelligence of the programmable controller. It allows any application program instructions to be interpreted and acted upon. It is transparent to the user and is almost never censidered to be included in the manufacturers rated memory sizes.

Scratch Pad. Also transparent to the user, this memory allows interim computations and some system configuration parameters to be established.

Input/Output Image Tables. This is one of the most basic and straightforward segments in the memory map. This section of memory contains a stored representation of both the internal and external I/O 'points.' An internal point is an input or output that is used only in an internal control logic process, and is not directly associated with the physical I/O modules. An external point is one that is directly associated or mapped to a physical I/O module, which in turn is physically connected to a sensor or actuator. These tables of the I/O are accessible and viewed by the programming device and some other programmable controller peripherals. They can then be observed or manipulated directly for program creation, editing, or later troubleshooting after the system has been installed. This memory segment is normally partitioned to some default value corresponding to the maximum I/O capacity of the programmable controller. The view seen on the programming device screen is the most current information on the status of the I/O, as it changes the application program instructions and real world environment.

Data Tables. Sometimes called the register tables, this segment of system memory contains the variable references used in the execution of the application program. Formatted in 16 bit words (8 bit in older systems), this word include storage of timer and counter accumulated values, in some cases timer and counter preset values, variable storage references for mathematical functions, storage of analog values converted to digital, storage of BCD or ASCII information, and so on. This segment, in controllers that allow it, is sized by the user to trade-off application memory size for register table capacity. This becomes a perplexing issue in systems that are particular data intensive at the expense of application program size.

Application Program. This segment contains the actual ladder logic control program. Hence it is sometimes called the logic memory section. Again variable in size for some systems, it is created, edited, and later viewed during operation with the help of the programming device. A section of ladder logic is created with the programming device using contacts, coils, and other references, and then is converted to machine level code for use by the central processing unit. There are many techniques and devices to accomplish this task.

11.1.6 Power Supply

As smart as the central processing unit is, it would be nothing without good, clean, reliable power. The manufacturer of the programmable

Foundation of PLC 255

controller system takes special design and manufacturing care with the system power supply. Some designs allow the power supply to be used external to the main CPU chassis, while others make it an integral part of the system chassis. In spite of the physical differences, the primary function remains the same: that is, to provide a consistent level of clean, low voltage direct current (DC) power to the system electronics, and protect the system from normal line voltage fluctuations.

Most of the programmable controllers used today employ alternating current (AC) with voltages of 115 or 230 as line voltages. In some unique applications, however, 24 V or 120 V DC is used. This is especially true in systems that utilize batteries to back-up an unreliable utility power system, or to suffice where normal utility lines do not exist. Examples of this include standby power generators used in remote areas to provide electrical power, and railroad trackside control applications where system availability and integrity is critical. Another interesting example is that of generating facilities that use 120 V DC to insure full-time control of the generation process in spite of power changes and fluctuations.

The power supplies on most programmable controller systems can operate and provide consistent power in spite of normal power line fluctuations. Typical supplies will provide "business as usual" for fluctuations in voltage of 95 ~ 130 V AC for a 115 V nominal system, 190 ~ 260 V AC for a 230 V system, and can accommodate frequencies from 47 ~ 63 Hz. In some extreme examples uninterruptable power supplies (UPS) or constant voltage transformers are used to guarantee constant power to the control system.

In a different environment, isolation transformer may be appropriate. Some installations may have fairly reliable power, but experience high incidents of electromagnetic interference (EMI) generated from adjacent equipment. Good judgment in the location of equipment and a control system is warranted of course, along with proper control cabinet choice.

Where this normal course does not suffice, however, an isolation transformer may prove to be the best solution. Connected between the programmable controller and the power source, the isolation transformer keeps most stray noise off the line to the controller.

11.1.7 Diagnostics

Central processing unit diagnostics are designed in most systems to allow the unit to detect and report a number of ills, some internal to itself, and some external. In some systems, these detected problems are used to close a hardwired power supply relay for alarm purposes, in other cases internal coils are set. Included in the list are:

Total scan time exceeds watchdog timer value

Unrecoverable communication error to subsystem

Memory backup battery low or failed

Parity error

CPU failed executive self-check

Input line voltage out of acceptable range

Depending on system size and construction, errors are announced on a board basis by front mounted light emitting diodes (LEDs). This allows rapid pinpointing of the likely problem, and quick replacement of the suspect board or power supply. The faulty board can then be repaired or returned to the manufacturer for replacement. In some extreme cases, emergency installation of a complete standby CPU with resident program may be more expedient than troubleshooting as board-swapping a CPU on line.

11.2 INSTALLATION AND MAINTENANCE

Today's programmable controller, properly installed, will provide a maximum of productivity with a minimum of maintenance. This section will cover the strength forward but critical areas of installation and maintenance of the programmable controller. It is intended to serve only as an overview on the subject, with the best guide for use being the documentation provided by the programmable controller manufacturer. This section will include rack installation for the CPU and I/O racks involved, line power, grounding, and signal cable consideration. Troubleshooting techniques as well as basic repair situations will be examined, and finally, training options will be presented.

11.2.1 Rack Installation

Depending on the size of the programmable controller being considered, the installation of the racks or chassis can be a simple or very complex task. Since most controllers are of open or partially enclosed design, it is assumed that the proper cabinet is chosen for the particular application area. Many times this is a NEMA 12 type enclosure. It provides an environment in which the controller can operate without exposure to the grime outside the enclosure. Most racks can be mounted in either a panel type mounting arrangement, or a 19 in(inch) rack mounting. This is not true of controllers of the very small variety, as they are normally a panel mount only design. Rack mounting is generally used where the equipment is installed in a control room where operators reside, or the environment is otherwise controlled. This type of installation is common where many instruments are mounted and used along with the programmable controller equipment. In either case, wire conductors must be routed in the rack; this is done with commercially available conduit that provides a means to bring in and out as many as 100 to 200 individual conductors from input and output points to real-world sensors and actuators. It is important that this phase of the design and installation be handled with care as it will dramatically affect the ability to maintain the system later. Good shop practices will provide carefully labeled and bundled conductors, routed through properly sized conduit systems. In addition to allowing any required system maintenance, this early care will make any system additions or modifications much easier.

11.2.2 Line Power and Grounding

Proper power to the programmable controller is critical. Today's systems are available in a wide variety of electrical configurations. Virtually all are designed for use in single phase power systems, and most are now beginning to be offered with the optional ability to operate in a DC supply environment. AC designs are offered in either single voltage supplies, such as 115 or 230 V AC; while some can be configured as either through a selection made on the power supply. Proper grounding of the power supply connection is required for a safe installation. Some programmable controller designs have individual grounding connections from rack to faceplates and other system components, so care must be taken to follow good electrical practice in system grounding during electrical installation. In certain applications, a 24 or 120 V DC power supply is required. This is common for installations that are made where no AC power is available, such as remote electrical generation stations. It is also found where AC power is unreliable and where loss of control is considered an unacceptable situation

11.2.3 Signal Cable Connections

The chain must be completed and have high integrity to provide the communication path for control signals to pass over. Depending on the specific design of the programmable control system, loss of communication to the I/O system will cause a critical failure, stopping the CPU scan. In other systems, configurations can be accomplished that allow the unaffected portions of the programmable controller system to continue to operate.

As we saw earlier, communication between chassis can either be parallel or serial. Parallel communication uses multiple conductors to pass all bits of a byte or word of data simultaneously. Serial communication provides a method for single bits of a byte or word of data simultaneously. Serial communication provides a method for signal bit of a byte or word to be transmitted sequentially. The difference this has on cable design and selection is significant. Parallel cables are made of as many as 16 or more pairs of twisted individual conductors, protected by a shielded external jacket. Multiple pin connectors are connected to one or both ends of the cable. The "D" type is popular, providing 25 or 39 pins in a standard configuration. Earlier design used a round type positive contact threaded design and certain manufactures still use this type of connector, although most have found the "D" type satisfactory. This cable is normally made available by the programmable controller manufacturer, and while it may seem expensive, the assurance of having a well designed and thoroughly tested cable is worth almost any price compared to tracking down an intermittent problem later during a critical production period. The programmable controller manufacturer will provide parallel cables designed to operate with its equipment in various lengths, from 2 ft(feet) up to as much as 500 ft. Serial cables on the other hand are generally easier to use and less expensive to purchase or build. Manufacturers may or may not provide these as an item to purchase, and may just refer the purchaser to a third party source. Serial signal cable is normally a single or dual twisted pair of conductors, and are often just connected directly to the I/O driver or receiver with screw terminals. The only major reason to use parallel over serial is the great communication speed available with parallel, which can be a factor of 10 to 1, or more.

11.2.4 Troubleshooting and Repair

Even the best of today's well-designed and manufactured programmable controllers require occasional preventative maintenance and repair. This section looks at some of the tools provided by the manufacturer and techniques for general maintenance.

Most of the medium- and large-sized programmable controller systems available today are designed to be maintained by individuals with a wide variety of skills, without the benefit of in-depth formal training of this piece of equipment. This is accomplished in the design by providing individual modules of functionality installed in a chassis serviced from the front (all module types including power supplies). Front access is critical to proper maintenance. This allows easy inspection and replacement of the suspected bad module. Module health is determined by inspecting the LED indicators normally provided on the front of each module. Typical indicators will be on or off depending on the design and individual condition of the module in question. Various CPU and I/O modules will have indicators showing I/O control communications status, memory integrity, power supply tolerance check, scan integrity, and others. On future controller designs, and even today on a few systems, it is likely that English language messages will be displayed on the controller advising the user or maintenance personnel that a particular failure has occurred and recommended actions to take.

The modular design and diagnostic indicators are, of course, important, but would be quite useless without well designed documentation provided by the manufacturer for the programmable controller system in question. Proper documentation will have sections dedicated to each major subsystem including CPU, I/O, and programming device. Each should explain in depth the step-by-step inspection of the system. All possible combinations of failure mode should be listed, along with suggested actions for repair. This will most often involve only the substitution of a replacement board for the suspected failed unit. The user is urged to purchase a set of spare modules for the system in question as recommended by the manufacturer. This is normally, at a minimum, a single replacement module for each CPU and programming device serviceable module, and spare I/O modules equal to 10% of the number in the system.

While the design of system and documentation provide an easy vehicle for system maintenance once trouble is detected, it is always better to perform preventative maintenance where possible. Some systems available today provide levels of predicted failure detection that allow excellent preventive maintenance. This can range from automatic singling of low battery conditions on the memory modules to predicting an output circuit failure before the circuit is energized. This particular phenomenon can be extremely valuable in performing predictive maintenance on critical systems. Examples of this would include emergency circuits for rapid shutdown of a machine sequence or plant process. Outputs that fail prior to their need may not be detected in time to provide this critical service.

The documented ladder logic diagram is a very useful tool for troubleshooting, especially on a complex system. It allows maintenance personnel or "walk through" the I/O segment in question, forcing transitions in specific inputs and outputs, while watching the system's reaction. Many times this can ferret out a tough system problem, and may help isolate problems external to the controller such as an open sensor wire.

The major manufacturers of programmable controller systems maintain 24 h telephone service numbers for users requiring emergency service. Their highly trained personnel can normally walk the user through his problem and determine what action he should take for repair.

11.2.5 Training Options

As with programming skill development, training is available for general maintenance and repair of the programmable controller. Most common is formal classroom training which provides an effective combination of class study and lab exercises that simulate problems for the student to detect and correct. Classroom training can be done at the programmable controller manufacturer's facility, or, in some cases, can be more efficiently done at the user's location. Supplementing this formal method are programmed instruction books, videotapes, and interactive computer-based instruction. This latter option is just now becoming available, but holds great promise for effective training, easily distributed and updated.

11.3 APPLICATIONS

Applying programmable controllers is as critical to the user, as is solving the problems that come with designing and operating efficient production processes. In fact, it is through its innovative applications that the programmable controller has excelled and attracted the large following it enjoys today. Continued development in the application area supported the evolution of certain features and capabilities that are common today. Now we will examine the current scope of programmable controller applications, briefly look at the steps involved in implementing a system for a typical application, and consider some logical groupings of applications common today, including basic, industry specific, and generic.

11.3.1 What a Programmable Controller Can Do

We have seen a partial listing of programmable controller applications, and while it was anything but complete, it did give a good overall look at the breadth and variety of use that programmable controllers enjoy. These systems, with such a simple and low technology heritage, have come to be capable of performing tasks that were previously considered impossible to accomplish, or at least very difficult and at great expense. We will look at a survey of applications by major industry groups, and while some of the application areas are common to many of the groups, it provides a structured method to categorize the wide variety of applications. The structure will consist of two major groups-discrete part manufacturing and process-and several subgroups in each major group.

(1) Discrete Part manufacturing Industries:

① Transportation. This industry group consists of automotive, aircraft, aerospace, railroad, and ship segments, as well as a number of smaller segments. Programmable controllers are used extensively in many of these segments, especially the automotive segment. Both the vehicle final assembly process and the various subassembly and part manufacturing processes make wide use of programmable controllers. The largest part of these are used for sequence and motion control applications, combined with a growing overlay of data management and communications applications. Almost all of these are driven by metal cutting, forming, and assembly needs, although a growing trend is on the plastic molding and forming area, as plastics and other engineered materials are replacing metal in some areas. The aircraft and aerospace segments share the use of programmable controllers for metal cutting and forming, but are lighter on assembly since many of the assembly processes are custom oriented, and hence cannot justify large capital outlays in hard automation. The need for factory floor data collection and analysis is very intense here, and programmable controllers play a major role in front line data is collection and concentration. Data is collected to document process integrity involving exotic and expensive metals, and for processes critical to design integrity or requiring regulatory agency documentation. The railroad and ship segments have less intense needs for programmable controllers, but one innovative use in the railroad industry involves the use of programmable controllers as trackside signal and switch control units, operating remotely and communicating with a central dispatching station over phone or microwave links.

② Fabricated Metal. The fabricated metal segment consists of a wide variety of sub-segments and processes, and as the name suggests, most involve the use of programmable controllers for metal forming and, to a lesser extent, metal cutting. The subsegments range from manufacturing metal doors and window to producing firearms. Controllers are most often found in sequencing and motion control applications, and much use is made to accomplish sophisticated material handing applications.

③ Nonelectical Machinery. This segment was designed to contain a very loose arrangement of machinery manufacturers, ranging from the general to the very specific. It includes both farm and construction equipment manufacturers, internal combustion engine manufacturers, manufacturers of machine tools, and an important category called special machinery manufactures, which includes companies that produce special purpose machinery such as tobacco, shoe, elevator, and plastic molding. As you might gather, such a variety of manufacturers use programmable controllers in very large numbers. The way in which they are used is relatively straightforward, and includes a large measure of sequence control and motion control. Larger facilities are also taking advantage of the communication and data management capabilities of the more sophisticated controllers. Elevators use the motion control and communication capabilities. Packaging machinery many times can use the smallest of today's programmable controllers as their sometimes limited application needs can be served by a basic featured, limited I/O controller. On the other hand, some packaging applications require the fastest and most powerful programmable controller features.

④ Electrical and Electronic. This segment is made up of manufacturers ranging from those that produce televisions and radios to those that make batteries. Machinery that is used in these manufacturing processes includes some batch processing, as well as a measure of sequential control (material handling), and motion control (component insertion). Other fertile areas include automatic assembly, automatic storage and retrieval systems, and testing systems. Again, as in the other segments we have examined so far, larger facilities are using local area networks to take advantage of the communication and data management features of the newer controllers. Also as with other segment, we find many, many stand-alone machine applications using small- to medium-sized controllers, including queueing conveyor systems and specially designed packaging machines.

(2) Process Industries:

① Food. The food processing industry is one that has a wide variety of programmable controller applications, ranging form the batch processing of fluid milk to the batch processing of beer, all the way to the packaging of both products. Material handling applications are common, and include both bulk (the controlled movement of a continuous stream of produce), and unit (the controlled movement of individual units of product). PID closed loop control is common with the need to regulate flow and level of foods in process, as well as the temperature regulation of certain cooking and sterilizing processes. Government regulation of many food-related processes calls for meticulous documentation and data gathering of process parameters to guarantee proper food quality. All of these application needs call on the natural strengths of programmable controllers, and use a board sample of control schemes.

② Chemical. The chemical industry consists of a number of related segments, including pharmaceuticals, paints, and engineered materials, such as plastics. This group relies on the programmable controller not for primary continuous process control needs, but is used in conjunction with the process computer. While the process computer has command of the many process loops involved in a continuous process, the programmable controller, connected through a communication interface, operates the various pump motors and supply valves involved in the process. In smaller facilities that produce products utilizing more batch processing, programmable controllers are sometimes used as the primary control devices. A perhaps surprisingly, large application area in the chemical segment is the packaging area. Programmable controllers, properly applied, make excellent control devices for high speed packaging processes.

③ Primary Metals. Primary metals are aluminum, steel, etc. The production of these metals relies on programmable controllers for many and various needs. Most of these relate to the sequencing and movement of the metal, in its liquid, semisolid, and finished states. Continuous casting processes, hot and cold rolling processes, and coding and in-line storage of finished materials all use sequence and motion control heavily. Integration with variable speed drives is common. Also common are uses of controllers for control of slitters and coilers. In some facilities, programmable controllers are also used for batch mixing and weighing of materials at the front of the process. This involves PID control and regulation of weights and flows, as well as the integration of bulk conveyor control.

④ Paper. Paper industry applications include both the original creation from wood fiber, and the conversion to finished goods such as corrugated boxes and stationary grade paper. Programmable controllers are used here in ways similar to those in the primary metals segment. This should come as no surprise since both are web processes. The "wet" end of the process is now experiencing more applications of programmable controllers for loop process control. The coordination of multiple variable speed drives on typical paper machine is accomplished by a combination of programmable controllers and special purpose controls. The converting process, normally asynchronous from the primary process, involves a number of cutting, folding, and assembly processes using motion and sequence control.

⑤ Electric Utilities. The electric utility industry, like many other process industries, uses a process computer for the actual control of the generation process, but use programmable controllers to perform ancillary functions. These include the bulk material handling of coal into the generation facility, the removal of waste ashes from the process, and the control of the scrubbers used to clean the by-product process air. These are connected to the main process computer by a communication link.

11.3.2 Implementing a Programmable Controller system

This section will describe the steps in the process of integrating the programmable controller and the control problem. The implementation phase of using programmable controllers is, by definition, the most important. It is through the successful implementation of the programmable controller that it is best allowed to solve the problems at hand. In addition, the proper implementation will also prepare the system to accommodate control process needs in the future.

Table 11.1 lists the steps involved in implementing a programmable controller system. Below, we will describe each briefly, and show how each contributes to the implementation.

Table 11.1 Steps Required to implement a Programmable Controller System

(1) Describe the control process
(2) Define the inputs and outputs
(3) Estimate memory requirements
(4) Determine man-machine interface
(5) Determine instruction set required
(6) Estimate response time required
(7) Document the program
(8) Write the program
(9) Test and debug the program

(1) Describe the Control Process. The very first operation required is to describe the control process in a comprehensive and detailed way. The end product of this exercise will be a functional description of the control solution as it relates to the control problem. It includes the diagrams and text that describes the relation of the programmable controller CPU, its Input and Output, and the man-machine interface to the controlled process. It also includes any other intelligent devices in the sys-

tem, including the basic connection to a host computer. The text going along with this segment should describe the process and all possible combinations.

(2) Define the Inputs and Outputs. The second step involves the detailed listing of the real world inputs and outputs of the programmable controller. Analog and discrete I/O needs are described and listed separately, and an individual listing group should be made for each field signal level, i.e., 12.5 V AC, and 24 V DC. Included on the listing should be slot address, circuit number, I/O point address, and circuit name. An accurately done job here will make the documentation process easier. In addition, logical grouping of the I/O points will make programming and use of the system much easier as well.

(3) Estimate Memory Requirements. As we saw in the chapter on the CPU, the programmable controller uses memory to store the control logic program. It also uses memory to store variable parameters, such as timer and counter accumulations and I/O status tables. Depending on the particular system used, memory sizing will require different approaches. As a rule of thumb, simple relay replacement applications utilize one I/O point for one control really equivalent. Assume also that the average application (if there is such a thing) uses inputs and outputs in the ratio of 6∶4, and that one control relay equals eight contact references. Since most 16 bit word systems use one word of memory for each contact and reference combination, each relay replaced requires an average of eight words of memory in the programmable controller logic memory. This suggests that a programmable controller system designed to replace a panel of 100 relays would require and average of 60 inputs, 40 outputs, and 800 sixteen-bit words of memory. Variable memory storage must be estimated separately, and will range form the minimum normally specified by programmable controller manufacturers for simple relay intensive applications to very large requirements (say 8 000 ~ 16 000 sixteen-bit registers) for

very data intensive applications such as automatic testing, and automatic storage and retrieval systems.

(4) Determine Man-Machine Requirements. Over and above the requirement above would be any I/O and memory intended for an operator interface panel. If this is a simple requirement, it may be handled with a few real-world I/O for pushbuttons and indicator lights. These devices would be mounted in a panel or cabinet for use by the operator and would be wired individually to discrete (and, in some cases, analog) I/O modules in the programmable controller system. For a more sophisticated CRT based interface, a data communication interface will normally be required. Also important is the determination of the functional requirements for the CRT system. For example, if the majority of the interface requirements are to be performed by the CRT, that system must have capacity in communication throughout, and screen quantity and complexity to support those needs.

(5) Determine Instruction Set Required. The application complexity also determines the choice of an instruction set. For small stand-alone machines, the basic instruction set provided by the manufacturer will probably suffice. However, for larger and more complex machines and processes, the enhanced instruction set is always a cost effective investment. Considering the trend demonstrated by programmable controller manufacturers so far, it is likely that more features will continue to evolve in the form of better instruction sets. These instruction sets will be found, more and more, in smaller, less expensive controllers.

(6) Estimate Response Time Required. For many applications the response time consideration is not a major issue since most programmable controllers available today are capable of handling a large number of I/O and logic solutions with sufficient speed. For some applications, however, the speed of the controllers is an essential consideration. Speed, in terms of solving problems, is measured as response time. Response time

is the total time required to convert the appropriate input to a given output, including the following components: input filter time delay, I/O service time delay, logic solution time, and output filter time delay. All of these components must be considered for time-critical circuits. To estimate normal expected throughput, the scan time can be doubled (or tripled for margin) to accommodate a worst case response time. Improvements in response time can be made through examination of the particular system being used. For example, the input filters, designed to provide switch 'debounce,' can be circumvented in some systems, This normally contributes greatly to improving throughput. Next comes the opportunity to make the logic used more efficient through optimization of ladder functions, and the increased use of enhanced functions where possible. This improves the logic solution time as the enhanced functions generally execute more rapidly than do the basic. Output filters are generally not a major contributor to system throughput, but can be examined if necessary. All of these actions taken together can improve throughput by 30% ~ 50%. In some rare systems, hardwired interrupt inputs are provided allowing the input process to be reduced to microseconds instead of milliseconds.

(7) Document the Program. While it may seem odd to show the documentation of the program prior to actually writing it, it is actually quite pragmatic. The program should be documented in term of its relationship to the controlled process, and the operation and maintenance of that process. This will naturally include diagrams, tables, and text, intended to provide the use with an easy to use road map of the controlled process. A flow diagram, timing diagrams for critical functions, annotated ladder diagrams (generated later), and data flow diagrams give a detailed look at the process. I/O definitions, wire lists, along with truth tables illustrate how the physical system comes together. And finally, complimenting text provides a common thread throughout for the documentation

of the system. The value of structuring the process should not be underestimated. A properly and thoughtfully designed structure becomes the basis for a better overall solution.

(8) Write the Program. Now is the logical time to actually begin writing the program. With the proper effort applied in the steps identified so far, the program writing task is indeed minimized. The process flow outline can be clothed with appropriate ladder logic programming. From a size and speed efficiency standpoint, enhanced instruction functions should be used wherever possible, except where doing so would make the programming needlessly complex to maintain later. Proper annotation and text comments go a long way to avoiding any confusion. Subroutines, available in some controllers, can be used to structure the programming effort, and to make execution more rapid. Special considerations must be made in the areas of power-up initialization, power-down impact, and safety. It may be important to provide logic to reset certain functions during a power-up cycle, and to predict a stable power-down routine. Safety circuits should be hardwired, in spite of the high reliability of the programmable controller. Status tables can be modified unintentionally, or remotely, causing an unsafe condition.

(9) Testing and Debugging the program. The most well designed program will still experience some flaws, some perhaps unpredictable. In light of this, it is important that the user or system integrator go through a series of steps prior to actually starting the machine or process. This includes testing the logic off-line in small sections to ensure that it responds predictably. Output wiring can be tested by forcing outputs on and off individually to ensure that field devices are wired properly. And finally, initialization routines and safety circuits must be thoroughly checked.

Vocabulary

1. configuration   *n.*   组态
2. Cyclic Redundancy Check   循环冗余检查

3. electromagnetic interference 电磁干扰
4. Longitudinal Redundancy Check 径向冗余检查
5. meticulous 详细的
6. nonvolatile *adj.* 非挥发的
7. parity 校验
8. peripheral *n.* 外设
9. pharmaceutical *n.* 药剂,药品
10. rack mounting 机架安装
11. resident program 驻留程序
12. spare *adj.* 备用的
13. standby *adj.* 后备的
14. volatile *adj.* 挥发的,易失的
15. watchdog timer 看门狗定时器

Notes:

1. This can be either volatile or nonvolatile in design, and can be configured and used in a variety of ways for both executive program storage, with which the system executes its instructions, and application program storage, for the actual control program.

它可以是采用挥发或非挥发设计,而且可以配置成不同的用途。一方面作为执行程序存储器,用于执行系统操作;另一方面作为应用程序存储器,用于实际的控制程序。

2. The last step of this basic scan process is to integrate the currently interpreted control logic program with the most current input statuses from the I/O scan, and to update the output statuses with the current results.

基本扫描过程的最后一步是把当前的控制逻辑程序运算和最新的 I/O 状态结合在一起,并用当前结果刷新输出状态。

3. It is this combination that makes RAM the memory of choice formats of today's programmable controller systems, especially for use in the application, data table, and portions of some scratch pad memories.

正是这个结合才使 RAM 成为现在可编程控制器系统存储器选择格式,

尤其是在应用、数表和随机缓存器中。

4. A section of ladder logic is created with the programming device using contacts, coils, and other references, and then is converted to machine level code for use by the central processing unit.

借助于使用触点、线圈和其它附注的编程设备建立梯形逻辑,然后转换成中央处理器可以使用的机器代码。

5. Serial signal cable is normally a single or dual twisted pair of conductors, and are often just connected directly to the I/O driver or receiver with screw terminals.

串行信号电缆通常是一对或两对双绞导线,利用螺丝端子它们被直接连接到 I/O 的驱动器或接受器上。

6. Most common is formal classroom training which provides an effective combination of class study and lab exercises that simulate problems for the student to detect and correct.

最常见的是常规课堂培训,它可以提供有效的课堂学习和实验练习。这些练习为学生模拟了要检查和修改的问题。

PART 4
AUTOMATIC CONTROL SYSTEMS

12

Electrical Distribution

12.1 PRIMARY DISTRIBUTION SYSTEMS

The wiring between the generating station and the final distribution point is called the primary distribution system. There are several methods used for transmitting the power between these two points. The two most common methods are the radial system and the loop system.

12.1.1 The Radial System

The term radial comes from the word radiate, which means to send out or emit from one central point. A radial system is an electrical transmission system which begins at a central station and supplies power to various substations.

In its simplest form, a radial system consists of a generating station which produces the electrical energy. This energy is transmitted from the generator(s) to the central station, which is generally part of, or adjacent to, the generating station. At the central station the voltage is stepped up to a higher value for long-distance transmission.

From the central station, several lines carry the power to various substations. At the substations the voltage is usually lowered to a value more suitable for distribution in populated areas. From the substations, lines carry the power to distribution transformers. These transformers lower the voltages to the value required by the consumer.

12.1.2 The Loop System

The loop system starts from the central station or a substation and makes a complete loop through the area to be served, and back to the starting point. This results in the area being supplied from both ends, allowing sections to be isolated in case of a breakdown. An expanded version of the loop system consists of several central stations joined together to form a very large loop.

12.2 CONSUMER DISTRIBUTION SYSTEMS

The type of distribution system that the consumer uses to transmit power within the premises depends upon the requirements of the particular installation. Residential occupancies generally use the simplest type. Commercial and industrial systems vary widely with load requirements.

12.2.1 Single-phase Systems

Most single-phase systems are supplied from a three-phase primary. The primary of a single-phase transformer is connected to one phase of the three-phase system. The secondary contains two coils connected in series with a midpoint tap to provide a single-phase, three-wire system. This rangement is generally used to supply power to residential occupancies and some commercial establishments. A schematic diagram is shown in Fig. 12.1.

For residential occupancies, the service conductors are installed either overhead or underground. Single-family and small multifamily dwellings have the kilowatt-hour meters installed on the outside of the building. From the kilowatt-hour meter, the conductors are connected to the main disconnect. Fig. 12.2(a) and 12.2(b) show this arrangement.

Three separate disconnecting means are used with one common ground.

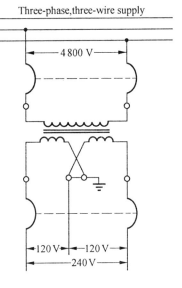

Fig. 12.1 Single-phase, three-wire, 120/240 V system

From the main disconnect, the conductors supply power to the branch circuit panels. For dwelling occupancies there are three basic types of branch circuits: general lighting circuits, small appliance and laundry circuits, and individual branch circuits. The individual branch circuits are frequently used to supply central heating and/or air-conditioning systems, water heaters, and other special loads.

12.2.2 Grounding Requirements

All AC services are required to be grounded on the supply side of the service disconnecting means. This grounding conductor runs from the combination system and equipment ground to the grounding electrode. For multifamily occupancies it is permitted to use up to six service disconnecting means. A single grounding conductor of adequate size should be used

Electrical Distribution 277

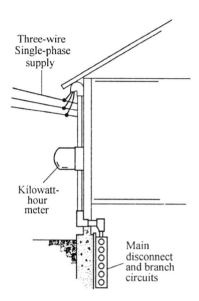

(a) Single-family residence with a three-wire, single-phase service

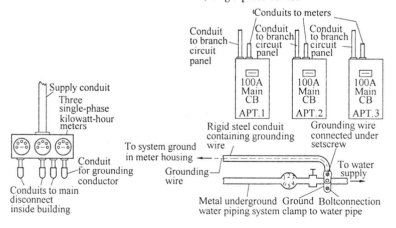

(b) Three-wire, single-phase service for a multifamily dwelling

Fig. 12.2

for the system ground (see Fig. 12.2(b)).

12.2.3 Commercial and Industrial Installations

Commercial and industrial installations are more complex than small residential installations. Large apartment complexes and condominiums, although classified as residential occupancies, often use commercial-style services. A single-phase, three-wire service or a three-phase, four-wire service may be brought into the building, generally from underground. The service-entrance conductors terminate in a main disconnect. From this point, the conductors are connected to the individual kilowatt-hour meters for each apartment and then to smaller disconnecting means and over-current protective devices. Branch-circuit panels are generally installed in each apartment. Feeder conductors connect the individual disconnecting means to the branch-circuit panels. Commercial and/or industrial buildings may have more than one kilowatt-hour meter, depending upon the number of occupancies. The service sizes vary according to the demand. The service is usually a three-phase, four-wire system. The available voltages may be 120/208 V or 277/480 V. If the system provides 277/480 V, a transformer must be installed in order to obtain 120 V. If the building covers a large area, it is recommended that the service be installed near the center of the building. This arrangement minimizes line loss on feeder and branch-circuit conductors. Some utilities supply a three-phase, three-wire or three-phase, four-wire delta system. The common voltages that may be obtained from the three-wire delta system are 240 V, 440 V, or 550 V. With this arrangement, a transformer must be used to obtain 120 V. The usual voltages supplied from the four-wire delta system are 240 V, three phase and 120 V, single phase.

Many large consumers purchase the electrical energy at the primary voltage, and transformers are installed on their premises. Three-phase voltages up to 15 kV are often used.

The service for this type of installation generally consists of metal cubicles called a substation unit. The transformers are either installed within the cubicle or adjacent to it. Isolation switches of the drawer type are installed within the cubicle. These switches are used to isolate the main switch or circuit breaker from the supply during maintenance or repair.

12.2.4 Consumer Loop Systems

Although the radial system of distribution is probably the most commonly used system of transmitting power on the consumer's property, the loop system is also employed. A block diagram of both system is illustrated in Fig. 12.3(a) and 12.3(b). There are several variations of these systems in use in the industry, but the systems illustrated here show the basic structure.

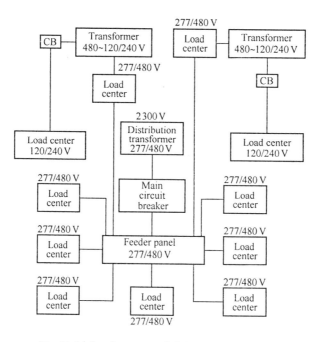

Fig. 12.3(a) Consumer radial distribution system

When installing any system, over-current protection and grounding

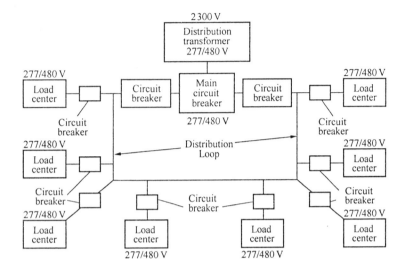

Fig. 12.3(b) Consumer loop distribution system. Disconnecting means may be installed anywhere in the distribution loop to provide for isolating sections

must be given primary consideration. Electrical personnel who design and install these systems must comply with the NEC® and local requirements.

12.2.5 Secondary High-voltage Distribution

Large industrial establishments may find it more economical to distribute power at voltages higher than 600 V. Depending upon the type of installation and the load requirements, voltages as high as 2 300 V may be used. Step-down transformers are installed in strategic locations to reduce the voltage to a practical working value. A diagram of a high-voltage radial system is shown in Fig. 12.4.

Sometimes the high-voltage (primary) system may be radial, and the low-voltage (secondary) system may be connected into a loop. Another method is to have both the primaries and secondaries connected to form a loop. Fig. 12.5(a) and Fig. 12.5(b) show these methods.

Electrical Distribution 281

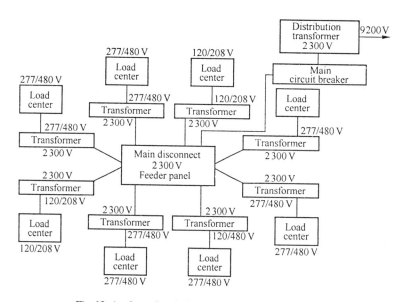

Fig. 12.4 Secondary high-voltage radial distribution system

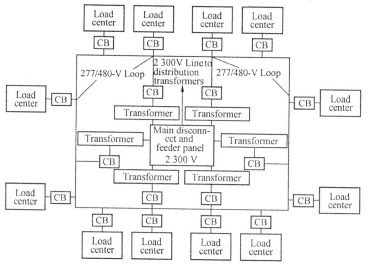

(a) Secondary high-voltage distribution system; high-voltage radical. low-voltage loop

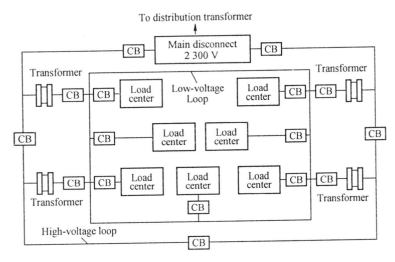

(b) Consumer distribution system with high-voltage and low-voltage loops

Fig. 12.5

12.2.6 Secondary Ties Loop System

It is frequently convenient to connect loads to the secondary conductors at points between transformers. These conductors are called secondary ties. Article 450 of the NEC© gives specific requirements regarding the conductor sizes and over-current protection.

12.3 GROUNDING OF ELECTRICAL SYSTEMS

In general, most electrical systems must be grounded. The purpose of grounding is to limit the magnitude of voltage caused by lightning, momentary surges, and accidental contact with higher voltages. System grounds must be arranged to provide a path of minimum impedance in order to ensure the operation of over-current devices when a ground fault occurs. Current should not flow through the grounding conductor during normal operation.

Direct-current system generally have the grounding conductor connected to the system at the supply station, and not at the individual service. Alternating-current systems, on the other hand, must be grounded on the supply side of the main disconnect at each individual service. For specific information on the location and method of grounding, refer to NEC®Article 250.

12.4 GROUNDING OF ELECTRICAL EQUIPMENT

Metal conduit and cases which enclose electrical conductors must be grounded. If the ungrounded (hot) conductor comes in contact with a metal enclosure which is not grounded, a voltage will be present between the enclosure and the ground. This presents a potential hazard. Persons coming in contact with the enclosure and ground will complete a circuit.

All non-current-carrying metal parts of electrical installations should be tightly bonded together and connected to a grounding electrode. Good electrical continuity should be ensured through all metal enclosures. The current caused by accidental grounds will be conducted through the enclosures, the grounding conductor, and the grounding electrode to the earth. If the current is large enough, it will cause the over-current device to open.

12.5 GROUND-FAULT PROTECTION

A ground-fault protector (GFP) is a device which senses ground faults and opens the circuit when the current to ground reaches a predetermined value. A ground-fault circuit interrupter (GFCI) is a device which opens the circuit when very small currents flow to ground.

There is no way to determine in advance the impedance of an accidental ground. Most circuits are protected by 15 A (ampere) or larger over-current devices. If the impedance of a ground fault is low enough, such devices will open the circuit. What about currents of less than 15 A? It has been proven that currents as small as 50 mA through the heart, lungs, or brain can be fatal.

Electrical equipment exposed to moisture or vibration may develop high-impedance grounds. Arcing between a conductor and the frame of equipment may cause a fire, yet the current may be less than 1 ampere. Leakage current caused by dirt and/or moisture may take place between the conductor and the frame. Portable tools are frequently not properly grounded, and the only path to ground is through the body of the operator.

The ground-fault circuit interrupter was developed to provide protection against ground-fault currents of less than 15 A. The GFCI is designed to operate on two-wire circuits in which one of the two wires is grounded. The standard circuit voltages are 120 V and 277 V. The time it takes to operate depends upon the value of the ground-fault current. Small currents of 10 mA or less may flow for up to 5 s before the circuit is opened. A current of 20 mA will cause the GFCI to operate in less than 0.04 s. This time/current element provides a sufficient margin of safety without nuisance tripping.

The GFCI operates on the principle that an equal amount of current is flowing through the two wires. When a ground fault occurs, some of the current flowing through the ungrounded (hot) wire does not flow through the grounded wire; it completes the circuit through the accidental ground. The GFCI senses the difference in the value of current between the two wires and opens the circuit. GFCIs may be incorporated into circuit breakers, installed in the

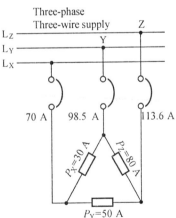

Fig. 12.6 Three-phase, unbalanced delta connection

line, or incorporated into a receptacle outlet or equipment.

Ground-fault protectors are generally designed for use with commercial and/or industrial installations. They provide protection against ground-fault currents from 2 A (special types go as low as 50 mA) up to 2 000 A. GFPs are generally installed on the main, submain, and/or feeder conductors. GFCIs are installed in the branch circuits. GFPs are generally used for three-wire, single-phase and for three-phase installations, while GFCIs are used for two-wire, single-phase circuits.

A ground-fault protector installed on supply conductors must enclose all the circuit conductors, including the neutral, if present. When operating under normal conditions, all the current to and from the load flows through the circuit conductors. The algebraic sum of the flux produced by these currents is zero. When a phase-to-ground fault occurs, the fault current returns through the grounding conductor. Under this condition an alternating flux is produced within the sensing device. When the fault current reaches a predetermined value, the magnetic flux causes a relay to actuate a circuit breaker.

Sometimes the GFP is installed on the grounding conductor of the system. Under this condition, the unit senses the amount of phase-to-ground current flowing in the grounding conductor. When the current exceeds the setting of the GFP, it will cause the circuit breaker to open.

The ground-fault protector is actually a specially designed current transformer connected to a solid-state relay.

12.6 THREE-PHASE SYSTEMS

The various three-phase systems in normal use will be described. Under ideal conditions, these systems operate in perfect balance, and if a neutral conductor is present it carries zero current. In actual practice, perfectly balanced systems are seldom encountered. The electrical worker, therefore, must be able to calculate values of current and voltage in unbalanced systems. Single-phase loads are frequently supplied from three-phase systems. The single-phase load requirements vary considerably, making it virtually impossible to maintain a perfect balance.

In a balanced three-phase system, the currents in the three lines are equal. The currents in the three phases are also equal. In other words, $I_{LX} = I_{LY} = I_{LZ}$ and $I_P = I_P = I_P$. If, however, $I_{LX} \neq I_{LY} \neq I_{LZ}$, then $I_{PX} \neq I_{PY} \neq I_{PZ}$ and the system is unbalanced(see Fig.12.6).

To calculate the line currents in an unbalanced three-phase system, the method in the following example may be used.

Example 1

Three pure resistance, single-phase loads are connected in a delta configuration across a three-phase supply, as illustrated in Fig. 12.6. Load X requires 30 A, load Y requires 50 A, and load Z requires 80 A. Calculate the current through each line wire.

(1) line $X = \sqrt{X^2 + Y^2 + (2XY\cos \Phi)}$

$X = \sqrt{30^2 + 50^2 + (2 \times 30 \times 50 \times 0.5)}$

$X = \sqrt{900 + 2\,500 + 1\,500}$

$X = \sqrt{4\,900}$

$X = 70$ A

(2) line $Y = \sqrt{X^2 + Z^2 + (2XZ\cos \Phi)}$

$Y = \sqrt{30^2 + 80^2 + (2 \times 30 \times 80 \times 0.5)}$

$Y = \sqrt{900 + 6\,400 + 2\,400}$

$Y = \sqrt{9\,700}$

$Y = 98.5$ A

(3) line $Z = \sqrt{Z^2 + Y^2 + (2ZY\cos \Phi)}$

$Z = \sqrt{80^2 + 50^2 + (2 \times 80 \times 50 \times 0.5)}$

$Z = \sqrt{6\,400 + 2\,500 + 4\,000}$

$Z = \sqrt{12\,900}$

$Z = 113.6$ A

Example 1 applies to loads of 100 percent power factor connected in delta. With loads of different power factors, the phase angle will vary from 120°. For a wye connection, the line current is equal to the phase current.

Some connections may be a combination of single-phase and three-phase loads. Under these conditions, the phase angle between the three-phase load and the single-phase load must be considered.

12.7 HARMONIC EFFECT OF FLUORESCENT LIGHTING FIXTURES

Most distribution systems in the United States and Canada operate on a frequency of 60 Hz. Certain types of electrical equipment produce secondary frequencies which are multiples of the supply frequency. These secondary frequencies are called harmonics. For example, the second harmonic of 60 Hz is 120 Hz, the third harmonic is 180 Hz, and so on.

The alternating flux developed by transformers, used in the ballasts of fluorescent lighting fixtures, produces a voltage which has a frequency of 180 hertz. This results in an additional current flowing in the supply conductors. The value of the current in the phase conductors is usually about 25 percent of the supply current. This third harmonic current adds to the supply current, causing a greater heating effect in the conductors. This increased heating effect is rather small, possibly in the vicinity of 3 ~ 5 percent.

The effect on the neutral conductor is quite different. The harmonic currents from the phase conductors add together, causing a large increase in the neutral current. The heating effect is 75% ~ 80% greater than if the third harmonic current did not exist.

CAUTION: When installing supply, feeder, and branch circuit conductors for heavy fluorescent loads, the size of the neutral conductor should be at least equal to that of the phase conductors.

Vocabulary

1. distribution	n.	分配,配电
2. primary	a.	最初的,基本的
	n.	初级线圈
3. radial	a.	径向的,辐射(状)的
4. premise	n.	上述各点,前言,根据
5. residential	a.	住宅的,居处的
6. residence	n.	住宅
7. occupancy	n.	占有,占用,居住
8. tap	n.	抽头
9. establishment	n.	组织,部门
10. dwelling	n.	住房
11. panel	n.	操纵台,面板
12. laundry	n.	洗衣房
13. means	n.	手段,工具
14. condominium	n.	(国际)共管
15. branch circuit		支路
16. transformer	n.	变压器
17. conduit	n.	导线,导线管
18. rigid	a.	刚性的,坚固的
19. clamp	n.	夹,钳
20. bolt	n.	螺栓
21. cubicle	n.	立方体
22. interrupter	n.	断续(流、电、路)器
23. margin	n.	余量,裕度
24. nuisance	n.	障碍,公害
25. receptacle	n.	插座,塞孔
26. algebraic	a.	代数的
27. virtually	ad.	实际上,实质上

28. fluorescent   a.   荧光的,有荧光性的
29. fixture   n.   设备,装置
30. vicinity   n.   附近,邻近,接近
31. ballast   n.   镇流器
32. feeder   n.   馈电线,电源线,馈电板
33. ground-fault protector(GFP)   接地故障保护器
34. ground-fault circuit interrupter(GFCI)   接地故障断路器

Notes:

1. A radial system is an electrical transmission system, which begins at a central station and supplies power to various substations.

辐射型系统是一类起源于主电站并向各种分电站传递电能的电力传输系统。

2. At the central station the voltage is stepped up to a higher value for long-distance transmission.

为长距离输电,在主电站将电压升高到较高的值。

3. At the substations the voltage is usually lowered to a value more suitable for distribution in populated areas.

为了在人口密集地区配电,在分电站将电压降低到合适的值。

4. The secondary contains two coils connected in series with a midpoint tap to provide a single-phase, three-wire system.

副边包含两个带中间接点的两个串联连接线圈以构成单相三线系统。

5. Commercial and/or industrial buildings may have more than one kilowatt-hour meter, depending upon the number of occupancies.

根据用户的数量,商业和(或)工业建筑可能有不止一个电度表。

6. Depending upon the type of installation and the load requirements, voltages as high as 2 300 volts may be used.

基于安装类型和负载需要,可以采用高达 2 300 V 的电压。

7. System grounds must be arranged to provide a path of minimum impedance in order to ensure the operation of over current devices when a ground fault occurs.

当接地故障发生时,为确保过流设备工作,必须设置系统接地以提供最小阻抗通路。

8. A ground-fault protector (GFP) is a device which senses ground faults and opens the circuit when the current to ground reaches a predetermined value.

GFP 是一种当接地电流达到预设值时能够检测接地故障并断开电路的设备。

9. It has been proven that currents as small as 50 milliamperes through the heart, lungs, or brain can be fatal.

已经证明小到 50 毫安的电流通过心脏、肺或大脑是致命的。

10. The GFCI is designed to operate on two-wire circuits in which one of the two wires is grounded.

GFCI 设计为按照双线电路工作,双线中的一根线接地。

11. GFPs are generally used for three-wire, single-phase and for three-phase installations, while GFCIs are used for two-wire, single-phase circuits.

GFP 通常用于三线单相和三相电路,而 GFCI 用于两线单相电路。

12. The harmonic currents from the phase conductors add together, causing a large increase in the neutral current.

各相线路来的三次谐波电流叠加在一起,使中线电流大幅度升高。

13

Introduction to Control Engineering

13.1 INTRODUCTION

Whenever energy is to be used purposefully, some form of control is necessary. In recent times there has been a considerable advance made in the art of automatic control. The art is, however, quite old, stemming back to about 1790 when James Watt invented the centrifugal governor to control the speed of his steam engines. He found that whilst in many applications an engine speed independent of load torque was necessary, in practice when a load was applied the speed fell and when the load was removed the speed increased.

A simple centrifugal governor is shown in Fig. 13.1. In this system, variations in engine speed are detected and used to control the pressure of the steam entering the engine. Under steady conditions the moment of the weight of the metal spheres balances that due to the centrifugal force and the steam valve opening is just sufficient to maintain the engine speed at the required level. When an extra load torque is applied to the engine, its speed will tend to fall, the centrifugal force will decrease and the metal spheres will tend to fall slightly. Their height controls the opening of the steam valve which now opens further to allow a greater steam pressure on the engine. The speed thus tends to rise, counteracting the original tendency for the speed to fall. If the extra load is removed, the reverse process takes place, the metal spheres tend to rise slightly, so tending to close the steam valve and counteracting any tendency for the speed to rise.

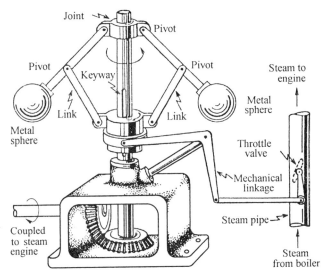

Fig. 13.1 Simple centrifugal governor

Typical responses of this system to load increase with and without the governor are shown in Fig. 13.2.

It is seen that without the governor the speed would fall considerably on load. However, in a correctly designed system with a governor the fall in speed would be very much less. An undesirable feature which accompanies a system which has been designed to be very sensitive to speed changes, is the tendency to 'hunt' or oscillate about the final speed. The real problem in the synthesis of all systems of this type is to prevent excessive oscillation but at the same time produce good 'regulation'. Regu-

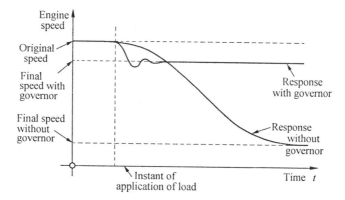

Fig. 13.2 Response of steam engine to suddenly applied load torque

lation is defined as the percentage change in controlled quantity on load relative to the value of the controlled quantity under condition of zero load. Regulators form an important class of control system, their object generally being to keep some physical quantity constant (e.g. speed, voltage, liquid level, humidity, etc.) regardless of load variation. A good regulator has only very small regulation.

The 1914 ~ 1918 war caused military engineers to realize that to win wars it is necessary to position heavy masses (e.g. ships and guns) precisely and quickly. Classic work was performed by N. Minorsky in the USA in the early 1920's on the automatic steering of ships and the automatic positioning of guns on board ships. In 1934 the word 'servomechanism' (derived from the Latin servus, meaning slave) was used in the literature for the first time by H. L. Hazen. He defined a servomechanism as 'a power amplifying device in which the amplifier element driving the output is actuated by the difference between the input to the servo and its output'. This definition can be applied to a wide variety of 'feedback control systems'. More recently it has been suggested that the term 'servomechanism' or 'servo' be restricted to a feedback control system in which the controlled variable is mechanical position.

The automatic control of various large-scale industrial processes, as encountered in the manufacture and treatment of chemicals, food and metals, has emerged during the last thirty years as an extremely important part of the general field of control engineering. In the initial stages of development it was scarcely realized that the theory of process control was intimately related to the theory of servomechanisms and regulators. Even nowadays complete academic design of process control systems is virtually impossible owing to our poor understanding of the dynamics of processes. In much of the theory introduced in this book, servomechanisms and regulators are used as examples to illustrate the methods of analysis. These methods are, however, often applicable to process control systems, which will be themselves introduced separately.

13.2 DEFINITIONS

In general there are two types of control systems, open loop and closed loop.

13.2.1 Open-loop System

In an open-loop system(see Fig.13.3) an input signal or command, is applied, amplified in a 'controller' and a power output is obtained from an 'output element'.

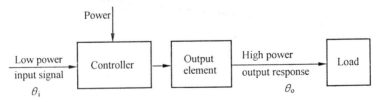

Fig.13.3 Open-loop system

The location of the output element is often remote from the input station. The input may be applied manually, as by turning a dial. The expected output is normally predetermined by calibration, and the input control may be accompanied by some sort of calibration chart. The actual output obtained depends on the validity of the calibration, and if components of the system are affected by time, temperature, humidity, lubrication, etc., the actual output may vary from the expected output. Such systems are also acutely affected by load variation.

A simple example of an open-loop control system is a steam engine without a governor. Such an arrangement is shown diagrammatically in Fig.13.4.

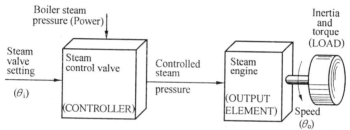

Fig.13.4 Schematic of steam engine without a governor

The speed is primarily affected by changes in load torque but will also be altered by changes in boiler steam pressure, the state of lubrication and wear in moving parts.

13.2.2 Closed-loop System

In a simple closed-loop system (see Fig.13.5), the controller is no longer actuated by the input but by the 'error'. The error is defined as the difference between the system input and its output. Such a system contains the same basic elements as the open-loop system, plus two extra features-an 'error detector' and a feedback loop. The error detector is a device which produces a signal proportional to the difference between input and output.

The open-loop system of Fig. 13.4 may be made 'manual closed loop' by means of an output speed indicator and a human operator. The

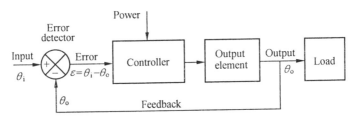

Fig.13.5 Simple closed-loop system

human operator must watch the engine speed continuously and make suitable adjustments to the steam valve opening when variations occur, in an attempt to keep the speed constant. The reasons why in many instances automatic control systems are preferred to human operators are given in Sec.13.6.

The steam-engine may be incorporated as part of a closed-loop speed control system as illustrated in Fig.13.6.

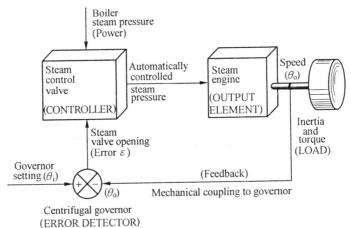

Fig.13.6 Schematic of steam engine with a governor

It has already been explained in Sec.13.1 how the governed steam engine regulates against speed changes due to alterations in load torque. Apart from this obvious advantage over the open-loop system, there is another more subtle advantage. The system possesses the ability to correct against its own defects. For instance, supposing the boiler steam pressure should decrease slightly. This would tend to make the speed fall; the error detector would sense this fall and cause the steam valve to open further, giving a corresponding increase in the controlled steam pressure. The speed would then tend to increase thus counteracting the original tendency for the speed to fall. The speed of response to changes in load is also very much faster than that of the open-loop system.

13.2.3 Control System Components

It is evident from the block schematic of the closed-loop system (see Fig. 13.5) that three basic components are required:

(1) The Error Detector. This is a device which receives the low-power input signal and the output signal which may be of different physical natures, converts them to a common physical quantity for the purposes of subtraction, performs the subtraction, and gives out a low-power error signal of the correct physical nature to actuate the controller. The error detector will usually contain 'transducers'; these are devices which convert signals of one physical form to another.

(2) The Controller. This is an amplifier which receives the low-power error signal, together with power from an external source. A controlled amount of power (of the correct physical nature) is then supplied to the output element.

(3) The Output Element. It provides the load with power of the correct physical nature in accordance with the signal received from the controller.

Other devices such as gear-boxes and 'compensating' devices are often featured in control systems, but these can usually be considered to form part of one of the other elements. A detailed description of some of the devices used in control systems will be given.

13.3 THE POSITION-CONTROL SYSTEMS

The regulator, whose object is to maintain the value of some physical quantity at a fixed level in spite of disturbances, is an important example of a closed-loop system. Equally important and certainly more challenging as an exercise in engineering design is the servomechanism whose object is to follow input commands. An example of such a device is the position-control servomechanism which must reproduce at some remote point the motion applied to a handwheel located at a local command station. The output motion might be used to drive a heavy object such as a missile launcher into a required position; power amplification of the command and accurate reproduction are thus necessary.

The signals can be transmitted by direct mechanical linkage or by hydraulic, pneumatic, or electric conduit. Apart from mechanical linkage the most rapid transmission may be achieved with electrical connection and this is often but not always used. Where it is used, the mechanical input and output signals are first converted into proportional electrical signals and then transmitted through wires to a subtracting device which produces a signal proportional to the error. A typical arrangement is shown in Fig.13.7.

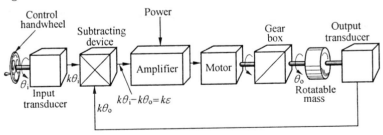

Fig.13.7 Position-control servomechanism

The low-power error signal is used to drive an amplifier which also receives power from an external source and delivers controlled power to

Introduction to Control Engineering 299

the motor.

The combination of transducers and subtracting element form the error detector, the amplifier is the controller and the motor together with its gear box form the output element.

The amplifier may be purely electrical if the motor is electrical but must be either electro-hydraulic or electro-pneumatic if the motor is either hydraulic or pneumatic.

It is emphasized that the object of the system is to make the rotatable mass copy as nearly as possible the motion of the hand-wheel. Let us consider what will happen if the position of the hand-wheel is turned very rapidly through an angle θ_i, the mass being initially at rest. Initially the mass has no velocity and the output position θ_o is zero, thus a signal $k\theta_i$ instantaneously appears at the terminals of the amplifier; power from the source is allowed to reach the motor which then begins to drive the mass so as to reduce the error. As θ_o approaches θ_i the error gets smaller and thus less power is allowed to reach the motor. Systems are usually designed so that the mass just overshoots the required position; since θ_o is then greater than θ_i, the error becomes negative and the motor forces the mass to stop and reverse direction. Some undershoots and further overshoots will then probably take place before the mass finally settles at the required position with θ_o equal to θ_i. Only when exact coincidence occurs does the amplifier receive zero signal and thus the motor is forced to move either one way or the other until all motion dies away. The motor can therefore only come to rest when the signal entering the amplifier is zero, i.e. when the output position is exactly equal to the command θ_i.

It becomes evident from the above discussion that unless very great care is taken in the design, it is quite possible that the oscillations about the desired position will build up instead of dying away quickly. A system in which oscillations build up is said to be unstable and much of the design work in control engineering is associated with producing a stable system. Adequate stability is, of course, only one of several requirements. Another requirement is faithful reproduction of a variety of input signals, and it has already been seen that the system of Fig. 13.7 is unlikely to reproduce a sudden change in input position with any degree of fidelity. Another type of input command might consist of hand-wheel motion of constant angular velocity. The system would then respond with an oscillatory transient and the mass would finally settle down with a velocity equal to the command but with a position lagging the command by a small angle. The slight difference between input and output positions would be of such magnitude as to produce an output torque from the motor sufficient to drive the mass at the required velocity against frictional torques. The error could not be zero otherwise the motor would stop and the error would then build up.

It is thus apparent that whilst the output θ_o will automatically align itself with the command θ_i under static conditions, under dynamic conditions the output motion only approximates to that of the command. The closeness of the approximation can however usually be made as good as is necessary to overcome most physical problems; for example, in certain types of automatically controlled profile milling machines a tracking accuracy to 0.000 1 inch has been achieved.

Another object of the position control system is that it must be capable of holding the output position equal to the command in the presence of severe load disturbances. For example, a launcher must remain pointing in the desired direction regardless of random gusts of wind. The position control system of Fig. 13.7, if correctly designed, would be able to achieve quite good regulation against load disturbances of this kind but a steady load disturbance would inevitably produce a small misalignment between output and command. In systems where such a misalignment would be intolerable, a more sophisticated type of controller must be used, having properties other than that of simple amplification. Design of a stable system is then correspondingly more difficult.

It should be appreciated that in a fully automatic system the 'hand-wheel' of Fig. 13.7 can be made to produce the necessary command signals without human aid. Indeed in many instances the hand-wheel may not even exist; the commands may be purely electrical in nature, having been derived directly from sensing elements. For example, in flight-control systems the control surfaces are normally actuated by servomechanisms which have command signals as directed by the pilot via the 'joy-stick', However, in airplanes containing auto-pilots, the pilot may switch to 'automatic', whereupon the command signals are generated directly from sensing gyroscopes which automatically detect deviations from the required path. Similarly some automatically-controlled machine tools have servomechanisms which react directly to electrical signals received from a digital computer. The computer usually acts partly as a memory which is able to reproduce a variety of complicated commands in a certain sequence and partly as arithmetic device to perform subtraction and produce highly accurate error signals on reception of digitized measurements of the output positions of the various servomechanisms under its control.

The position control servomechanism has many applications amongst which are:

Machine-tool position-control systems

Tracking radar systems

Gun directors and missile launchers

Positioners for radio and optical telescopes

Constant-tension control of sheet rolls in paper mills

Control of sheet metal thickness in hot-rolling mills

Missile guidance systems

Automatic pilots for aircraft

Automatic ship steering

Roll stabilization of ships

Recording instruments and servo-multipliers
Inertial guidance systems
Automatic handling of materials
Assisted braking and steering devices in motor vehicles

13.4 PROCESS-CONTROL SYSTEMS

It should be understood that any division of control engineering into 'regulators', 'servomechanisms' and 'process-control systems' is very artificial and is really due to historic rather than logical reasons. A process-control system is often fundamentally a regulator. However, a complicated process-control system may possibly contain several devices which could be defined as servomechanisms when considered individually. However, the following are examples of control problems usually classified as process control:

Control of chemical concentration in liquids
Control of liquid level
Control of rate of flow of fluids
Electrolytic plating control
Distillation process control
Gas-blending control
Reaction controls in nuclear reactors
Boiler plant control
Control of furnace temperature
Heat exchange process control

The philosophy of the design of process-control systems is rather different from that of the design of servomechanisms. However, many of the analytical problems involved are similar and most of the techniques of analysis and synthesis and methods of test are common to all branches of control engineering. In the past the controllers and motoring elements used in process control have been mainly pneumatic; electro-pneumatic

Introduction to Control Engineering 303

devices have become rather more popular recently and there is considerable evidence that this trend will continue and that in the future large plants will be controlled by means of electronic digital computers.

An example of a typical process control system will now be considered. A schematic diagram of the arrangement is shown in Fig. 13.8.

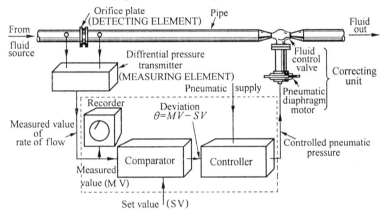

Fig. 13.8   Process-control system for controlling rate of flow of fluid

Process-Control Systems	Simple Closed-loop Control System
Measured value	Output θ_o
Set value	Input θ_i
Deviation	Minus error ($-\epsilon = \theta_o - \theta_i$)
Orifice plate Differential pressure transmitter Comparator	Error detector
Controller	Controller
Pneumatic motor Control valve	Output element
Process	Load

The object of the system is to maintain the rate of flow of fluid at a fixed value in accordance with a fixed command termed the 'set value', regardless of disturbances in supply pressure and back pressure. The actual rate of flow is detected by means of an orifice plate; the pressure difference across the plate is then a function of the rate of flow. A signal (termed the 'measured value') which is proportional to the pressure difference and hence to a function of the rate of flow of fluid is then transmitted by means of a 'differential pressure transmitter' to the recorder-controller. The method of transmission can be mechanical, electrical or pneumatic. The measured value is usually recorded continuously on a chart recorder which forms an integral part of the recorder-controller unit. The measured value is also compared with the set value in a 'comparing element' which generates the 'deviation' θ representing the difference between the measured value and the set value. The nature of the comparing element depends largely upon the method of transmission of the measured value and the nature of the controller; in a pneumatic system a simple differential mechanical linkage is often used to produce a mechanical signal proportional to the deviation, the controller which is either pneumatic or electro-pneumatic responds to the deviation by producing a pneumatic pressure which is a function of the deviation. This pressure is used to control a pneumatic motor which moves so as to actuate a control valve placed in the fluid supply pipe, the control valve will be moved automatically in such a way as to keep the deviation at a minimum level. The rate of flow of fluid is thus held reasonably constant in accordance with the set value.

It is usually possible to vary the set value in such a system by manual adjustment of a control knob or by means of an auxiliary automatic control system.

Whilst the nomenclature associated with process control (as recommended in B. S. 1523 Section 2: 1960) is somewhat different from that popularly used for the description of servomechanisms, both types of system are essentially closed loop; it is therefore of interest to compare the process-control system of Fig. 13.8 with the general block diagram for a simple closed-loop system shown in Fig. 13.5.

Definitions and symbols are always a source of disagreement and difficulty in a fast-moving field such as control engineering. As far as possible this book will adhere to the recommended symbols of the British Standards Institution but where these are liable to give rise to ambiguities, or they are not in popular use, exceptions will be made.

A particularly useful definition is that of a feedback control system as specified by the Institution of Radio Engineers (USA) in their Standards on Terminology for Feedback Control Systems (proceedings I.R.E. January 1956).

A feedback control system is a control system comprising one or more feedback control loops, which combines functions of the controlled signals with functions of the commands to tend to maintain prescribed relationships between the commands and the controlled signals···A servomechanism is a feedback control system in which one or more of the system signals represent mechanical motion.

13.5 AUTONOMIC CONTROL SYSTEMS

The performance of a control system having a controller with fixed parameters will always depend to some extent on the parameters of the plant or system being controlled. Now the design of a controller having fixed parameters to produce optimum performance in a control system will depend on an accurate knowledge of the plant parameters and environmental conditions. In systems where the variation of plant parameters and environmental conditions is severe, the controller cannot be designed in such a way as to produce the desired performance at all times.

An autonomic or self-adaptive or self-optimizing system may, however, be used to give the best possible performance. In this type of device, of which there are several classes, the parameters of the controller are automatically adjusted so that the system gives an optimum performance according to some in-built criterion of merit. Such systems are more complex than ordinary feedback control systems and require much additional equipment. The idea of autonomic control was conceived by Draper and Li and was first published in 1951.

A wealth of theoretical work related to autonomic control systems now exists and a textbook covering many aspects of the subject has now been published. Due to their considerable expense, autonomic control systems have only, as yet, found application in fields where conventional systems are grossly unsatisfactory. For instance in aircraft designed to fly at high speeds, the effectiveness of the control surfaces can vary greatly from low to high altitudes and from low to high speeds. The pilot can adapt his own behavior at the controls to a certain extent to counteract this but a greatly improved performance has been shown to be possible with a self-adaptive control system.

13.6 REASONS WHY CONTROL SYSTEMS ARE PREFERRED TO HUMAN OPERATIONS

Apart from the ideological issue that it is morally wrong to employ human beings to do laborious, soul-destroying, repetitive work which requires no judgment, and is far better done by machines, there are a number of very sound engineering reasons why automatic control systems are preferred to human operators, some of which are:

(1) The effect of human reaction time (0.3 s) prevents manual control being used where high response speed is required (e.g. A. A. guns or radar sets which are required to engage high-speed targets).

(2) Continuous operation over long periods causes boredom and fatigue in human operators with subsequent deterioration of performance.

Also great tress or danger to operator causes a rapid falling off in efficiency.

(3) It is impossible to standardize the behavior of human operators unless very simple tasks are undertaken.

(4) It is often uneconomical to use manual control.

(5) For many applications it is physically impossible for human operators to carry out an operation because of power and speed limitations, severe ambient conditions, the presence of harmful radiations, etc.

13.7 CONCLUDING REMARKS

The analysis and synthesis of practical control systems are not simple and they lean heavily on physical principles together with mathematical technique. The author rates the importance of these topics so highly that several chapters of this book are devoted exclusively to 'essential mathematics and physics'. Some readers may feel that their grasp of these subjects is already perfectly adequate and may wish to progress to topics directly related to control problems; it should be possible for them to merely scan through chapters 2, 3, and 5. The work introduced in chapters 4 and 6, is however, regarded as absolutely essential. The author wishes to emphasize that most courses in mathematics are often so totally unrelated to control engineering that a real barrier can exist to a full understanding of the problems of control unless symbols, units, definitions, and simple mathematical techniques are initially brought on to a common level which is completely suited to control requirements. The chapters on essential mathematics and physics have been designed with this object in mind; they are not in any way intended as a substitute for full courses in these subjects.

Vocabulary

1. centrifugal $a.$ 离心的; $n.$ 离心力,离心
2. whilst = while
3. sphere $n.$ 球体

4. counteract　　　　　v. 　　抵抗,抵消,消除
5. joint　　　　　　　　n. 　　关节,铰链
6. keyway　　　　　　n. 　　键槽
7. pivot　　　　　　　n. 　　轴,支点
8. link　　　　　　　　n. 　　连杆
9. throttle　　　　　　n. 　　节流(气)阀,风门
10. synthesis　　　　　n. 　　综合(物)
11. mass　　　　　　　n. 　　物质,块,堆
12. classic　　　　　　a. 　　古典的,经典的,传统的
13. steer　　　　　　　v. 　　驾驶,操纵,引导
14. servomechanism　　n. 　　伺服机构,伺服系统
15. actuate　　　　　　v. 　　激励,驱动
16. intimately　　　　　ad. 　 紧密地,直接的
17. academic　　　　　a. 　　纯理论的
18. dial　　　　　　　　n. 　　刻度盘,调节控制盘
19. calibration　　　　　n. 　　标定,标准化
20. lubrication　　　　　n. 　　润滑,注油
21. arrangement　　　　n. 　　结构
22. wear　　　　　　　n. 　　磨损,耗损
23. subtle　　　　　　　a. 　　微妙的,巧妙的
24. transducer　　　　　n. 　　变送器
25. hand-wheel　　　　　　　　手轮,驾驶盘,操纵盘
26. hydraulic　　　　　　a. 　　液压的; n. 液压传动装置
27. pneumatic　　　　　a. 　　气动的,气体力学的
28. electro-hydraulic　　　a. 　　电动液压的
29. electro-pneumatic　　a. 　　电动气动的
30. coincidence　　　　　n. 　　一致,相等
31. faithful　　　　　　　a. 　　正确的,可靠的
32. fidelity　　　　　　　n. 　　重现精度,真实,正确
33. oscillatory　　　　　a. 　　振动的,摆动的

34. align   v.   调准,调整
35. profile   n.   轮廓,仿行
36. milling machines   铣床
37. gyroscope   n.   陀螺仪
38. launcher   n.   发生器,启动装置
39. inertial   a.   惯性的,惯量的
40. electrolytic   a.   电解的
41. plate   v.   (电)镀
42. distillation   n.   蒸馏
43. blend   v.   混合,调和,配料
44. philosophy   n.   基本原理
45. analytical   a.   分析的,分解的
46. orifice   n.   测流孔,隔板
47. diaphragm   n.   膜,隔板
48. knob   n.   钮,圆形把手
49. nomenclature   n.   术语
50. liable   a.   有责任的
51. ambiguity   n.   模糊,多义
52. autonomic   a.   自治的
53. grossly   ad.   大概,大体上
54. ideological   a.   思想的
55. morally   ad.   道德上,道义上
56. boredom   n.   讨厌,无趣
57. deterioration   n.   变化,降低品质
58. ambient   a.   环境的
59. remarks   n.   附注,要点
60. differential pressure transducer   差压变送器

Notes:

1. In recent times there has been a considerable advance made in the art of automatic control.

近期,在自动控制策略方面已经取得了很大的进步。

2. Regulation is defined as the percentage change in controlled quantity on load relative to the value of the controlled quantity under condition of zero load.

调节作用定义为负载条件下被控量相对空载条件下被控量数值的变化百分比。

3. In a simple closed-loop system, the controller is no longer actuated by the input but by the 'error'.

在简单的闭环系统里,控制器不再受输入而是受"偏差"激励。

4. The speed of response to changes in load is also very much faster than that of the open-loop system.

对负载变化的响应速度也比开环系统的响应速度快得多。

5. A detailed description of some of the devices used in control systems will be given.

后面将给出用于控制系统的一些部件的详细说明。

6. The regulator, whose object is to maintain the value of some physical quantity at a fixed level in spite of disturbances, is an important example of a closed – loop system.

调节器是闭环系统的一个重要例子,其目标是即使有扰动也要将某些物理量维持为恒值。

7. The low-power error signal is used to drive an amplifier which also receives power from an external source and delivers controlled power to the motor.

小功率的误差信号用于驱动放大器,放大器还是从外部电源获取功率并将被控功率传输到电动机。

8. Only when exact coincidence occurs does the amplifier receive zero signal and thus the motor is forced to move either one way or the other until all motion dies away.

只有当(给定和反馈)完全一致时,放大器接收零值信号,从而使电动机向某个方向或反方向旋转直至运动消失。

9. A system in which oscillations build up is said to be unstable and much of the design work in control engineering is associated with producing a stable system.

工作于振荡状态的系统称为不稳定系统,控制工程的许多设计工作都与建立一个稳定系统相关。

10. The slight difference between input and output positions would be of such magnitude as to produce an output torque from the motor sufficient to drive the mass at the required velocity against frictional torques.

输入与输出位置的轻微差别能够达到如此的幅度,足以产生足够的电动机输出转矩,能够克服摩擦转矩后以所需速度拖动控制对象。

11. Another object of the position control system is that it must be capable of holding the output position equal to the command in the presence of severe load disturbances.

位置控制系统的另一个目标是它在恶劣的负载扰动下保证输出位置和命令相同。

12. However, a complicated process-control system may possibly contain several devices which could be defined as servomechanisms when considered individually.

但复杂的过程控制系统可能包含多个部件,当分别考虑时可以把它们定义为伺服机构。

13. The rate of flow of fluid is thus held reasonably constant in accordance with the set value.

这样,流体流速按照设定值维持在合理的恒值。

14. An autonomic or self-adaptive or self-optimizing system may, however, be used to give the best possible performance.

而自动或自适应或自寻优系统可以用来给出可能的最好性能。

14

Speed Control of DC Motor

14.1 REGULATOR SYSTEMS

A regulator system is one which normally provides output power in its steady-state operation.

For example, a motor speed regulator maintains the motor speed at a constant value despite variations in load torque. Even if the load torque is remove, the motor must provide sufficient torque to over-come the viscous friction effect of the bearings. Other forms of regulator also provide output power; a temperature regulator must maintain the temperature of, say, an oven constant despite the heat loss in the oven. A voltage regulator must also maintain the output voltage constant despite variation in the load current. For any system to provide an output, e.g., speed, temperature, voltage, etc., an error signal must exist under steady-state conditions.

14.2 ELECTRICAL BRAKING

In many speed control systems, e.g., rolling mills, mine winders, etc., the load has to be frequently brought to a standstill and reversed.

Speed Control of DC Motor 313

The rate at which the speed reduces following a reduced speed demand is dependent on the stored energy and the braking system used. A small speed control system (sometimes known as a velodyne) can employ mechanical braking, but this is not feasible with large speed controllers since it is difficult and costly to remove the heat generated.

The various methods of electrical braking available are:

(1) Regenerative braking.
(2) Eddy current braking.
(3) Dynamic braking.
(4) Reverse current braking (plugging).

Regenerative braking is the best method, though not necessarily the most economic. The stored energy in the load is converted into electrical energy by the work motor (acting temporarily as a generator) and is returned to the power supply system. The supply system thus acts as a 'sink' into which the unwanted energy is delivered. Providing the supply system has adequate capacity, the consequent rise in terminal voltage will be small during the short periods of regeneration. In the Ward-Leonard method of speed control of DC motors, regenerative braking is inherent, but thyristor drives have to be arranged to invert to regenerate. Induction motor drives can regenerate if the rotor shaft is driven faster than the speed of the rotating field. The advent of low-cost variable-frequency supplies from thyristor inverters have brought about considerable changes in the use of induction motors in variable speed drives.

Eddy current braking can be applied to any machine, simply by mounting a copper or aluminum disc on the shaft and rotating it in a magnetic field. The problem of removing the heat generated is severe in large systems as the temperature of the shaft, bearings, and motor will be raised if prolonged braking is applied.

In dynamic braking, the stored energy is dissipated in a resistor in the circuit. When applied to small DC machines, the armature supply is disconnected and a resistor is connected across the armature (usually by a relay, contactor, or thyristor). The field voltage is maintained, and braking is applied down to the lowest speeds. Induction motors require a somewhat more complex arrangement, the stator windings being disconnected from the AC supply and reconnected to a DC supply. The electrical energy generated is then dissipated in the rotor circuit. Dynamic braking is applied to many large AC hoist systems where the braking duty is both severe and prolonged.

Any electrical motor can be brought to a standstill by suddenly reconnecting the supply to reverse the direction of rotation (reverse current braking). Applied under controlled conditions, this method of braking is satisfactory for all drives. Its major disadvantage is that the electrical energy consumed by the machine when braking is equal to the stored energy in the load. This increases the running costs significantly in large drives.

14.3 DC MOTOR SPEED CONTROL

The basis of all methods of DC motor speed control is derived from the equations:

$$E \propto \Phi \omega$$
$$U = E + I_a R_a$$

the terms having their usual meanings. If the $I_a R_a$ drop is small, the equations approximate to

$$U \propto \Phi \omega$$

or

$$\omega \propto \Phi / U$$

Thus, control of armature voltage and field flux influences the motor speed. To reduce the speed to zero, either $U = 0$ or $\Phi = \infty$. The latter is inadmissible; hence control at low speed is by armature voltage variation. To increase the speed to a high value, either U is made very large or Φ is reduced. The latter is the most practical way and is known as field weakening. Combinations of the two are used where a wide range of speed is required.

14.4 A SINGLE-QUADRANT SPEED CONTROL SYSTEM USING THYRISTORS

A single-quadrant thyristor converter system is shown in Fig. 14.1. For the moment the reader should ignore the rectifier BR2 and its associated circuitry (including resistor R in the AC circuit), since this is needed only as a protective feature and is described in Sec. 14.5.

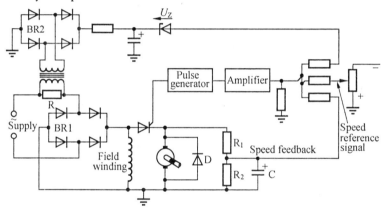

Fig. 14.1 Thyristor speed control system with current limitation on the AC side

Since the circuit is a single-quadrant converter, the speed of the motor shaft (which is the output from tie system) can be controlled in one direction of rotation only. Moreover, regenerative braking can not be applied to the motor; in this type of system, the motor armature can suddenly be brought to rest by dynamic braking (i.e. when the thyristor gate pulses are phased back to 180°, a resister can be connected across the armature by a relay or some other means).

Rectifier BR1 provides a constant voltage across the shunt field winding, giving a constant field flux. The armature current is controlled by a thyristor which is, in turn, controlled by the pulses applied to its gate. The armature speed increases as the pulses are phased forward (which reduces the delay angle of firing), and the armature speed reduces as the gate pulses are phased back.

The speed reference signal is derived from a manually operated potentiometer (shown at the right-hand side of Fig. 14.1), and the feedback signal or output speed signal is derived from the resistor chain R_1 R_2, which is connected across the armature. (Strictly speaking, the feedback signal in the system in Fig. 14.1 is proportional to the armature voltage, which is proportional to the shaft speed only if the armature resistance drop, $I_a R_a$, is small. Methods used to compensate for the $I_a R_a$ drop are discussed in Sec. 14.6.) Since the armature voltage is obtained from a thyristor, the voltage consists of a series of pulses, these pulses are smoothed by capacitor C. The speed reference signal is of the opposite polarity to the armature voltage signal to ensure that overall negative feedback is applied.

A feature of DC motor drives is that the load presented to the supply is a mixture of resistance, inductance, and back EMF Diode D in Fig. 14.1 ensures that the thyristor current commutates to zero when its anode potential falls below the potential of the upper armature connection, in the manner outlined before. In the drive shown, the potential of the thyristor cathode is equal to the back EMF of the motor while it is in a blocking state. Conduction can only take place during the time interval when the instantaneous supply voltage is greater than the back EMF Inspection of Fig. 14.2 shows that when the motor is running, the peak inverse voltage applied to the thyristor is much greater than the peak forward voltage. By connecting a diode in series with the thyristor, as shown, the reverse blocking capability of the circuit is increased to allow low-voltage thyristors to be used.

The waveforms shown in Fig. 14.2 are idealized waveforms inasmuch as they ignore the effects of armature inductance, commutator ripple, etc.

Typical armature voltage waveforms are shown in Fig. 14.3. In this waveform the thyristor is triggered at point A, and conduction continues to point B when the supply voltage falls below the armature back EMF. The effect of armature inductance is to force the thyristor to continue to con-

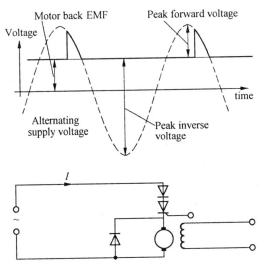

Fig. 14.2 Illustrating the effect of motor back EMF on the peak inverse voltage applied to the thyristor

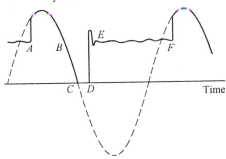

Fig. 14.3 Armature voltage waveforms

duct until point C, when the fly-wheel diode prevents the armature

318 English in Electric Automation

voltage from reversing. When the inductive energy has dissipated (point D), the armature current is zero and the voltage returns to its normal level, the transients having settled out by point E. The undulations on the waveform between E and F are due to commutator ripple.

The reason for BR2 and its associated circuitry is described in Sec. 14.5.

14.5 PROTECTION CIRCUITS OR LIMITING CIRCUITS

To withstand the mechanical shock of suddenly applied torques, large DC motors for control applications are designed with oversize shafts and bearings, and specially constructed commutators. This does not, however, eliminate the possibility of serious damage to the machine and associated equipment. In order to limit the maximum values of speed, torque, current, acceleration, etc., it is necessary to build protective circuits into the closed-loop system.

The basic principle is shown in Fig. 14.4. The quantity to be limited is converted into a voltage, and is fed to the limit circuit together with a constant voltage U_L. Under normal working conditions, the input to the limit circuit is less than U_L and the output U_X is zero. Under conditions of excessive loading, the input voltage exceeds U_L and the output from the limit circuit rises. The output voltage is subtracted from the error signal, so reducing the net input to the amplifier. This has the effect of reducing not only the output of the system but also the magnitude of the quantity to be limited.

The thyristor circuit in Fig. 14.1 incorporates electronic current limit protection (and it therefore provides motor shaft torque limitation since, in the case of a shunt machine which has fixed excitation, the torque is proportional to armature current). Resistor R in Fig. 14.1 has a low value of resistance, and for normal values of operating current the RMS. voltage across R is less than about 1.0 V. It is arranged that the current limiting

Speed Control of DC Motor 319

circuit comes into operation when the voltage across R reaches about 1.0 V.

For the purpose of comparing the current limiting circuit in Fig. 14.1 with the block diagram in Fig. 14.4, the voltage from the rectifier BR2 is equivalent to the signal from the transducer in Fig. 14.4, and the Zener diode voltage U_Z in Fig. 14.1 corresponds to the 'limit' voltage U_L in Fig. 14.4.

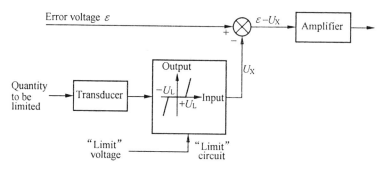

Fig. 14.4 Block diagram of one method of limiting quantities to a safe level in a control system

When the motor current in Fig. 14.1 is less than its limiting value, the alternating voltage across R gives rise to a rectified voltage across BR2 which is less than U_Z. Consequently, no current flows through the Zener diode. However, when the motor current exceeds its limiting value, the voltage produced by rectifier BR2 is greater than U_Z, and a current flows into the summing resistors of the amplifier. The direction of this current is such as to cause the pulse generator to phase back the thyristor gate pulses, so that the armature current is reduced to a safe value.

14.6 THE CLOSED-LOOP WARD-LEONARD METHOD OF SPEED CONTROL

Named after its American, the system contains a motor whose speed is to be controlled (known as the work motor) together with a motor generator set. The work motor usually has a constant excitation and its armature is fed by the generator of the motor generator set (the latter operating at constant speed). The general arrangement is shown in Fig. 14.5.

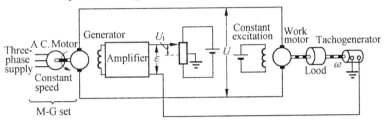

Fig. 14.5 Closed-loop Ward-leonard speed control system.

Before describing the operating of the circuit in detail, it is worth while explaining the need to introduce the Ward-Leonard method at a time when thyristor drives are almost universally used. The Ward-Leonard method of speed control allows the user to smoothly control the speed of the work motor from standstill to full speed in either direction of rotation. Moreover, regenerative braking is inherent for both directions of drive, so that electrical braking is available from full speed in either direction of rotation down to 'creep' speed (the work motor must finally be stopped by some form of mechanical braking). That is, the Ward-Leonard method of speed control is the forerunner of an ideal four-quadrant thyristor drive, and serves as an excellent model of speed control.

The AC motor drives the generator at a constant speed, and the armature voltage U is approximately proportional to the generator field flux in accordance with the equations developed earlier. The flux, in turn, is dependent on the error voltage at the amplifier terminals. To a first approximation, neglecting the effects of loading and saturation, $U \propto \varepsilon$. Since the work motor excitation is constant, its flux is constant and

$$\omega \propto U \qquad (14.1)$$

Combining the above equations shows that

$$\omega \propto \varepsilon \qquad (14.2)$$

i.e., the system is error-actuated and the work motor shaft speed is proportional to the error voltage.

The direction of rotation of the work motor shaft is reversed by reversing the polarity of the speed reference voltage U_1. This reverses the polarity of the generated voltage and current, reversing the work motor torque.

In Fig. 14.5, the speed is measured by a tachogenerator, but from Eq. (14.1) the armature voltage could be used as the speed signal, providing that the load current is small. With a large value of load current, the $I_a R_a$ drop makes Eq. (14.1) inaccurate. For accurate speed control, the voltage fed back must be proportional to the motor back EMF $E = (U - I_a R_a)$. A simple circuit which compensates for the armature voltage drop is shown in Fig. 14.6. The PD across R is $I_a R$, and the voltage at B relative to A is $[R_2 U/(R_1 + R_2) - I_a R]$, which is of similar form to the equation for the back EMF. By a suitable choice of values, the voltage between A and B is proportional to the back EMF, eliminating the need for a tachogenerator. In practice, the resistor R is not always necessary, as the PD across the interpoles of the work motor may be utilized.

It can be shown that, for a motor of armature resistance R_a, which is used in a circuit of the type in Fig. 14.6, $I_a R_a$ drop compensation is obtained if

$$R_1 R = R_2 R_a \qquad (14.3)$$

If any three of the above values are known, then the fourth can be calculated.

While the circuit in Fig. 14.6 is satisfactory for Ward-Leonard type drives in which the workmotor armature voltage is supplied by a DC generator, it may be unsuitable for a thyristor drive (see, for example, the speed control system in Fig. 14.1) in which the armature supply is obtained from a thyristor. The reason is that the output from a thyristor supply is rich in harmonics, and even when the condition in Eq. (14.3) is satisfied, the voltage between point A and point B in Fig. 14.6 is very distorted, even when the work motor is running at constant speed. To reduce the harmonics in the voltage between A and B, it is necessary to shunt resistor R_2 by capacitor C, as shown by the dotted connection in Fig. 14.6. The value of capacitor C can be calculated from the equation.

$$C = L / (R_1 R) \qquad (14.4)$$

where L is the inductance of the work motor armature. In a thyristor drive, Eq. (14.3) and (14.4) must be satisfied to give $I_a R_a$ compensation.

The work motor may be directly coupled to the drive as shown in Fig. 14.5, particularly in large low-speed installations, or it may be coupled through a speed-reducing gearbox, so permitting a high-speed low-inertia motor to be used. If a very wide speed range is required, the basic system is modified to allow field weakening of the work motor to give the higher values of speed. This technique is employed in many machine tool applications.

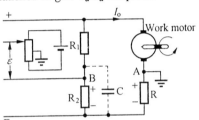

Fig. 14.6 Armature voltage drop compensation

A feature of the Ward-Leonard system is that regenerative braking is inherent. When the reference signal is reduced, the generator voltage falls, but the work motor speed (and back EMF) is maintained for a short time by the stored energy in the load. Momentarily, the work motor back EMF is greater than the generator voltage and the direction of the current through the two DC machine armatures reverses, causing the work motor to function as a generator (driven by the stored energy of the load). The DC generator now operates as a motor, forcing the AC motor to operate as a generator returning energy to the power supply system. Regenerative braking down to the work motor 'creep' speed is obtained in this way.

14.7 TYPES OF PHASE-CONTROLLED THYRISTOR DC DRIVES

The following is a brief summary of the basic types of DC drive in popular use. To remind the reader of the meaning of one-, two-, and four-quadrant control, they are defined below:

One-quadrant control is speed control in one direction of rotation only (indicated by the diode in Fig.14.7(a)).

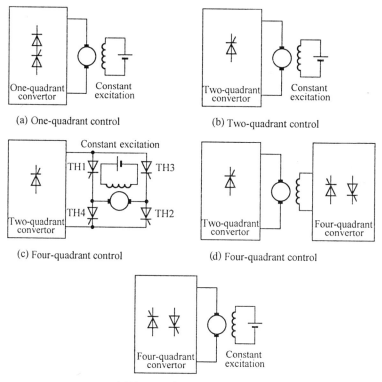

(a) One-quadrant control

(b) Two-quadrant control

(c) Four-quadrant control

(d) Four-quadrant control

(e) Four-quadrant control

Fig.14.7 Thyristor drives

Two-quadrant control is speed control and regenerative braking for one direction of rotation (see Fig. 14.7(b)).

Four-quadrant control is speed control and regenerative braking in both directions of rotation (equivalent to the Ward-leonard method of speed control) (see Fig. 14.7 (c), (d), (e)).

The block diagram in Fig. 14.7(a) corresponds to the speed control system in Fig. 14.1, in which the rotation of the armature of the motor is controlled in one direction.

The block diagram in Fig. 14.7(b) provides two quadrant control in which the motor rotation is controlled in one direction, and regenerative braking can also be obtained.

The diagram in Fig. 14.7(c) is a four-quadrant converter in which motoring and regenerative braking is obtained for both directions of rotation. This arrangement uses a bridge circuit comprising thyristors TH1 to TH4, inclusive, to provide a means of reversing the armature current.

For one direction of rotation, current flows through thyristors TH1 and TH2, and for the other direction of rotation, through TH3 and TH4. The main power supply is from a two-quadrant converter which enables either motoring or regenerative braking to be obtained. One disadvantage of this system is that each of the thyristor TH1 to TH4 must be rated to carry the full armature current. Another disadvantage is that when armature current reversal is required, there is a small time delay while the armature current is transferred from one pair of thyristors in the armature bridge to the other. In the case of the thyristor bridge shown this delay is small, but if the thyristors are replaced by a reversing contactor the time delay (typically 0.1s) may not be tolerated in some systems. During the time that it takes to operate the armature current-reversing circuit, the armature 'coasts' and is not under the control of the converter.

Fig. 14.7(d) shows a four-quadrant converter which incorporates field current reversal. The time constant of the field circuit is usually a few seconds, and to speed up the process of field current reversal it is usually necessary to use a 'forcing' voltage which is greatly in excess of the normal field voltage.

Fig.14.7(e) uses two 'back-to-back' converters to provide a four-quadrant drive. This type of system enables very rapid reversal of armature speed and torque with no 'dead time' between reversals. This type of drive is also known as a dual-converter drive, a Fig.8 drive, an inverse-parallel drive, or a twin-bridge drive.

14.8 DUAL-CONVERTER DRIVE

The basic block diagram of a dual-converter drive is shown in Fig. 14.8(a), and comprises two two-quadrant converters connected back to back with one another. The bridges are arranged to operate so that when one bridge is rectifying, the other bridge is inverting. The speed reference signal, which can be obtained either from a manually operated potentiomerter or from a computer via a digital-to-analogue converter, is compared with the output speed signal. The resulting error signal controls the gate pulse generator electronics which, in turn, provide firing pulses which are appplied to the gates of the thyristors.

The gate pulse generator ensures that when one bridge is operating as a rectifier, the other bridge operates as an inverter. A simplified block diagram is shown in Fig.14.8(b). For the machine to operate as a motor in Fig.14.8(b), the gate pulses cause converter A to operate as a rectifier and converter B as an inverter. The delay angles of the firing pulses of the converters ensure that the mean value, Vd, of the 'internal' voltage of each converter is equal to one another. This ensures that, theoretically at any rate, no current circulates between the two converters. Under the conditions shown in Fig.14.8(b), and when $U_a < U_{D1}$, converter A provides power via D1 to the armature which rotates, say, in a clockwise direction. The relationship between the gate delay angles of the two converters is shown in Fig.14.8(c), and the operating condition described

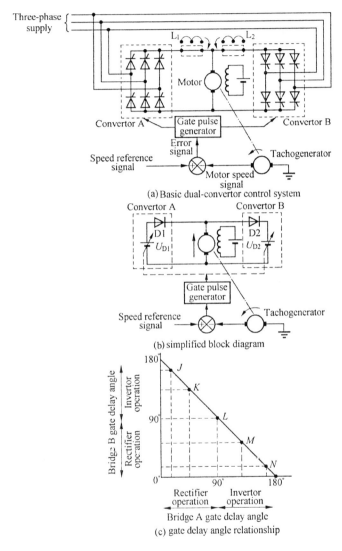

Fig.14.8

above could correspond to operating point J on the characteristics.

When it is necessary to slow down the work motor, the reference voltage is reduced; this reduces the error signal, which causes the operating point on diagram(c) to move to, say, point K. This has the effect of simultaneously reducing the value of U_{D1} and U_{D2} (see Fig. 14.8(b)). However, due to the inertia of the motor and load, the armature voltage U_a remains unchanged until the speed reduces. The net result is that momentarily diode D1 is reverse-biased and stops conducting and that diode D2 is forward-biased and starts conducting. That is, energy is extracted from the work motor (which now acts as a generator) and the system regeneratively brakes the motor to a lower speed. In this way the armature speed is quickly reduced to the lower value demanded by the lower reference signal. Once the lower speed is reached, diode D1 in Fig. 14.8(b) begins conducting once more and diode D2 is reverse-biased. When the converters are triggered with a delay angle of 90° (point L in Fig. 14.8 (c)), the mean output voltage is zero, causing the work motor to stop. When the speed reference polarity is reversed, the operating point on the delay angle characteristic (see Fig. 14.8(c)) moves, say, to point M; at this point, converter B provides power to the armature, causing it to rotate in the reverse direction. Under this condition the polarities of U_{D1} and U_{D2} in Fig. 14.8(b) are reversed. A further increase in the (reverse) speed reference signal results in operation at, say, point N on the delay angle characteristic (see Fig. 14.8(c)). When the speed reference signal is reduced once more to cause the motor to slow down, converter A momentarily operates in its inverter mode and provides regenerative braking to slow the motor down.

In the above discussion it has been assumed that, under normal circumstances, current cannot circulate between the two converters. However, since there are inevitable instantaneous potential differences between the waveforms of U_{D1} and U_{D2}, current will circulate between the two converters in Fig. 14.8. Moreover, if the diodes D1 and D2 are 'perfect', the resistance of the loop between the two bridges is practically zero; the result is that the instantaneous value of the circulating current can be very high. Two alternative methods are used to overcome this problem, and will be discussed.

14.8.1 Circulating current-free mode of operation

In this mode, the converter which is shown as being in its inverting mode in Fig. 14.8 is 'blocked' out of operation by the gate pulse circuit, i.e., it is switched off. This very clearly prevents the flow of circulating current. Should the converter be needed for inversion purposes when the work motor speed is reduced, the normally rectifying converter is blocked by the gate pulses and the inverting converter is brought into operation. While this arrangement appears to be a simple solution, there are many control problems which are introduced due to discontinuous load current.

14.8.2 Circulating current mode of operation

In this mode, a limited amount of circulating current is allowed to flow. The value of the circulating current is limited by means of reactors L_1 and L_2 which are connected as indicated in Fig. 14.8(a); these reactors allow a smooth transfer of control between the two converters without the associated problems with discontinuous current. A disadvantage of this system is the need for expensive current-limiting reactors.

14.9 COMPUTER MONITORING OF SPEED PROFILE

Many speed control systems require the work motor speed to follow a particular 'profile'. For example, a mine-winder speed control system must allow the conveyance in the shaft to accelerate at a certain rate and, when it reaches a certain speed, it must maintain a constant speed. Towards the end of the winding cycle, the conveyance must decelerate steadily until it stops at the bottom of the shaft. Moreover, the conveyance must be allowed to accelerate and decelerate at a greater rate when it is conveying coal and material than when it is conveying men.

Typical speed-depth profiles are shown in Fig. 14.9(a); these profiles are stored in ROM in the form of binary numbers representing the maximum speed at various distances in the shaft.

The work motor may, typically, be a dual-converter drive of the type in Fig. 14.8, with the speed reference signal being obtained from a potentiometer.

In the application considered here, the speed profile is used in a monitoring situation rather than in a speed control system. Basically, the computer monitors the speed of the winder and compares it with the speed profile in ROM. Emergency action is taken only if the speed of the conveyance exceeds the speed profile at any point in the shaft.

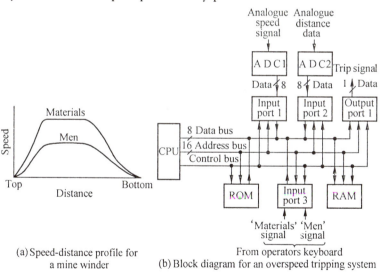

(a) Speed-distance profile for a mine winder
(b) Block diagram for an overspeed tripping system

Fig. 14.9

Referring to Fig. 14.9, a signal would be initially sent to the CPU via input port 3 to say if men or materials are being wound; the winder operator then moves his control lever to set the conveyance in operation. The CPU then monitors the distance that the conveyance has moved in the shaft via analogue-to-digital converter ADC2 and input port 2. (The system described here assumes that the distance measurement is obtained by analogue means, i.e., a potentiometer geared to the motor shaft. However, if the distance measurement is digital, then the need for ADC2 is eliminated, and the digital data can be input directly to the CPU via port 2.) The CPU then uses the speed profile to 'look up' the maximum speed corresponding to that distance. The speed of the conveyance at that instant of time is converted into its digital equivalent by ADC1, and the CPU 'reads' the digital value of speed via input port 1. The next step in the computer program will call for the CPU to compare the actual speed of the conveyance with the maximum allowable speed. If the actual speed is less than the maximum value, no action is taken; If the conveyance speed is too great, the CPU sends out a signal to a trip mechanism via output port 1, causing the conveyance to stop.

14.10 PULSE-WIDTH MODULATION SPEED CONTROL OF DC MOTORS

Pulse-width modulation (PWM) control or duty cycle control, when applied to DC drives, is a method of control in which pulses of direct current of variable width are applied to the motor armature. The basis of one system is shown in Fig. 14.10. The armature speed would be measured by means of, for example, the voltage from a tachogenerator which is compared with a speed reference signal. The resuming signal is used to control the thyristor gate pulses, the operation of the circuit is described below.

When TH1 is conducting and TH2 is turned off, the right-hand plate of C is charged to $-U_s$. By

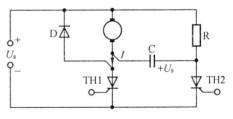

Fig. 14.10 Capacitor-commutated thyristor circuit

triggering TH2 to the 'on' state, the capacitor is connected across TH1, applying a reverse voltage to it. This results in TH1 being rapidly turned off. Commutating diode D is necessary with an inductive load. When TH2 conducts, the capacitor charges to the reverse polarity, and the next gate pulse applied to TH1 turns it on and TH2 off. The minimum value of capacitance is set by the maximum load current (including overload) and the thyristor turn-off time. For most thyristors if

$$U_s \, C \, / \, I \geqslant 30 \, \mu s$$

satisfactory commutation is achieved. To ensure positive turn-off, C must be fully charged in the time interval between TH1 being triggered on and the switch-off time. This time interval must be greater than 5RC seconds. If the time interval is large, the calculated value R will be large, but it should not be greater than 10 times the forward blocking resistance of TH2. Since TH2 carries the capacitor discharge current only momentarily, it has a current rating less than that of TH1.

By applying pulses alternately to the two thyristor gates, the load current is switched on and off repeatedly. This affords a simple method of regulating the average value of current, and has the great advantage that the power loss in the circuit is very small. On the debit side, the current is passed in a series of pulse, giving rise to commutation problems.

The average armature voltage, and therefore motor speed, depends on the relative length of time that TH1 is on and off, giving approximately

Armature voltage = supply voltage·on time / (on + off) times

Owing to the pulsating nature of the armature current, the inductance of the armature circuit may have to be increased by additional inductance to ensure adequate smoothing.

Vocabulary

1. viscous   *a*.   粘稠的
2. viscous friction   粘滞摩擦
3. bearing   *n*.   轴承
4. rolling mill   轧钢机
5. mine minder   矿坑卷扬机
6. velodyne   *n*.   伺服积分器
7. feasible   *a*.   可行的
8. regenerative braking   回馈制动
9. eddy current braking   涡流制动
10. dynamic braking   能耗制动
11. reverse current braking   反接制动
12. advent   *n*.   出现
13. prolong   *v*.   延长
14. armature   *n*.   电枢
15. contactor   *n*.   接触器
16. hoist   *n*.   起重机,升降机
17. field winding   励磁绕组
18. commutator   *n*.   换向器
19. ripple   *n*.   纹波
20. creep   *v*.   蠕动
21. tachogenerator   *n*.   测速发电机
22. quadrant   *n*.   象限
23. coast   *n*.   跟踪惯性
24. profile   *n*.   轮廓
25. conveyance   *n*.   运输工具
26. lever   *n*.   手柄,控制杆

Notes:

1. A regulator system is one which normally provides output power in its steady-state operation.
调节系统是一类通常在稳态运行下提供输出功率的系统。

2. Regenerative braking is the best method, though not necessarily the most economic.
虽然不一定是最经济的方式,但回馈制动是最好的方式。

3. Providing the supply system has adequate capacity, the consequent rise in terminal voltage will be small during the short periods of regeneration.
假设电源系统具有足够的容量,短时回馈过程引起的端电压升高很小。

4. Combinations of the two are used where a wide range of speed is required.
需要宽范围调速的场合采用两者的结合。

5. In the drive shown, the potential of the thyristor cathode is equal to the back e.m.f. of the motor while it is in a blocking state.
在所示的拖动系统中,在晶闸管关断状态下,晶闸管的阴极电位与电动机反电动势相同。

6. This has the effect of reducing not only the output of the system but also the magnitude of the quantity to be limited.
它具有不但减小系统输出而且减小被限幅量幅值的作用。

7. This reverses the polarity of the generated voltage and current, reversing the work motor torque.
它改变产生的电压和电流的极性,从而使工作电动机的转矩反向。

8. By a suitable choice of values, the voltage between A and B is proportional to the back E M F, eliminating the need for a tachogenerator.
通过合理取值,A 和 B 点间电压正比于反电动势,从而不需测速机。

9. A feature of the Ward-Leonard system is that regenerative braking is inherent.
Ward-Leonard 系统的一个特点是本身具有回馈制动。

10. The gate pulse generator ensures that when one bridge is operating as a rectifier, the other bridge operates as an invertor.
触发器保证当一组整流器工作于整流状态时,另一组整流器工作在逆变状态。

11. On the debit side, the current is passed in a series of pulse, giving rise to commutation problems.
对应的不利方面,电流是一系列脉冲,加重换流问题。

15

Frequency Controls for Ac Motors

15.1 ADJUSTABLE-FREQUENCY CONCEPTS

Let's review for a moment the concepts of line and forced commutation as they are used to obtain adjustable frequency to be applied to an AC squirrel cage induction motor. Fig. 15.1 illustrates what the controller is

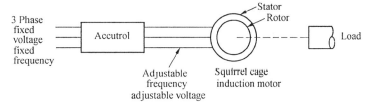

Fig. 15.1 Conversion functions of adjustable-frequency controllers applied to AC motors

supposed to do: create an adjustable voltage and adjustable frequency from fixed line voltage and fixed line frequency. Let's first decide what we need to put in the box. The circuit using six thyristors will not work. It can create an adjustable voltage to the motor, but the line frequency passes straight on through. Therefore, we need a means of creating an adjustable frequency as well as an adjustable voltage. The simplest way of doing this is by means of a 'DC link'. The DC link is then controlled by one of several means to create the adjustable frequency. In some cases the DC link is also controlled to create the adjustable voltage. To form the DC link, the incoming AC voltage must somehow be changed to a DC voltage, after which the DC is changed back to AC for applying to the AC motor.

Fig. 15.2 shows a generalized frequency controller with a DC link. The input uses six semiconductors to provide the DC, and the output uses six semiconductors to provide the adjustable frequency. Which type of semiconductor should be selected for each box? Since the AC line is always connected to the first box, the input devices can be line commutated. They can therefore be diodes, thyristors, GTOs, transistors, or triacs. GTOs are quite costly, and transistors and triacs may not have the desired ampere capacity and voltage capabilities. Therefore, the input power devices will be diodes or thyristors or perhaps a combination.

Again the devices in the output box of Fig. 15.2 must utilize forced commutation because there is no natural or line means to turn off the power semiconductors. This means that they must be thyristors, transistors, or GTOs. Triacs could be used but are limited in capacity.

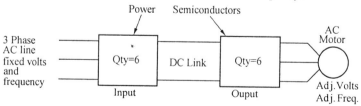

Fig. 15.2 Generalized adjustable-frequency controller with DC link

Let's start with diodes in the input box. With diodes, there is no means of adjusting the DC link voltage. Therefore, both the adjustable frequency and the adjustable voltage must be created in the output stage.

This is actually done in the real case. The resulting system is called pulse-width modulation (PWM).

If the input box were to use thyristors instead of diodes, they can be controlled to provide adjustable DC link voltage. The output stage then needs only to create the adjustable frequency from the DC link and pass the adjustable voltage on through to the AC motor, together with the adjustable frequency. The output stage can therefore be less complex than for a PWM system, but the input stage must be more complex. However, this method is also in popular use for frequency controllers, in one of two arrangements. One is known as the adjustable voltage inverter (AVI). The other is known as the current source inverter (CSI).

Table 15.1 is a summary of power devices as used in these three most common types of frequency controllers.

Table 15.1 Summary of Power Semiconductors as Used with the Three Basic Types of Adjustable-Frequency Controllers

Type of controller	Input devices	DC link voltage	Output devices
PWM	Diodes	Constant	Thyristors
AVI	Thyristors	Adjustable	or Diodes
CSI	Thyristors	Adjustable	or GTOs

15.2 TERMINOLOGY

Let's review for a moment some of the various terms as they are used to describe solid-state frequency controllers. There are rigid technical definitions as well as generally used terminology. First, the technical definitions as suggested by organizations such as IEC. NEMA, and IEEE (Institute of Electrical and Electronics Engineers):

Converter : an operative unit for electronic power conversion comprising one or more valve devices (power semiconductors, for example).

Self-commutated converter: a converter in which the commutation voltages are supplied by components within the converters.

Rectifier: a converter for conversion from AC to DC.

Inverter: a converter for conversion from DC to AC.

Indirect AC converter: a converter comprising a rectifier and an inverter with a DC link.

If we look at Fig. 15.2, all definitions above apply to solid-state frequency controllers in one form or another, and that definition 5 covers the complete system. However, general usage in the United States is to call the configuration of Fig. 15.2 an ' inverter': PWM inverter, adjustable voltage inverter, or current source inverter [also called an adjustable-current inverter (ACI)].

For the rest of this chapter we use the terms 'adjustable-frequency controller' and 'inverter' interchangeably, recognizing, of course, that we can have the whistle blown on us at any time for not using correct technical terminology.

15.3 PWM VERSUS AVI VERSUS CSI

All three of the most commonly used adjustable-frequency controllers consist of three basic sections, as shown in Fig. 15.2. The input section converts the incoming AC power to DC. The center section, or DC link, smoothes out or filters the DC voltage. The output section inverts the DC into AC of the desired frequency.

The differences among these three types of controllers are (a) the manner in which the adjustable voltage is obtained, and (b) the techniques used to create the adjustable frequency.

15.3.1 PWM

Pulse-width modulation (PWM) utilizes diodes in the input stage to provide a fixed-voltage DC bus. The output, or inverter stage, creates a series of pulses of constant voltage with the pulse widths and pulse quantities varying as required by the desired output frequency and voltage. The output section supplies and controls both parameters, adjustable frequency and adjustable voltage.

15.3.2 AVI

Adjustable-voltage inverters (AVIs) use thyristors in the input stage to obtain adjustable voltage in the DC link. The output stage switches this DC voltage with thyristors or transistors or GTOs to obtain a square-wave voltage whose width and timing sequence are proportional to the desired frequency. Voltage control is obtained in the first stage. Frequency control is obtained in the second stage.

15.3.3 CSI

Current source inverters (CSIs) are similar to AVIs, except that the control is arranged to provide a series of square waves of current output.

15.3.4 Comparison of PWM, AVI, and CSI

Fig. 15.3 shows the three types of adjustable-frequency controllers, with power circuits and resulting theoretical output voltage and current waveforms. There are numerous variations within these three basic systems, such as sine-wave modulation with PWM, chopper techniques, and output circuitry that provides a form of load commutation. These refinements are beyond the scope of this book and are covered in the references.

Frequency Controls for Ac Motors 339

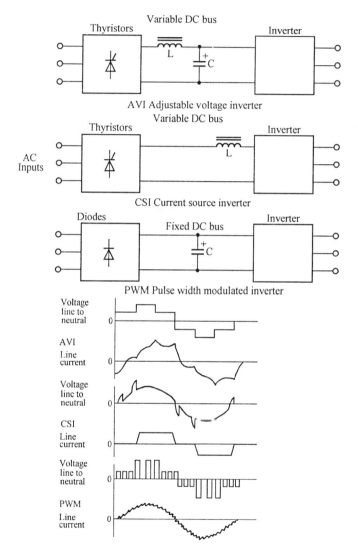

Fig.15.3 Power circuit and output waveforms of the basic types of adjustable-frequency controllers

15.4 PERFORMANCE COMPARISONS OF PWM, AVI, AND CSI

Each of these types of inverters are usually designed to allow operation within these motor constraints. The differences are in the techniques used to generate volts/hertz, adjustable frequency, and any inherent design limitations on minimum and maximum frequency.

It is not the intent of this book to take sides or to pass judgment on the relative merits or pros and cons of the three types of inverters. They all do a good job when properly applied and properly designed. Some manufacturers offer two designs, and in some cases, all three designs, depending on horsepower ranges and application requirements.

For the moment, however, the most frequently stated advantages and disadvantages of these three most commonly used types of inverters are listed as follows:

15.4.1 AVI Advantages

(1) Basic simplicity: it has simple logic and can be operated open loop. (No feedback of amperes or volts is required for steady-state operation)

(2) A single controller can be used with more than one motor.

(3) Reliability is good, somewhat better than for PWM types.

(4) Voltage stresses on motor insulation are relatively low.

(5) Can be designed for up to 500 Hz operation.

15.4.2 AVI Disadvantages

(1) Speed range is limited because of motor cogging at 6 Hz and below.

(2) DC link stability can be a problem at low speeds because of motor interaction with DC link filter elements.

(3) Requires an additional set of power devices in the input stage if regeneration back to the AC line is desired.

(4) To obtain extended ride-through capability on incoming power loss, a DC chopper must be added to the DC link.

(5) Input power factor is poor below base speed.

15.4.3 PWM Advantages

(1) A wider speed range (below rated frequency) is possible.

(2) Can be used with more than one motor.

(3) Input power factor is good at all frequencies.

(4) Diode input stage allows ride-through on input power interruption.

15.4.4 PWM Disadvantages

(1) Logic circuitry is relatively complex.

(2) Operation above 120 ~ 150 Hz is difficult.

15.4.5 CSI Advantages

(1) Capable of regeneration back to the AC line because DC link bus polarity can be reversed.

(2) Large DC link filter inductor and regulated power supply acts as a current limiter, making it easier to apply protective fuses.

(3) Ability to ride through power-line interruptions.

(4) Thyristors in output stage can be commercial grade.

15.4.6 CSI Disadvantages

(1) Cogging can occur at speeds below 6 Hz.

(2) DC link filter inductor is large, costly, and contributes to losses and enclosure size.

(3) Can cause high-voltage spikes on motor terminals.

(4) Usually not possible to use with more than one motor.

(5) Motor power factor appears on the incoming line to the controller.

(6) Voltage clamping devices lower overall efficiency.

(7) May require special tuning to motor parameters.

15.4.7 Summary of Performance Comparisons

The technical references cover the various advantages and disadvantages of the different types of inverters in more detail. For purposes of this book it is sufficient to state that the great majority of items that must be considered when selecting an inverter to be applied to a particular application are the same, regardless of the type of inverter. In other words, 90% of the problem is in proper selection of the motor and operating options, and 10% of the problem is whether to select PWM or AVI or CSI.

15.5 APPLICATIONS OF GENERAL-PURPOSE INVERTERS

The applications for inverters and their associated AC induction drive motors fall generally into three basic categories: ① in place of or as retrofits for DC motor drives, ② instead of or as retrofits for mechanical speed changers, and ③ to regulate or control fluid flow (e.g., air or liquids) by speed instead of restrictive devices such as vanes, dampers, and modulating valves. Each of these is discussed in the following sections.

15.5.1 Instead of DC Drives

Many existing DC drives are being used because of historic preference and performance. Users were (and are) willing to put up with the space, cost, and, maintenance inherent in a DC drive because it was, so to speak, 'the only game in town.' The great majority of stand-alone single-motor DC drive applications can be supplied or replaced by an inverter and an AC induction motor.

This is not to say, however, that all DC systems are replaceable with general-purpose inverters. We will discuss some of the pitfalls that can be encountered when DC drives are indiscriminately replaced by inverters and AC motors.

Which DC drives are candidates for replacement by general-purpose invert? Typical examples would be those applications with performance requirements that were available only from DC drives, now available with general-purpose inverters, such as :

(1) Operation of several motors and inverters from a master reference, with individually adjustable vernier speeds among the motors.

(2) Individual start-stop control of each motor.

(3) Independently adjustable acceleration and deceleration adjustments of each inverter-driven motor, as well as for group control of the same functions.

(4) Reversing capability, either as groups of motors or as individual motors.

(5) Jog or thread operation, individually or in groups.

(6) Individual torque- or current-limiting control.

(7) Controlled slowdown by dynamic braking in the DC link.

(8) Accuracies on the order of ± 1/2% of rated speed.

(9) Up to a 2 : 1 range at constant horsepower, allowing for increased torque at lower speeds.

Plus features of inverter drives include the capability of the AC motor to survive in hostile environments: chemical, temperature, moisture, and explosive. The higher-speed capability of an AC motor results in even less space at the driven process.

Examples of using inverters with AC motors instead of DC drives include, both for new installations and retrofits, paper mill washer drives, metal saws, conveyors, textile range drives, metal industry runout tables, certain helper drives on paper machines, clinker-cooler drives in cement plants, various types of kilns, centrifuges, and high-speed grinders. Today's general-purpose inverters should always be evaluated whether in justifying a new DC drive or simply in trying to justify the continued investment in shelf spares for an existing DC drive.

15.5.2 Instead of Mechanical Speed Changers

Mechanical speed changers are devices that use mechanisms such as movable belts, cone pulleys, or variable-pitch pulleys to provide an adjustable-speed output from an AC motor that runs at constant speed. An item seldom evaluated in the total operating expense of these devices is the inventory cost of spares. This should be added to the cost of lost production for changeout periods, loss of production space at the driven machine, lower AC line-to-shaft efficiency, and annual budgets for maintenance costs. It is of interest to note that many power transmission distribution houses, the historical source of mechanical speed changers, are also making available to their customers one or more lines of inverters, a product far removed from the normal world of power transmission hardware.

15.5.3 Flow Control

The concept of controlling flow (air or fluids) has always been recognized as being more efficient and less complex when the speed of the flow generator (pump or fan) is the controlled variable. However, it has only been with the escalation of energy costs and the cost-effective availability of inverters that this method of flow control is being taken seriously in the 2 ~ 373 kW range of flow power requirements. Examples of recent and current marriages of inverters to flow control in these horsepower ranges include:

(1) New paper mills with all pumps now controlled by inverters for flow control instead of the historic modulating valves.

(2) New and retrofit heating, ventilating, and air conditioning (HVAC) systems in institutional and office buildings, particularly those with variable air volume (VAV) control, are using inverters for air-handling units, cooling-tower fans, chillers, and compressors. There are numerous examples where up to 100 or more inverters are being installed in a single building. The energy savings generally will pay for the initial first-cost difference within a year or less.

(3) The sequencing and maintenance of vanes and dampers of the forced-draft (FD) and induced-draft (ID) fans of power boilers has always been an operating headache, not to mention the sometimes total disregard of the efficiency losses. Utilities and large industrial plants have long recognized and have gone to the use of adjustable-speed drives on these fans. The advent of cost-effective inverters in the range 37 ~ 373 kW is leading to their use on FD and ID fans in institutional buildings as well as in smaller industrial plants. Combinations of inverter-driven FD and ID fans, programmable controllers, and sensors for flow and ignition are resulting in energy savings, smoother ignition cycles, and reduced maintenance.

(4) Many industrial processes use fans to exhaust heat and fumes, to remove excess material, and to control incoming air or other gaseous fluids. These processes seldom operate at full capacity at all times. However, the fans are seldom, if ever, shut down or slowed down when their full-load capacity is not required. Most of these process fans are ideal candidates for energy savings by applying adjustable-frequency controllers to the fan drive motors, with automatic slow down when full capacity is not required. Typical examples are:

① Exhaust fans on continuous steel casters and basic oxygen processes

② Trim blowers on paper-mill winders

③ Fume exhaust (and possible heat and material recovery) in printing plants

④ Exhaust fans in drying processes

(5) The chemical and petroleum refining industries are large users of cooling towers. In many cases these cooling towers will use a multitude of fans for cooling air, with sequenced on-off operation of the fans to obtain the desired cooling effects. Also, it is not unusual to adjust the pitches on the fans on initial startup for the worst-case conditions, which is in itself a waste of energy. Inverters are being applied to these cooling towers not only to save energy, but to provide closer control of the process itself.

15.5.4 Specific Example of Pump Selection

The following example illustrates how looking at the overall concept of flow control instead of optimum selection of individual components (pump, piping, motor and valve) can lead to dramatic savings in first costs as well as operating and energy costs. Fig. 15.4 shows a typical selection of a pumping system. For simplicity we will assume that feet of head and the resultant required horse-power are of the same numerical magnitude (50 ft of head = 37 kW, etc.). The basic requirement of Fig. 15.4 is to pump a fluid to 50 ft, which in this case corresponds to 50 kW. Ten horse-power is required for losses in the piping, including the additional pipe length and elbows required to place the modulating valve in position so that it can be maintained. 11 kW is required to overcome losses in the modulating valve, even though it is assumed to be wide open for maximum flow. The

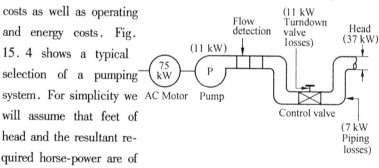

Fig. 15.4 Pump and constant-speed motor selection with modulating valve.

pump is estimated to be approximately 85% efficient, which is quite optimistic. The net result is that a 75 kW motor is selected. Ac line-to-required head efficiency is on the order of 50%. The efficiency will drop off rapidly when the modulating valve is called upon to reduce flow, both because of increased valve losses and because the pump operates at reduced efficiency when flow is reduced at constant speed. Fig.15.5 shows what happens when flow control is obtained by speed control of the pump drive motor instead of with the modulating valve. Piping losses are reduced because there is no need to supply additional piping and elbows for access to the valve. Valve losses are eliminated. A smaller pump and motor can be used. AC line-to-required head efficiency is improved at full flow from 50% ~ 66%, with additional efficiency improvements over the range of flow control.

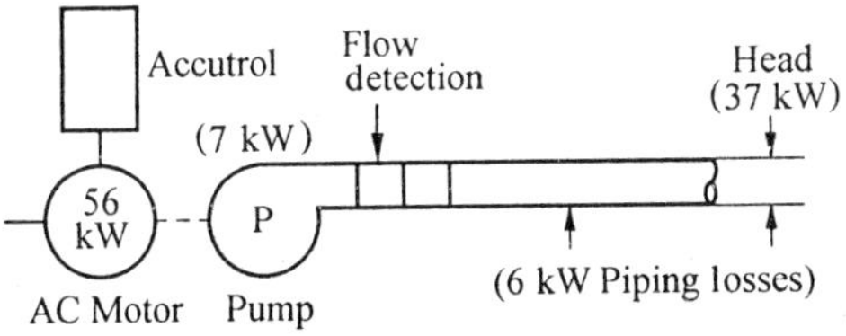

Fig.15.5 Pump and motor selection with inverter instead of modulating valve

Another hidden energy cost in the selection and rating of systems is the tendency to oversize each element. The net result of this oversizing is that the entire process must be 'turned down' on initial production by setting the valve so that flow is restricted and energy wasted continuously from the very first day of usage. With an inverter-driven pump, this initial turndown can be achieved by operating the motor at the required speed, either above or below base frequency.

Vocabulary

1. forced commutation   强迫换流
2. ac squirrel cage induction motor   交流笼型感应电动机
3. accutrol   n.   控制器
4. stator   n.   定子
5. rotor   n.   转子

6. DC link 直流环节
7. Triac   *n.* 双向晶闸管
8. Adjustable-voltage inverter 电压型逆变器
9. Current source inverter 电流型逆变器
10. refinement   *n.* 明确表达
11. pros and cons 优缺点
12. cogging   *n.* 齿槽效应
13. retrofit   *n.* 改型
14. vane   *n.* 节气阀
15. damper   *n.* 减速器
16. pitfall   *n.* 缺陷
17. vernier   *n.* 游标尺
18. jog 啮合
19. runout table 输出轨道
20. clinker-cooler 熟料冷却器
21. kiln   *n.* 炉
22. grinder   *n.* 磨床
23. pitch   *n.* 齿轮
24. inventory   *n.* 存货
25. cone pulley 塔轮,快慢轮
26. escalation   *n.* 升级,提高
27. forced-draft 强制通风
28. induced-draft fan 吸风机
29. elbow   *n.* 弯头

Notes:

1. Therefore, we need a means of creating an adjustable frequency as well as an adjustable voltage.
所以,我们需要产生可调频率和可调电压的装置。

2. To form the DC link, the incoming AC voltage must somehow be changed to a DC voltage, after which the DC is changed back to AC for applying to the AC motor.

为构成直流环节,进线交流电压必须通过某种方式变为直流电压,然后该直流电压反变为交流以驱动交流电动机。

3. If the input box were to use SCRs instead of diodes, they can be controlled to provide adjustable DC link voltage.

如果输入框采用晶闸管而非二极管,可以控制晶闸管以提供可变的直流环节电压。

4. Current source inverters (CSIs) are similar to AVIs, except that the control is arranged to provide a series of square waves of current output.

电流源逆变器与电压源逆变器相似,只是采用的控制方式是提供一系列方波输出电流。

5. These refinements are beyond the scope of this book and are covered in the references.

这些细节超出本书范围,详见参考文献。

6. The differences are in the techniques used to generate volts/hertz, adjustable frequency, and any inherent design limitations on minimum and maximum frequency.

差别在于采用的发生一定压/频比的变频电源的方法和固有的最高、最低设计频率限制。

7. For purposes of this book it is sufficient to state that the great majority of items that must be considered when selecting an inverter to be applied to a particular application are the same, regardless of the type of inverter.

从本书的目的出发,足以肯定:不管逆变器的类型如何,对特定应用场合选择逆变器时,需要考虑的主要方面是相同的。

8. Inverters are being applied to these cooling towers not only to save energy, but to provide closer control of the process itself.

在这些冷却塔采用逆变器不仅是为了节省能量,还是为了提供对过程自身的合理控制。

9. The efficiency will drop off rapidly when the modulating valve is called upon to reduce flow, both because of increased valve losses and because the pump operates at reduced efficiency when flow is reduced at constant speed.

当要求调节阀减小流量时效率迅速降低,这是由于阀门损耗增加,并且当流量减小为恒值时泵工作在较低的效率下。